Jesus

ALSO BY MAX LUCADO

INSPIRATIONAL
3:16
A Gentle Thunder
A Love Worth Giving
And the Angels Were Silent
Anxious for Nothing
Because of Bethlehem
Before Amen
Come Thirsty
Cure for the Common Life
Facing Your Giants
Fearless
Glory Days
God Came Near
Grace
Great Day Every Day
He Chose the Nails
He Still Moves Stones
In the Eye of the Storm
In the Grip of Grace
It's Not About Me
Just Like Jesus
Max on Life
More to Your Story
Next Door Savior
No Wonder They Call Him the Savior
On the Anvil
Outlive Your Life
Six Hours One Friday
The Applause of Heaven
The Great House of God
Traveling Light
When Christ Comes
When God Whispers Your Name
You'll Get Through This

FICTION
Christmas Stories
The Christmas Candle
Miracle at the Higher Grounds Café

BIBLES (GENERAL EDITOR)
Grace for the Moment Daily Bible
The Lucado Life Lessons Study Bible
Children's Daily Devotional Bible

CHILDREN'S BOOKS
A Max Lucado Children's Treasury
Do You Know I Love You, God?
God Forgives Me, and I Forgive You
God Listens When I Pray
Grace for the Moment: 365 Devotions for Kids
Hermie, a Common Caterpillar
Itsy Bitsy Christmas
Just in Case You Ever Wonder
Lucado Treasury of Bedtime Prayers
One Hand, Two Hands
Thank You, God, for Blessing Me
Thank You, God, for Loving Me
The Boy and the Ocean
The Crippled Lamb
The Oak Inside the Acorn
The Tallest of Smalls
You Are Mine
You Are Special

YOUNG ADULT BOOKS
3:16
It's Not About Me
Make Every Day Count
Wild Grace
You Were Made to Make a Difference

GIFT BOOKS
Fear Not Promise Book
For the Tough Times
God Thinks You're Wonderful
Grace for the Moment
Grace Happens Here
His Name Is Jesus
Let the Journey Begin
Live Loved
Mocha with Max
Safe in the Shepherd's Arms
This Is Love
You Changed My Life

Jesus

MAX LUCADO

THOMAS NELSON
Since 1798

Published in Nashville, Tennessee, by Thomas Nelson. Thomas Nelson is a registered trademark of HarperCollins Christian Publishing, Inc.

Thomas Nelson titles may be purchased in bulk for educational, business, fund-raising, or sales promotional use. For information, please e-mail SpecialMarkets@ThomasNelson.com.

Any Internet addresses, phone numbers, or company or product information printed in this book are offered as a resource and are not intended in any way to be or to imply an endorsement by Thomas Nelson, nor does Thomas Nelson vouch for the existence, content, or services of these sites, phone numbers, companies, or products beyond the life of this book.

Scripture quotations marked AMPC are from the Amplified® Bible, Classic Edition. Copyright © 1954, 1958, 1962, 1964, 1965, 1987 by The Lockman Foundation. Used by permission. (www.Lockman.org). Scripture quotations marked CEV are from the Contemporary English Version. Copyright © 1991, 1992, 1995 by American Bible Society. Used by permission. Scripture quotations marked ESV are from the ESV® Bible (The Holy Bible, English Standard Version®). Copyright © 2001 by Crossway, a publishing ministry of Good News Publishers. Used by permission. All rights reserved. Scripture quotations marked GNT are from the Good News Translation in Today's English Version—Second Edition. Copyright 1992 by American Bible Society. Used by permission. Scripture quotations marked HCSB are from the Holman Christian Standard Bible®. Copyright © 1999, 2000, 2002, 2003, 2009 by Holman Bible Publishers. Used by permission. HCSB® is a federally registered trademark of Holman Bible Publishers. Scripture quotations marked KJV are from the King James Version. Public domain. Scripture quotations marked THE MESSAGE are from *The Message*. Copyright © by Eugene H. Peterson 1993, 1994, 1995, 1996, 2000, 2001, 2002. Used by permission of NavPress. All rights reserved. Represented by Tyndale House Publishers, Inc. Scripture quotations marked NAB are from the *New American Bible, revised edition.* © 2010, 1991, 1986, 1970 Confraternity of Christian Doctrine, Washington, DC. Used by permission of the copyright owner. All rights reserved. No part of the New American Bible may be reproduced in any form without permission in writing from the copyright owner. Scripture quotations marked NASB are from New American Standard Bible®. Copyright © 1960, 1962, 1963, 1968, 1971, 1972, 1973, 1975, 1977, 1995 by The Lockman Foundation. Used by permission. (www.Lockman.org). Scripture quotations marked NCV are from the New Century Version®. © 2005 by Thomas Nelson. Used by permission. All rights reserved. Scripture quotations marked NEB are from the New English Bible. © Cambridge University Press and Oxford University Press 1961, 1970. All rights reserved. Scripture quotations marked NIV are from the Holy Bible, New International Version®, NIV®. Copyright © 1973, 1978, 1984, 2011 by Biblica, Inc.® Used by permission of Zondervan. All rights reserved worldwide. www.Zondervan.com. The "NIV" and "New International Version" are trademarks registered in the United States Patent and Trademark Office by Biblica, Inc.®. Scripture quotations marked NKJV are from the New King James Version®. © 1982 by Thomas Nelson. Used by permission. All rights reserved. Scripture quotations marked NLT are from the Holy Bible, New Living Translation. © 1996, 2004, 2007, 2013, 2015 by Tyndale House Foundation. Used by permission of Tyndale House Publishers, Inc., Carol Stream, Illinois 60188. All rights reserved. Scripture quotations marked NRSV are from New Revised Standard Version Bible. Copyright © 1989 National Council of the Churches of Christ in the United States of America. Used by permission. All rights reserved. Scripture quotations marked PHILLIPS are from The New Testament in Modern English by J. B. Phillips. Copyright © 1960, 1972 J. B. Phillips. Administered by the Archbishops' Council of the Church of England. Used by permission. Scripture quotations marked RSV are from Revised Standard Version of the Bible. Copyright 1946, 1952, and 1971 National Council of the Churches of Christ in the United States of America. Used by permission. All rights reserved. Scripture quotations marked TLB are from The Living Bible. Copyright © 1971. Used by permission of Tyndale House Publishers, Inc., Carol Stream, Illinois 60188. All rights reserved. Scripture quotations marked THE VOICE are from The Voice™. © 2012 by Ecclesia Bible Society. Used by permission. All rights reserved. Note: Italics in quotations from The Voice are used to "indicate words not directly tied to the dynamic translation of the original language" but that "bring out the nuance of the original, assist in completing ideas, and . . . provide readers with information that would have been obvious to the original audience" (The Voice, preface).

ISBN 978-1-4041-0695-6 (custom)

Printed in the United States of America

18 19 20 21 22 LSC 10 9 8 7 6 5 4 3 2 1

Contents

A Word from Max vii

1. Creator 1
2. Immanuel 17
3. Friend 34
4. Example 51
5. Teacher 67
6. Healer 83
7. Provider 98
8. Victor 113
9. Life 126
10. Forgiver 142
11. Intercessor 159
12. Servant Leader 173
13. Sacrifice 188
14. Savior 205
15. Hope 222

Notes 236
Sources Index 241

A Word from Max

My wife's family is a repository of great stories. When I am with them, I keep a notebook handy because I know someone will share something worth retelling. Among my favorite is the account of a trip from Tulsa to Los Angeles. The primary characters in the episode are Uncle Ellis and his son-in-law Pat. Back in the early '90s, as the story goes, they drove Pat's son to Los Angeles so the boy could take a shot at an acting career.

Uncle Ellis was in his sixties at the time and pretty set in his ways. He didn't take to being away from home. The idea was to travel nonstop from Tulsa to LA, spend one night in the big city, and head back.

Turned out, even one night was too many. Ellis saw the hustle of Los Angeles and changed his mind. He and Pat dropped the young man at his destination and turned the truck around with every intent of driving nonstop to Oklahoma. But as the sun began to set, their eyelids grew heavy. They made it as far as Arizona before they decided to spend the night.

About 5:00 p.m. they found a hotel with an adjacent diner. They checked into a room with two beds. Ellis called his wife and informed her of their plans. The two men then went to the restaurant. They found an open booth and ordered breakfast for supper. By 6:30 they had eaten, cleaned up, gone to bed, and fallen fast asleep.

Thirty minutes later Pat rolled over and noticed that the time on the digital clock said 7:00. He mistakenly assumed that it was 7:00 a.m. not

7:00 p.m. and that it was time to get out of bed and hit the road. He woke up his father-in-law and told him it was time to leave. Ellis grumbled something about the short night. Still, he climbed out of bed.

They checked out of the hotel and decided it would be prudent to eat breakfast before getting on the highway. (After all, they thought it was 7:00 a.m.) They entered the same restaurant, sat at the same booth, were served by the same attendant, and ordered the same breakfast. It didn't occur to them to ask why she was still on duty. It didn't occur to her to ask why the same two men were ordering the same meal she had served them an hour earlier.

By now it was 8:00 p.m., though Ellis and Pat thought it was 8:00 a.m. As they drove toward Tulsa one told the other, "The sky seems to be getting darker, not brighter." By 9:00 p.m. (or 9:00 a.m. in their imaginations) the sky was black and the stars were out and Ellis and Pat were spooked. They pulled over to the side of the road. Ellis called his wife and told her to get her stuff ready because the world was about to end and the Battle of Armageddon was about to begin.

"Honey," she replied, "you just called three hours ago. What are you doing back out on the road?" Only then did Ellis realize they'd misinterpreted the time.

They aren't the first to make such a mistake. This journey toward home can bewilder the best of us. Truth be told, we've all lost track of time. We've lost our bearings. We've lost our perspective. At one time or another, we've all needed help. We need to be reminded where we are and where we're headed. For Ellis and Pat, it was a voice from home.

For us, it's the name of Jesus, sweetest name ever spoken.

I know, I know. The name Jesus has been derided and mocked, turned into a curse word and a scapegoat for everything from a hammered thumb to medieval Crusades. Peeling back all the layers from the name is no easy task. But it is one worth the effort.

To see me is to see God, Jesus said. His voice, God's voice. His tears,

God's tears. Want to know what matters to God? Find out what matters to Jesus. Want to know what in the world God is doing? Ponder the words of Jesus. Need to know where history is headed? He wrote the time line.

It could be that your experience with the name of Jesus has been less than positive. Did someone ram some frosty ideas about right and wrong down your throat and tell you they started with Jesus? Did a circle of high and mighty folks keep you out because you weren't good enough? Or maybe no one needs to tell you anything. You've fumbled enough footballs in life to know that no one like Jesus would have a spot for someone like you.

Reconsider, won't you?

What if he really is who he claims to be? The image of the invisible God. And what if he can do what he claimed to do? Lead wayward travelers like you and me onto the right road. Maybe it's time to pull over to the side of the road and make a call.

1

Creator

Jesus was "in very nature God." Before Bethlehem, Jesus had every advantage and benefit of deity. He was boundless, timeless, and limitless. "All things were made through Him, and without Him nothing was made that was made" (John 1:3 NKJV).

Every rock, tree, and planet needs a stamp that says "Made by Jesus." He gets credit for the Whirlpool Galaxy. It contains more than a hundred billion stars.[1] He created our sun. More than a million Earths could fit inside the sun.[2] Jesus fashioned Betelgeuse, which if it were placed at the center of the Earth's solar system would extend out to the orbit of Jupiter.[3] The star Betelgeuse is approximately a thousand times bigger than our sun.[4] Jesus spoke and the bespangled sky happened. He calls each star by name and can fold up the skies as a bedouin would pack his tent.

—Because of Bethlehem

Christ is running the show. Right now. A leaf just fell from a tree in the Alps. Christ caused it to do so. A newborn baby in India inhaled for the first time. Jesus measured the breath. The migration of the belugas through the oceans? Christ dictates their itinerary. He is the firstborn of all creation. For by Him all things were created, both in the heavens and on earth, visible and invisible, whether thrones or dominions or rulers or authorities—all things have been created through Him and for Him. (Col. 1:15–16 NASB)

What a phenomenal list! Heavens and earth. Visible and invisible. Thrones, dominions, rulers, and authorities. No thing, place, or person omitted. The scale on the sea urchin. The hair on the elephant hide. The hurricane that wrecks the coast, the rain that nourishes the desert, the infant's first heartbeat, the elderly person's final breath—all can be traced back to the hand of Christ. . . .

The Christ of the galaxies is the Christ of your Mondays. The Starmaker manages your travel schedule. Relax. You have a friend in high places. Does the child of Arnold Schwarzenegger worry about tight pickle-jar lids? Does the son of Nike founder Phil Knight sweat a broken shoestring? If the daughter of Bill Gates can't turn on her computer, does she panic?

No. Nor should you. The universe's Commander in Chief knows your name. He has walked your streets.

—Next Door Savior

*B*ehind it all was a choice. A deliberate decision. An informed move. He didn't have to do it. But he chose to. He knew the price. He saw the implications. He was aware of the consequences.

We don't know when he decided to do it. We can't know. Not just because we weren't there. Because time was not there. *When* did not exist. Nor did *tomorrow* or *yesterday* or *next time*. For there was no time.

We don't know when he thought about making the choice. But we do know that he made it. He didn't have to do it. He chose to.

He chose to create.

"In the beginning God created . . ."[5]

With one decision, history began. Existence became measurable.

Out of nothing came light.

Out of light came day.

Then came sky . . . and earth.

And on this earth? A mighty hand went to work.

Canyons were carved. Oceans were dug. Mountains erupted out of flatlands. Stars were flung. A universe sparkled.

Our sun became just one of millions. Our galaxy became just one of thousands. Planets invisibly tethered to suns roared through space at breakneck speeds. Stars blazed with heat that could melt our planet in seconds.

The hand behind it was mighty. He is mighty.

And with this might, he created. As naturally as a bird sings and a fish swims, he created. Just as an artist can't not paint and a runner can't not run, he couldn't not create. He was the Creator. Through and through, he was the Creator. A tireless dreamer and designer.

From the pallet of the Ageless Artist came inimitable splendors. Before there was a person to see it, his creation was pregnant with wonder. Flowers didn't just grow; they blossomed. Chicks weren't just born; they hatched. Salmons didn't just swim; they leaped.

Mundaneness found no home in his universe.

He must have loved it. Creators relish creating. I'm sure his commands were delightful! "Hippo, you won't walk . . . you'll waddle!" "Hyena, a bark is too plain. Let me show you how to laugh!" "Look, raccoon, I've made you a mask!" "Come here, giraffe, let's stretch that neck a bit." And on and on he went. Giving the clouds their puff. Giving the oceans their blue. Giving the trees their sway. Giving the frogs their leap and croak. The mighty wed with the creative, and creation was born.

He was mighty. He was creative.

And he was love. Even greater than his might and deeper than his creativity was one all-consuming characteristic:

Love.

Water must be wet. A fire must be hot. You can't take the wet out of water and still have water. You can't take the heat out of fire and still have fire.

In the same way, you can't take the love out of this One who lived before time and still have him exist. For he was . . . and is . . . Love.

Probe deep within him. Explore every corner. Search every angle. Love is all you find. Go to the beginning of every decision he has made and you'll find it. Go to the end of every story he has told and you'll see it.

Love.

No bitterness. No evil. No cruelty. Just love. Flawless love. Passionate love. Vast and pure love. He is love.

As a result, an elephant has a trunk with which to drink. A kitten has a mother from which to nurse. A bird has a nest in which to sleep. The same God who was mighty enough to carve out the canyon is tender enough to put hair on the legs of the Matterhorn fly to keep it warm. The same force that provides symmetry to the planets guides the baby kangaroo to its mother's pouch before the mother knows it is born.

And because of who he was, he did what he did.

He created a paradise. A sinless sanctuary. A haven before fear. A home before there was a human dweller. No time. No death. No hurt. A gift built by God for his ultimate creation. And when he was through, he knew "it was very good."[6]

But it wasn't enough.

His greatest work hadn't been completed. One final masterpiece was needed before he would stop.

Look to the canyons to see the Creator's splendor. Touch the flowers and see his delicacy. Listen to the thunder and hear his power. But gaze on this—the zenith—and witness all three . . . and more.

Imagine with me what may have taken place on that day.

He placed one scoop of clay upon another until a form lay lifeless on the ground.

All of the garden's inhabitants paused to witness the event. Hawks hovered. Giraffes stretched. Trees bowed. Butterflies paused on petals and watched.

"You will love me, nature," God said. "I made you that way. You will obey me, universe. For you were designed to do so. You will reflect my glory, skies, for that is how you were created. But this one will be like me. This one will be able to choose."

All were silent as the Creator reached into himself and removed something yet unseen. A seed. "It's called 'choice.' The seed of choice."

Creation stood in silence and gazed upon the lifeless form.

An angel spoke, "But what if he . . ."

"What if he chooses not to love?" the Creator finished. "Come, I will show you."

Unbound by today, God and the angel walked into the realm of tomorrow.

"There, see the fruit of the seed of choice, both the sweet and the bitter."

The angel gasped at what he saw. Spontaneous love. Voluntary devotion. Chosen tenderness. Never had he seen anything like these. He felt the love of the Adams. He heard the joy of Eve and her daughters. He saw the food and the burdens shared. He absorbed the kindness and marveled at the warmth.

"Heaven has never seen such beauty, my Lord. Truly, this is your greatest creation."

"Ah, but you've only seen the sweet. Now witness the bitter."

A stench enveloped the pair. The angel turned in horror and proclaimed, "What is it?"

The Creator spoke only one word: "Selfishness."

The angel stood speechless as they passed through centuries of repugnance. Never had he seen such filth. Rotten hearts. Ruptured promises. Forgotten loyalties. Children of the creation wandering blindly in lonely labyrinths.

"This is the result of choice?" the angel asked.

"Yes."

"They will forget you?"

"Yes."

"They will reject you?"

"Yes."

"They will never come back?"

"Some will. Most won't."

"What will it take to make them listen?"

The Creator walked on in time, further and further into the future, until he stood by a tree. A tree that would be fashioned into a cradle. Even then he could smell the hay that would surround him.

With another step into the future, he paused before another tree. It stood alone, a stubborn ruler of a bald hill. The trunk was thick, and the wood was strong. Soon it would be cut. Soon it would be trimmed. Soon it would be mounted on the stony brow of another hill. And soon he would be hung on it.

He felt the wood rub against a back he did not yet wear.

"Will you go down there?" the angel asked.

"I will."

"Is there no other way?"

"There is not."

"Wouldn't it be easier to not plant the seed? Wouldn't it be easier to not give the choice?"

"It would," the Creator spoke slowly. "But to remove the choice is to remove the love."

He looked around the hill and foresaw a scene. Three figures hung on three crosses. Arms spread. Heads fallen forward. They moaned with the wind.

Men clad in soldiers' garb sat on the ground near the trio. They played games in the dirt and laughed.

Men clad in religion stood off to one side. They smiled. Arrogant, cocky. They had protected God, they thought, by killing this false one.

Women clad in sorrow huddled at the foot of the hill. Speechless. Faces tear streaked. Eyes downward. One put her arm around another and tried to lead her away. She wouldn't leave. "I will stay," she said softly. "I will stay."

All heaven stood to fight. All nature rose to rescue. All eternity poised to protect. But the Creator gave no command.

"It must be done . . . ," he said, and withdrew.

But as he stepped back in time, he heard the cry that he would someday scream: "My God, my God, why have you forsaken me?"[7] He wrenched at tomorrow's agony.

The angel spoke again. "It would be less painful . . ."

The Creator interrupted softly. "But it wouldn't be love."

They stepped into the garden again. The Maker looked earnestly at the clay creation. A monsoon of love swelled up within him. He had died for the creation before he had made him. God's form bent over the sculptured face and breathed. Dust stirred on the lips of the new one. The chest rose, cracking the red mud. The cheeks fleshened. A finger moved. And an eye opened.

But more incredible than the moving of the flesh was the stirring of the spirit. Those who could see the unseen gasped.

Perhaps it was the wind who said it first. Perhaps what the star saw that moment is what has made it blink ever since. Maybe it was left to an angel to whisper it:

"It looks like . . . it appears so much like . . . it is him!"

The angel wasn't speaking of the face, the features, or the body. He was looking inside—at the soul.

"It's eternal!" gasped another.

Within the man, God had placed a divine seed. A seed of his self. The God of might had created earth's mightiest. The Creator had created, not a creature, but another creator. And the One who had chosen to love had created one who could love in return.

Now it's our choice.

—In the Eye of the Storm

$\mathcal{T}$he town may have been common, but his attention to it was not. The city of Nazareth sits on a summit. Certainly no Nazarene boy could resist an occasional hike to the crest to look out over the valley beneath. Sitting six hundred feet above the level of the sea, the young Jesus could examine this world he had made. Mountain flowers in the spring. Cool sunsets. Pelicans winging their way along the streams of Kishon to the Sea of Galilee. Thyme-besprinkled turf at his feet. Fields and fig trees in the distance. Do you suppose moments here inspired these words later? "Observe how the lilies of the field grow" (Matt. 6:28 NASB) or "Look at the birds of the air" (Matt. 6:26 NASB). The words of Jesus the rabbi were born in the thoughts of Jesus the boy.

—Next Door Savior

$\mathcal{H}$e looked around the carpentry shop. He stood a moment in the refuge of the little room that housed so many sweet memories. He balanced the hammer in his hand. He ran his fingers across the sharp teeth of the saw.

He stroked the smoothly worn wood of the sawhorse. He had come to say good-bye.

It was time for him to leave. He had heard something that made him know it was time to go. So he came one last time to smell the sawdust and lumber. . . .

You can almost see the tools of the trade in his words as he spoke. You can see the trueness of a plumb line as he called for moral standards. You can hear the whistle of the plane as he pleads for religion to shave away unnecessary traditions. You can picture the snugness of a dovetail as he demands loyalty in relationships. You can imagine him with a pencil and a ledger as he urges honesty.

It was here that his human hands shaped the wood his divine hands had created.

—God Came Near

*J*esus and the disciples are in a boat crossing the Sea of Galilee. A storm arises suddenly, and what was placid becomes violent—monstrous waves rise out of the sea and slap the boat. Mark described it clearly: "A furious squall came up, and the waves broke over the boat, so that it was nearly swamped" (Mark 4:37 NIV).

It's very important that you get an accurate picture, so I'm going to ask you to imagine yourself in the boat. It's a sturdy vessel but no match for these ten-foot waves. It plunges nose first into the wall of water. The force of the waves dangerously tips the boat until the bow seems to be pointing straight at the sky, and just when you fear flipping over backward, the vessel pitches forward into the valley of another wave. A dozen sets of hands join yours in clutching the mast. All your shipmates have wet heads and wide eyes. You tune your ear for a calming voice, but all you hear are screams and prayers. All of a sudden it hits you—someone is missing.

Where is Jesus? He's not at the mast. He's not grabbing the edge. Where is he? Then you hear something—a noise . . . a displaced sound . . . like someone is snoring. You turn and look, and there curled in the stern of the boat is Jesus, sleeping!

You don't know whether to be amazed or angry, so you're both. How can he sleep at a time like this? Or as the disciples asked, "Teacher, don't you care if we drown?" (Mark 4:38 NIV).

If you're a parent of a teenager, you've been asked similar questions. The time you refused to mortgage your house so your daughter could buy the latest style tennis shoes, she asked, "Don't you care if I look out-of-date?"

When you insisted that your son skip the weekend game and attend his grandparents' golden anniversary, he asked, "Don't you care if I have a social life?"

When you limited the ear piercing to one hole per lobe, the accusation came thinly veiled as a question, "Don't you care if I fit in?"

Do the parents care? Of course they do. It's just that they have a different perspective. What the teenager sees as a storm, mom and dad see as a spring shower. They've been around enough to know these things pass.

So had Jesus. The very storm that made the disciples panic made him drowsy. What put fear in their eyes put him to sleep. The boat was a tomb to the followers and a cradle to Christ. How could he sleep through the storm? Simple, he was in charge of it.

The same happens with you and televisions. Ever doze off with the TV on? Of course you have. But put the same television in the grass hut of a primitive Amazonian Indian who has never seen one and, believe me, he won't sleep. How could anyone sleep in the presence of a talking box! As far as he knows, those little people behind the glass wall might climb out of the box and come after him. There is no way he's going to sleep. And there is no way he's going to let you sleep either. If you doze off, he'll wake you up. Don't you care that we're about to be massacred? Rather than argue with him, what do you do? You just point the remote at the screen and turn it off.

Jesus didn't even need a remote. "He got up, rebuked the wind and said to the waves, 'Quiet! Be still!' Then the wind died down, and it was completely calm. He said to his disciples, 'Why are you so afraid? Do you still have no faith?'" (Mark 4:39–40 NIV).

Incredible. He doesn't chant a mantra or wave a wand. No angels are called; no help is needed. The raging water becomes a stilled sea, instantly. Immediate calm. Not a ripple. Not a drop. Not a gust. In a moment the sea goes from a churning torrent to a peaceful pond. The reaction of the disciples? Read it in verse 41: "They were in absolute awe, staggered. 'Who is this, anyway?' they asked. 'Wind and sea at his beck and call!'" (MSG).

They'd never met a man like this. The waves were his subjects, and the winds were his servants. And that was just the beginning of what his sea mates would witness. Before it was over, they would see fish jump into the boat, demons dive into pigs, cripples turn into

dancers, and cadavers turn into living, breathing people. "He even gives orders to evil spirits and they obey him," the people proclaimed (Mark 1:27 NIV).

Is it any wonder the disciples were willing to die for Jesus? Never had they seen such power, never had they seen such glory. It was like, well, like the whole universe was his kingdom. You wouldn't have needed to explain this verse to them; they knew what it meant: "Thine is the kingdom and the power and the glory forever."

In fact, it was two of these rescued fishermen who would declare his authority most clearly. Listen to John: "Greater is he that is in you, than he that is in the world" (1 John 4:4 KJV). Listen to Peter: "Jesus has gone into heaven and is at God's right side ruling over angels, authorities, and powers" (1 Pet. 3:22 NCV).

It's only right that they declare his authority. And it's only right that we do the same. And that is exactly what this phrase is, a declaration. A declaration of the heart. A declaration God deserves to hear. Doesn't he? Doesn't he deserve to hear us proclaim his authority? Isn't it right for us to shout from the bottom of our hearts and at the top of our voice, "Thine is the kingdom and the power and the glory forever!" Isn't it right for us to stare at these mountain peaks of God and worship him?

Of course it is. Not only does God deserve to hear our praise, but we also need to give it.

—The Great House of God

*O*n earth, Jesus was an artist in a gallery of his own paintings. He was a composer listening as the orchestra interpreted his music. He was a poet hearing his own poetry. Yet his works of art had been defaced. Creation after battered creation.

He had created people for splendor. They had settled for mediocrity. He had formed them with love. They had scarred each other with hate.

When he saw businessmen using God-given intelligence to feed
    Satan-given greed . . .
When he saw tongues he had designed to encourage used as daggers
    to cut . . .
When he saw hands that had been given for holding used as
    weapons for hurting . . .
When he saw eyes into which he'd sprinkled joy now burning with
    hatred . . .

I wonder, did it weary him to see hearts that were stained, even discarded?

—Six Hours One Friday

*J*esus is presented with a man who is deaf and has a speech impediment. Perhaps he stammered. Maybe he spoke with a lisp. Perhaps, because of his deafness, he never learned to articulate words properly.

Jesus, refusing to exploit the situation, took the man aside. He looked him in the face. Knowing it would be useless to talk, he explained what he was about to do through gestures. He spat and touched the man's tongue, telling him that whatever restricted his speech was about to be removed. He touched his ears. They, for the first time, were about to hear.

But before the man said a word or heard a sound, Jesus did something I never would have anticipated.

He sighed.

I might have expected a clap or a song or a prayer. Even a "Hallelujah!" or a brief lesson might have been appropriate. But the Son of God did none of these. Instead, he paused, looked into heaven, and sighed. From the depths of his being came a rush of emotion that said more than words.

Sigh. The word seemed out of place.

I'd never thought of God as one who sighs. I'd thought of God as one who commands. I'd thought of God as one who weeps. I'd thought of God as one who called forth the dead with a command or created the universe with a word . . . but a God who sighs? . . .

Man was not created to be separated from his creator; hence he sighs, longing for home. The creation was never intended to be inhabited by evil; hence she sighs, yearning for the Garden. And conversations with God were never intended to depend on a translator; hence the Spirit groans on our behalf, looking to a day when humans will see God face to face.

And when Jesus looked into the eyes of Satan's victim, the only appropriate thing to do was sigh. "It was never intended to be this way," the sigh said. "Your ears weren't made to be deaf, your tongue wasn't made to stumble." The imbalance of it all caused the Master to languish.

So, I found a place for the word. You might think it strange, but I placed it beside the word *comfort*, for in an indirect way, God's pain is our comfort.

And in the agony of Jesus lies our hope. Had he not sighed, had he not felt the burden for what was not intended, we would be in a pitiful condition. Had he simply chalked it all up to the inevitable or washed his hands of the whole stinking mess, what hope would we have?

But he didn't. That holy sigh assures us that God still groans for his people. He groans for the day when all sighs will cease, when what was intended to be will be.

—God Came Near

*Y*ou wonder, *I believe in God. Is he aware? Does he care?*

Deism says no. God created the universe and then abandoned it.

Pantheism says no. Creation has no story or purpose unto itself; it is only a part of God.

Atheism says no. Not surprisingly, the philosophy that dismisses the existence of a god will, in turn, dismiss the possibility of a divine plan.

Christianity, on the other hand, says, "Yes, there is a God. Yes, this God is personally and powerfully involved in his creation."

"The Son is the radiance of God's glory and the exact representation of his being, sustaining all things by his powerful word" (Heb. 1:3 NIV). The Greek word that is translated "sustaining" is a term commonly used in the New Testament for "carrying" or "bringing."[8] The friends carried the paralyzed man to Jesus, and the servants brought wine to the master of the wedding. They "sustained" the man and the wine (Luke 5:18; John 2:8). They guaranteed the safe delivery.

To say Jesus is "sustaining all things by his powerful word" is to say he is directing creation toward a desired aim. The use of the present participle implies that Jesus is continually active in his creation. He exercises supremacy over all things.

Distant? Removed? Not God. "He is before all things, and in him all things hold together" (Col. 1:17 NIV). Were he to step back, the creation would collapse. His resignation would spell our evaporation. "For in him we live and move and have our being" (Acts 17:28 NIV).

Because of him, the water stays wet and the rocks remain firm. The laws of gravity and thermodynamics don't change from generation to generation. With his hand at the helm of creation, spring still follows winter, and winter follows autumn. There is an order to the universe. He sustains everything.

And this is crucial: he uses everything to accomplish his will. He "works out everything in conformity with the purpose of his will" (Eph. 1:11 NIV). The phrase "works out" comes from the Greek word *energeō*.[9] God is the energy and energizing force behind everything. No moment, event, or detail falls outside of his supervision. He stands before the universe like a symphony conductor before the orchestra, calling forth the elements to play their part in the divine reprise.

> He makes grass grow for the cattle,
> and plants for people to cultivate—
> bringing forth food from the earth:
> wine that gladdens human hearts,
> oil to make their faces shine,
> and bread that sustains their hearts. (Ps. 104:14–15 NIV)

God is the one who "causes his sun to rise on the evil and the good, and sends rain on the righteous and the unrighteous" (Matt. 5:45 NIV). God is the one who feeds the birds and watches the sparrows (Matt. 6:26; 10:29). God is the one in charge of everything, even the details of our lives.

He isn't making up this plan as he goes along. And he didn't wind up the clock and walk away. "The Most High God rules the kingdom of men, and sets over it whom he will" (Dan. 5:21 RSV). He "executes judgment, putting down one and lifting up another" (Ps. 75:7 NRSV). "The fierce anger of the LORD will not turn back until he has executed and accomplished the intents of his mind" (Jer. 30:24 NRSV).

Such starchy verbs: God "rules," "sets," "executes," "accomplished." These terms attest to the existence of a heavenly Architect and blueprint, and his blueprint includes you.

—Anxious for Nothing

2

Immanuel

$\mathcal{G}$abriel must have scratched his head at this one.

He wasn't one to question his God-given missions. Sending fire and dividing seas were all in an eternity's work for this angel. When God sent, Gabriel went.

And when word got out that God was to become man, Gabriel was enthused. He could envision the moment:

The Messiah in a blazing chariot.
The King descending on a fiery cloud.
An explosion of light from which the Messiah would emerge.

That's what he expected. What he never expected, however, was what he got: a slip of paper with a Nazarene address. "God will become a baby," it read. "Tell the mother to name the child Jesus. And tell her not to be afraid."

Gabriel was never one to question, but this time he had to wonder.

God will become a baby? Gabriel had seen babies before. He had been platoon leader on the bulrush operation. He remembered what little Moses looked like.

That's okay for humans, he thought to himself. *But God?*

The heavens can't contain him; how could a body? Besides, have you seen what comes out of those babies? Hardly befitting for the Creator of the universe. Babies must be carried and fed, bounced and bathed. To imagine some mother burping God on her shoulder—why, that was beyond what even an angel could imagine.

And what of this name—what was it—*Jesus?* Such a common name. There's a Jesus in every cul-de-sac. Come on, even *Gabriel* has more punch to it than Jesus. Call the baby *Eminence* or *Majesty* or *Heaven-sent.* Anything but *Jesus.*

So Gabriel scratched his head. What happened to the good ol' days? The Sodom and Gomorrah stuff. Flooding the globe. Flaming swords. That's the action he liked.

But Gabriel had his orders. Take the message to Mary. *Must be a special girl,* he assumed as he traveled. But Gabriel was in for another shock. One peek told him Mary was no queen. The mother-to-be of God was not regal. She was a Jewish peasant who'd barely outgrown her acne and had a crush on a guy named Joe.

And speaking of Joe—what does this fellow know? Might as well be a weaver in Spain or a cobbler in Greece. He's a carpenter. Look at him over there, sawdust in his beard and nail apron around his waist. You're telling me God is going to have dinner every night with him? You're telling me the source of wisdom is going to call this guy "Dad"? You're telling me a common laborer is going to be charged with giving food to God?

What if he gets laid off?

What if he gets cranky?

What if he decides to run off with a pretty young girl from down the street? Then where will we be?

It was all Gabriel could do to keep from turning back.

"This is a peculiar idea you have, God," he must have muttered to himself.

—When God Whispers Your Name

The noise and the bustle began earlier than usual in the village. As night gave way to dawn, people were already on the streets. Vendors were positioning themselves on the corners of the most heavily traveled avenues. Store owners were unlocking the doors to their shops. Children were awakened by the excited barking of the street dogs and the complaints of donkeys pulling carts.

The owner of the inn had awakened earlier than most in the town. After all, the inn was full, all the beds taken. Every available mat or blanket had been put to use. Soon all the customers would be stirring and there would be a lot of work to do.

One's imagination is kindled thinking about the conversation of the innkeeper and his family at the breakfast table. Did anyone mention the arrival of the young couple the night before? Did anyone ask about their welfare? Did anyone comment on the pregnancy of the girl on the donkey? Perhaps. Perhaps someone raised the subject. But, at best, it was raised, not discussed. There was nothing that novel about them. They were, possibly, one of several families turned away that night.

Besides, who had time to talk about them when there was so much excitement in the air? Augustus did the economy of Bethlehem a favor when he decreed that a census should be taken. Who could remember when such commerce had hit the village?

No, it is doubtful that anyone mentioned the couple's arrival or wondered about the condition of the girl. They were too busy. The day was upon them. The day's bread had to be made. The morning's chores had to be done. There was too much to do to imagine that the impossible had occurred.

God had entered the world as a baby.

Yet, were someone to chance upon the sheep stable on the outskirts of Bethlehem that morning, what a peculiar scene they would behold.

The stable stinks like all stables do. The stench of urine, dung, and sheep reeks pungently in the air. The ground is hard, the hay scarce. Cobwebs cling to the ceiling and a mouse scurries across the dirt floor.

A more lowly place of birth could not exist.

Off to one side sit a group of shepherds. They sit silently on the floor; perhaps perplexed, perhaps in awe, no doubt in amazement. Their night watch had been interrupted by an explosion of light from heaven and a symphony of angels. God goes to those who have time to hear him—so on this cloudless night he went to simple shepherds.

Near the young mother sits the weary father. If anyone is dozing, he is. He can't remember the last time he sat down. And now that the excitement has subsided a bit, now that Mary and the baby are comfortable, he leans against the wall of the stable and feels his eyes grow heavy. He still hasn't figured it all out. The mystery of the event puzzles him. But he hasn't the energy to wrestle with the questions. What's important is that the baby is fine and that Mary is safe. As sleep comes, he remembers the name the angel told him to use . . . Jesus. "We will call him Jesus."

Wide awake is Mary. My, how young she looks! Her head rests on the soft leather of Joseph's saddle. The pain has been eclipsed by wonder. She looks into the face of the baby. Her son. Her Lord. His Majesty. At this point in history, the human being who best understands who God is and what he is doing is a teenage girl in a smelly stable. She can't take her eyes off him. Somehow Mary knows she is holding God. So this is he. She remembers the words of the angel. "His kingdom will never end."[1]

He looks like anything but a king. His face is prunish and red. His cry, though strong and healthy, is still the helpless and piercing cry of a baby. And he is absolutely dependent upon Mary for his well-being.

Majesty in the midst of the mundane. Holiness in the filth of sheep manure and sweat. Divinity entering the world on the floor of a stable, through the womb of a teenager and in the presence of a carpenter.

She touches the face of the infant-God. How long was your journey!

This baby had overlooked the universe. These rags keeping him warm were the robes of eternity. His golden throne room had been abandoned in favor of a dirty sheep pen. And worshiping angels had been replaced with kind but bewildered shepherds.

Meanwhile, the city hums. The merchants are unaware that God has visited their planet. The innkeeper would never believe that he had just sent God into the cold. And the people would scoff at anyone who told them the Messiah lay in the arms of a teenager on the outskirts of their village. They were all too busy to consider the possibility.

Those who missed His Majesty's arrival that night missed it not because of evil acts or malice; no, they missed it because they simply weren't looking.

Little has changed in the last two thousand years, has it?

—God Came Near

*T*here is one word that describes the night he came—ordinary.

The sky was ordinary. An occasional gust stirred the leaves and chilled the air. The stars were diamonds sparkling on black velvet. Fleets of clouds floated in front of the moon.

It was a beautiful night—a night worth peeking out your bedroom window to admire—but not really an unusual one. No reason to expect a surprise. Nothing to keep a person awake. An ordinary night with an ordinary sky.

The sheep were ordinary. Some fat. Some scrawny. Some with barrel bellies. Some with twig legs. Common animals. No fleece made of gold. No history makers. No blue-ribbon winners. They were simply sheep—lumpy, sleeping silhouettes on a hillside.

And the shepherds. Peasants they were. Probably wearing all the clothes they owned. Smelling like sheep and looking just as woolly. They were conscientious, willing to spend the night with their flocks. But you won't find their staffs in a museum nor their writings in a library. No one asked their opinion on social justice or the application of the Torah. They were nameless and simple.

An ordinary night with ordinary sheep and ordinary shepherds. And were it not for a God who loves to hook an "extra" on the front of the ordinary, the night would have gone unnoticed. The sheep would have been forgotten, and the shepherds would have slept the night away.

But God dances amidst the common. And that night he did a waltz.

The black sky exploded with brightness. Trees that had been shadows jumped into clarity. Sheep that had been silent became a chorus of curiosity. One minute the shepherd was dead asleep, the next he was rubbing his eyes and staring into the face of an alien.

The night was ordinary no more.

The angel came in the night because that is when lights are best seen and that is when they are most needed. God comes into the common for the same reason.

His most powerful tools are the simplest.

—The Applause of Heaven

*P*eople have always wondered about the image of God. Societies have speculated. Tribes have cogitated. And we've reached a variety of conclusions. God has been depicted as a golden calf and a violent wind and an angry volcano. He wears wings, breathes fire, eats infants, and demands penance. We've fancied God as ferocious, magical, fickle, and maniacal. A god to be avoided, dreaded, and appeased. But never in mankind's wildest imaginings did we consider that God would enter the world as an infant.

"The Word became flesh and dwelt among us" (John 1:14 NKJV). The Word became not a whirlwind or a devouring fire but a single cell, a fertilized egg, an embryo—a baby. Placenta nourished him. An amniotic sac surrounded him. He grew to the size of a fist. His tiny heart divided into chambers. God became flesh.

Jesus entered our world not *like* a human but *as* a human. He endured puberty, pimples, hot weather, and cranky neighbors. God became human down to his very toes. He had suspended the stars and ladled out the seas, yet he suckled a breast and slept in hay. . . .

Why such a journey? Why did God go so far?

A chief reason is this: he wants you to know that he gets you. He understands how you feel and has faced what you face. Jesus is not "out of touch with our reality. He's been through weakness and testing, experienced it all—all but the sin. So let's walk right up to him and get what he is so ready to give. Take the mercy, accept the help" (Heb. 4:15–16 MSG).

Since you know he understands, you can boldly go to him. Because of Bethlehem's miracle, you can answer these fundamental questions: Does God care if I'm sad? Look at the tear-streaked face of Jesus as he stands near Lazarus's tomb. Does God notice when I'm afraid? Note the resolve in the eyes of Jesus as he marches through the storm to rescue his friends. Does God know if I am ignored or rejected? Find the answer in the compassionate eyes of Christ as he stands to defend the adulterous woman.[2]

"[Jesus] radiates God's own glory and expresses the very character of God" (Heb. 1:3 NLT). Jesus himself stated, "Anyone who has seen me has seen the Father" (John 14:9 NIV).

"Anyone who has seen me weep has seen the Father weep."

"Anyone who has seen me laugh has seen the Father laugh."

"Anyone who has seen me determined has seen the Father determined."

Would you like to see God? Take a look at Jesus.

—*Because of Bethlehem*

*I*mmanuel. The name appears in the same Hebrew form as it did two thousand years ago. "Immanu" means "with us." "El" refers to Elohim, or God. Not an "above us God" or a "somewhere in the neighborhood God." He came as the "with us God." God with us.

Not "God with the rich" or "God with the religious." But God with *us*. All of us. Russians, Germans, Buddhists, Mormons, truckdrivers and taxi drivers, librarians. God with *us*.

God *with* us. Don't we love the word "with"? "Will you go *with* me?" we ask. "To the store, to the hospital, through my life?" God says he will. "I am *with* you always," Jesus said before he ascended to heaven, "to the very end of the age" (Matt. 28:20 NIV). Search for restrictions on the promise; you'll find none. You won't find "I'll be with you if you behave . . . when you believe. I'll be with you on Sundays in worship . . . at mass." No, none of that. There's no withholding tax on God's "with" promise. He is *with* us.

God is with us.

Prophets weren't enough. Apostles wouldn't do. Angels won't suffice. God sent more than miracles and messages. He sent himself; he sent his Son. "The Word became flesh and dwelt among us" (John 1:14 NKJV). . . .

For thousands of years, God gave us his voice. Prior to Bethlehem, he gave his messengers, his teachers, his words. But in the manger, God gave us himself.

Many people have trouble with such a teaching. Islam sees God as one who sends others. He sends angels, prophets, books, but God is too holy to come to us himself. For God to touch the earth would be called a "shirk."[3] People who claim that God has touched the earth shirk God's holiness; they make him gross. They blaspheme him.

Christianity, by contrast, celebrates God's surprising descent. His nature does not trap him in heaven, but leads him to earth. In God's great gospel, he not only sends, he becomes; he not only looks down, he lives among; he not only talks to us, he lives with us as one of us.

He swims in Mary's womb.
Wiggles in the itchy manger straw.
Totters as he learns to walk.
Bounces on the back of a donkey.
God with us.

—Cure for the Common Life

*H*oliday travel. It isn't easy. Then why do we do it? Why cram the trunks and endure the airports? You know the answer. We love to be with the ones we love.

The four-year-old running up the sidewalk into the arms of Grandpa.

The cup of coffee with Mom before the rest of the house awakes.

That moment when, for a moment, everyone is quiet as we hold hands around the table and thank God for family and friends and pumpkin pie.

We love to be with the ones we love.

May I remind you? So does God. He loves to be with the ones he loves. How else do you explain what he did? Between him and us there was a distance—a great span. And he couldn't bear it. He couldn't stand it. So he did something about it.

Before coming to the earth, "Christ himself was like God in everything. . . . But he gave up his place with God and made himself nothing. He was born to be a man and became like a servant" (Phil. 2:6–7 NCV).

Why? Why did Jesus travel so far?

I was asking myself that question when I spotted the squirrels outside my window. A family of black-tailed squirrels has made its home amid the roots of the tree north of my office. We've been neighbors for three years now. They watch me peck the keyboard. I watch them store their nuts and climb the trunk. We're mutually amused. I could watch them all day. Sometimes I do.

But I've never considered becoming one of them. The squirrel world holds no appeal to me. Who wants to sleep next to a hairy rodent with beady eyes? (No comments from you wives who feel you already do.) Give up the Rocky Mountains, bass fishing, weddings, and laughter for a hole in the ground and a diet of dirty nuts? Count me out.

But count Jesus in. What a world he left. Our classiest mansion would be a tree trunk to him. Earth's finest cuisine would be walnuts on heaven's table. And the idea of becoming a squirrel with claws and tiny teeth and a furry tail? It's nothing compared to God becoming an embryo and entering the womb of Mary.

But he did. The God of the universe kicked against the wall of a womb, was born into the poverty of a peasant, and spent his first night in the feed trough of a cow. "The Word became flesh and lived among us" (John 1:14 NRSV). The God of the universe left the glory of heaven and moved into the neighborhood. Our neighborhood! Who could have imagined he would do such a thing.

Why? He loves to be with the ones he loves.

—*Next Door Savior*

"*C*hrist the Incarnate One." The One who made everything "made himself nothing." Christ made himself small. He made himself dependent upon lungs, a larynx, and legs. He experienced hunger and thirst. He went through all the normal stages of human development. He was taught to walk, stand, wash his face, and dress himself. His muscles grew stronger; his hair grew longer. His voice cracked when he passed through puberty. He was genuinely human.

When he was "full of joy" (Luke 10:21 NIV), his joy was authentic. When he wept for Jerusalem (Luke 19:41), his tears were as real as yours or mine. When he asked, "How long must I put up with you?"

(Matt. 17:17 NLT), his frustration was honest. When he cried out from the cross, "My God, my God, why have you forsaken me?" (Matt. 27:46 NIV), he needed an answer. He knew only what the Father revealed to him (John 12:50). If the Father did not give direction, Jesus did not claim to have it.

He took "the very nature of a servant" (Phil. 2:7 NIV). He became like us so he could serve us! He entered the world not to demand our allegiance but to display his affection.

—Because of Bethlehem

It all happened in a moment, a most remarkable moment. As moments go, that one appeared no different than any other. If you could somehow pick it up off the timeline and examine it, it would look exactly like the ones that have passed while you have read these words. It came and it went. It was preceded and succeeded by others just like it. It was one of the countless moments that have marked time since eternity became measurable.

But in reality, that particular moment was like none other. For through that segment of time a spectacular thing occurred. God became a man. While the creatures of earth walked unaware, Divinity arrived. Heaven opened herself and placed her most precious one in a human womb.

The omnipotent, in one instant, made himself breakable. He who had been spirit became pierceable. He who was larger than the universe became an embryo. And he who sustains the world with a word chose to be dependent upon the nourishment of a young girl.

God as a fetus. Holiness sleeping in a womb. The creator of life being created.

God was given eyebrows, elbows, two kidneys, and a spleen. He stretched against the walls and floated in the amniotic fluids of his mother.

God had come near.

He came, not as a flash of light or as an unapproachable conqueror, but as one whose first cries were heard by a peasant girl and a sleepy carpenter. The hands that first held him were unmanicured, calloused, and dirty.

No silk. No ivory. No hype. No party. No hoopla.

Were it not for the shepherds, there would have been no reception. And were it not for a group of star-gazers, there would have been no gifts.

Angels watched as Mary changed God's diaper. The universe watched with wonder as The Almighty learned to walk. Children played in the street with him. And had the synagogue leader in Nazareth known who was listening to his sermons . . .

Jesus may have had pimples. He may have been tone-deaf. Perhaps a girl down the street had a crush on him or vice-versa. It could be that his knees were bony. One thing's for sure: he was, while completely divine, completely human.

For thirty-three years he would feel everything you and I have ever felt. He felt weak. He grew weary. He was afraid of failure. He was susceptible to wooing women. He got colds, burped, and had body odor. His feelings got hurt. His feet got tired. And his head ached.

To think of Jesus in such a light is—well, it seems almost irreverent, doesn't it? It's not something we like to do; it's uncomfortable. It is much easier to keep the humanity out of the incarnation. Clean the manure from around the manger. Wipe the sweat out of his eyes. Pretend he never snored or blew his nose or hit his thumb with a hammer.

He's easier to stomach that way. There is something about keeping him divine that keeps him distant, packaged, predictable.

But don't do it. For heaven's sake, don't. Let him be as human as he intended to be. Let him into the mire and muck of our world. For only if we let him in can he pull us out.

Listen to him.

"Love your neighbor" was spoken by a man whose neighbors tried to kill him.[4]

The challenge to leave family for the gospel was issued by one who kissed his mother good-bye in the doorway.[5]

"Pray for those who persecute you" came from the lips that would soon be begging God to forgive his murderers.[6]

"I am with you always" are the words of a God who in one instant did the impossible to make it all possible for you and me.[7]

It all happened in a moment. In one moment . . . a most remarkable moment. The Word became flesh.

There will be another. The world will see another instantaneous transformation. You see, in becoming man, God made it possible for man to see God. When Jesus went home he left the back door open. As a result, "we shall all be changed—in a moment, in the twinkling of an eye."[8]

The first moment of transformation went unnoticed by the world. But you can bet your sweet September that the second one won't. The next time you use the phrase "just a moment, . . ." remember that's all the time it will take to change this world.

—*God Came Near*

*Y*ou know the coolest thing about the coming of Christ? You know the most remarkable part of the incarnation?

Not just that he swapped eternity for calendars. Though such an exchange deserves our notice.

Scripture says that the number of God's years is unsearchable (Job 36:26 NCV). We may search out the moment the first wave slapped on a shore or the first star burst in the sky, but we'll never find the first moment when God was God, for there is no moment when God was not God. He has never not been, for he is eternal. God is not bound by time.

But when Jesus came to the earth, all this changed. He heard for the first time a phrase never used in heaven: "Your time is up." As a child, he had to leave the Temple because his time was up. As a man, he had to leave Nazareth because his time was up. And as a Savior, he had to die because his time was up. For thirty-three years, the stallion of heaven lived in the corral of time.

That's certainly remarkable, but there is something even more so.

You want to see the brightest jewel in the treasure of incarnation? You might think it was the fact that he lived in a body. One moment he was a boundless spirit; the next he was flesh and bones. Remember these words of King David? "Where can I go to get away from your Spirit? Where can I run from you? If I go up to the heavens, you are there. If I lie down in the grave, you are there. If I rise with the sun in the east and settle in the west beyond the sea, even there you would guide me" (Ps. 139:7–10 NCV).

Our asking "Where is God?" is like a fish asking "Where is water?" or a bird asking "Where is air?" God is everywhere! Equally present in Peking and Peoria. As active in the lives of Icelanders as in the lives of Texans. The dominion of God is "from sea to sea and from the River to the ends of the earth" (Ps. 72:8 NIV). We cannot find a place where God is not.

Yet when God entered time and became a man, he who was boundless became bound. Imprisoned in flesh. Restricted by weary-prone muscles and eyelids. For more than three decades, his once limitless reach would be limited to the stretch of an arm, his speed checked to the pace of human feet.

I wonder, was he ever tempted to reclaim his boundlessness? In the middle of a long trip, did he ever consider transporting himself to the next city? When the rain chilled his bones, was he tempted to change the weather? When the heat parched his lips, did he give thought to popping over to the Caribbean for some refreshment?

If ever he entertained such thoughts, he never gave in to them. Not once. Stop and think about this. Not once did Christ use his supernatural powers for personal comfort. With one word he could've transformed the hard earth into a soft bed, but he didn't. With a wave of his hand, he could've boomeranged the spit of his accusers back into their faces, but he didn't. With an arch of his brow, he could've paralyzed the hand of the soldier as he braided the crown of thorns. But he didn't.

Remarkable. But is this the most remarkable part of the coming? Many would argue not. Many, perhaps most, would point beyond the surrender of timelessness and boundlessness to the surrender of sinlessness. It's easy to see why.

Isn't this the message of the crown of thorns?

An unnamed soldier took branches—mature enough to bear thorns, nimble enough to bend—and wove them into a crown of mockery, a crown of thorns.

Throughout Scripture thorns symbolize, not sin, but the consequence of sin. Remember Eden? After Adam and Eve sinned, God cursed the land: "So I will put a curse on the ground. . . . The ground will produce thorns and weeds for you, and you will eat the plants of the field" (Gen. 3:17–18 NCV). Brambles on the earth are the product of sin in the heart.

This truth is echoed in God's words to Moses. He urged the Israelites to purge the land of godless people. Disobedience would result in difficulties. "But if you don't force those people out of the land, they will bring you trouble. They will be like sharp hooks in your eyes and thorns in your sides" (Num. 33:55 NCV).

Rebellion results in thorns. "Evil people's lives are like paths covered with thorns and traps" (Prov. 22:5 NCV). Jesus even compared the lives of evil people to a thornbush. In speaking of false prophets, he said, "You will know these people by what they do. Grapes don't come from thornbushes, and figs don't come from thorny weeds" (Matt. 7:16 NCV).

The fruit of sin is thorns—spiny, prickly, cutting thorns.

I emphasize the "point" of the thorns to suggest a point you may have never considered: If the fruit of sin is thorns, isn't the thorny crown on Christ's brow a picture of the fruit of our sin that pierced his heart?

What is the fruit of sin? Step into the briar patch of humanity and feel a few thistles. Shame. Fear. Disgrace. Discouragement. Anxiety. Haven't our hearts been caught in these brambles?

The heart of Jesus, however, had not. He had never been cut by the thorns of sin. What you and I face daily, he never knew. Anxiety? He never worried! Guilt? He was never guilty! Fear? He never left the presence of God! Jesus never knew the fruits of sin . . . until he became sin for us.

And when he did, all the emotions of sin tumbled in on him like shadows in a forest. He felt anxious, guilty, and alone. Can't you hear the emotion in his prayer? "My God, my God, why have you rejected me?" (Matt. 27:46 NCV). These are not the words of a saint. This is the cry of a sinner.

And this prayer is one of the most remarkable parts of his coming. But I can think of something even greater. Want to know what it is? Want to know the coolest thing about the coming?

Not that the One who played marbles with the stars gave it up to play marbles with marbles. Or that the One who hung the galaxies gave it up to hang doorjambs to the displeasure of a cranky client who wanted everything yesterday but couldn't pay for anything until tomorrow.

Not that he, in an instant, went from needing nothing to needing air, food, a tub of hot water and salts for his tired feet, and, more than anything, needing somebody—anybody—who was more concerned about where he would spend eternity than where he would spend Friday's paycheck.

Or that he resisted the urge to fry the two-bit, self-appointed hall monitors of holiness who dared suggest that he was doing the work of the devil.

Not that he kept his cool while the dozen best friends he ever had felt the heat and got out of the kitchen. Or that he gave no command to the angels who begged, "Just give the nod, Lord. One word and these demons will be deviled eggs."

Not that he refused to defend himself when blamed for every sin of every slut and sailor since Adam. Or that he stood silent as a million guilty verdicts echoed in the tribunal of heaven and the giver of light was left in the chill of a sinner's night.

Not even that after three days in a dark hole he stepped into the Easter sunrise with a smile and a swagger and a question for lowly Lucifer—"Is that your best punch?"

That was cool, incredibly cool.

But want to know the coolest thing about the One who gave up the crown of heaven for a crown of thorns?

He did it for you. Just for you.

—He Chose the Nails

3

Friend

*M*any of the names in the Bible that refer to our Lord are nothing less than palatial and august: Son of God, The Lamb of God, The Light of the World, The Resurrection and the Life, The Bright and Morning Star, He that Should Come, Alpha and Omega.

They are phrases that stretch the boundaries of human language in an effort to capture the uncapturable, the grandeur of God. And try as they might to draw as near as they may, they always fall short. Hearing them is somewhat like hearing a Salvation Army Christmas band on the street corner play Handel's *Messiah*. Good try, but it doesn't work. The message is too majestic for the medium.

And such it is with language. The phrase "There are no words to express . . ." is really the only one that can honestly be applied to God. No names do him justice.

But there is one name which recalls a quality of the Master that bewildered and compelled those who knew him. It reveals a side of him that, when recognized, is enough to make you fall on your face.

It is not too small, nor is it too grand. It is a name that fits like the shoe fit Cinderella's foot.

Jesus.

In the gospels it's his most common name—used almost six hundred times. And a common name it was. Jesus is the Greek form of Joshua, Jeshua, and Jehoshua—all familiar Old Testament names. There were at least five high priests known as Jesus. The writings of the historian Josephus refer to about twenty people called Jesus. The New Testament speaks of Jesus Justus, the friend of Paul,[1] and the sorcerer of Paphos is called Bar-Jesus.[2] Some manuscripts give Jesus as the first name of Barabbas. "Which would you like me to release to you—Jesus Barabbas or Jesus called the Messiah?"[3]

What's the point? Jesus could have been a "Joe." If Jesus came today, his name might have been John or Bob or Jim. Were he here today, it is doubtful he would distance himself with a lofty name like Reverend Holiness Angelic Divinity III. No, when God chose the name his son would carry, he chose a human name.[4] He chose a name so typical that it would appear two or three times on any given class roll.

"The Word became flesh," John said, in other words.

He was touchable, approachable, reachable. And, what's more, he was ordinary. If he were here today you probably wouldn't notice him as he walked through a shopping mall. He wouldn't turn heads by the clothes he wore or the jewelry he flashed.

"Just call me Jesus," you can almost hear him say.

He was the kind of fellow you'd invite to watch the Rams-Giants game at your house. He'd wrestle on the floor with your kids, doze on your couch, and cook steaks on your grill. He'd laugh at your jokes and tell a few of his own. And when you spoke, he'd listen to you as if he had all the time in eternity.

And one thing's for sure, you'd invite him back.

It is worth noting that those who knew him best remembered him as Jesus. The titles Jesus Christ and Lord Jesus are seen only six times. Those who walked with him remembered him not with a title or designation, but with a name—Jesus.

Think about the implications. When God chose to reveal himself to mankind, what medium did he use? A book? No, that was secondary.

A church? No. That was consequential. A moral code? No. To limit God's revelation to a cold list of dos and don'ts is as tragic as looking at a Colorado road map and saying that you'd seen the Rockies.

When God chose to reveal himself, he did so (surprise of surprises) through a human body. The tongue that called forth the dead was a human one. The hand that touched the leper had dirt under its nails. The feet upon which the woman wept were calloused and dusty. And his tears . . . oh, don't miss the tears . . . they came from a heart as broken as yours or mine ever has been.

"For we do not have a high priest who is unable to sympathize with our weaknesses."[5]

So, people came to him. My, how they came to him! They came at night; they touched him as he walked down the street; they followed him around the sea; they invited him into their homes and placed their children at his feet. Why? Because he refused to be a statue in a cathedral or a priest in an elevated pulpit. He chose instead to be Jesus.

There is not a hint of one person who was afraid to draw near him. There were those who mocked him. There were those who were envious of him. There were those who misunderstood him. There were those who revered him. But there was not one person who considered him too holy, too divine, or too celestial to touch. *There was not one person who was reluctant to approach him for fear of being rejected.*

Remember that. No reason to fear rejection

Remember that the next time you find yourself amazed at your own failures.

Or the next time acidic accusations burn holes in your soul.

Or the next time you see a cold cathedral or hear a lifeless liturgy.

Remember. It is man who creates the distance. It is Jesus who builds the bridge.

"Just call me Jesus."

—*God Came Near*

FRIEND ❧

*W*hy does Jesus endure thirst?

While we are asking this question, add a few more. Why did he grow weary in Samaria (John 4:6), disturbed in Nazareth (Mark 6:6), and angry in the Temple (John 2:15)? Why was he sleepy in the boat on the Sea of Galilee (Mark 4:38), sad at the tomb of Lazarus (John 11:35), and hungry in the wilderness (Matt. 4:2)? . . .

Why? Why did he endure all these feelings? Because he knew you would feel them too. He knew you would be weary, disturbed, and angry.

He knew you'd be sleepy, grief-stricken, and hungry. He knew you'd face pain. If not the pain of the body, the pain of the soul . . . pain too sharp for any drug. He knew you'd face thirst. If not a thirst for water, at least a thirst for truth, and the truth we glean from the image of a thirsty Christ is—he understands.

And because he understands, we can come to him.

Wouldn't his lack of understanding keep us from him? Doesn't the lack of understanding keep us from others? Suppose you were discouraged at your financial state. You need some guidance from a sympathetic friend. Would you go to the son of a zillionaire? (Remember, you're asking for guidance, not a handout.) Would you approach someone who inherited a fortune? Probably not. Why? He would not understand. He's likely never been where you are, so he can't relate to how you feel.

Jesus, however, has and can. He has been where you are and can relate to how you feel. And if his life on earth doesn't convince you, his death on the cross should. He understands what you are going through. Our Lord does not patronize us or scoff at our needs. He responds "generously to all without finding fault" (James 1:5 NIV). How can he do this? No one penned it more clearly than did the author of Hebrews.

Jesus understands every weakness of ours, because he was tempted in every way that we are. But he did not sin! So whenever we are in need, we should come bravely before the throne of our merciful God. There we will be treated with undeserved kindness, and we will find help. (Heb. 4:15–16 CEV)

Why did the throat of heaven grow raw? So we would know that he understands; so all who struggle would hear his invitation: "You can trust me."

—He Chose the Nails

*L*et me state something important. There is never a time during which Jesus is not speaking. Never. There is never a place in which Jesus is not present. Never. There is never a room so dark . . . a lounge so sensual . . . an office so sophisticated . . . that the ever-present, ever-pursuing, relentlessly tender Friend is not there, tapping gently on the doors of our hearts— waiting to be invited in.

Few hear his voice. Fewer still open the door.

But never interpret our numbness as his absence. For amidst the fleeting promises of pleasure is the timeless promise of his presence.

"Surely I am with you always, to the very end of the age."[6]

"'Never will I leave you; never will I forsake you.'"[7]

There is no chorus so loud that the voice of God cannot be heard . . . if we will but listen.

—In the Eye of the Storm

*A*ccording to the Bible he can [understand us]: "For we have no super-human High Priest to whom our weaknesses are unintelligible—he himself has shared fully in all our experience of temptation, except that he never sinned" (Heb. 4:15 PHILLIPS).

The writer of Hebrews is adamant almost to the point of redundancy. It's as if he anticipates our objections. It's as if he knows that we will say, "God, it's easy for you up there. You don't know how hard it is from down here." So he boldly proclaims Jesus' ability to understand. Look at the wording again.

He himself. Not an angel. Not an ambassador. Not an emissary. But Jesus himself.

Shared fully. Not partially. Not nearly. Not to a large degree. Entirely! Jesus shared fully.

In all our experience. Every hurt. Each ache. All the stresses and all the strains. No exceptions. No substitutes. Why? So he could sympathize with our weaknesses.

Every page of the Gospels hammers home this crucial principle: God knows how you feel. From the funeral to the factory to the frustration of a demanding schedule. Jesus understands. When you tell God that you've reached your limit, he knows what you mean. When you shake your head at impossible deadlines, he shakes his too. When your plans are interrupted by people who have other plans, he nods in empathy.

He has been there.

He knows how you feel.

—Max on Life

*R*ead these truths and tell me, who am I describing?

Jesus . . . or you?

Born to a mother.
Acquainted with physical pain.

Enjoys a good party.
Rejected by friends.
Unfairly accused.
Loves stories.
Reluctantly pays taxes.
Sings.
Turned off by greedy religion.
Feels sorry for the lonely.
Unappreciated by siblings.
Stands up for the underdog.
Kept awake at night by concerns.
Known to doze off in the midst of trips.
Accused of being too rowdy.
Afraid of death.

You?
Jesus?
Both?
Seems you, like David, have much in common with Jesus.
Big deal? I think so.

Jesus understands you. He understands small-town anonymity and big-city pressure. He's walked pastures of sheep and palaces of kings. He's faced hunger, sorrow, and death and wants to face them with you. Jesus "understands our weaknesses, for he faced all of the same temptations we do, yet he did not sin. So let us come boldly to the throne of our gracious God. There we will receive his mercy, and we will find grace to help us when we need it" (Heb. 4:15–16 NLT).

He became one of us. And he did so to redeem all of us.

—Facing Your Giants

*W*hen everyone else rejects you, Christ accepts you. When everyone else leaves you, Christ finds you. When no one else wants you, Christ claims you. When no one else will give you the time of day, Jesus will give you the words of eternity. . . .

What is the work of God? Accepting people. Loving before judging. Caring before condemning.

Look before you label.

—A Gentle Thunder

"*A*s Jesus was going down the road, he saw Matthew sitting at his tax-collection booth. 'Come, be my disciple,' Jesus said to him. So Matthew got up and followed him" (Matt. 9:9 NLT).

The surprise in this invitation is the one invited—a tax collector. Combine the greed of an embezzling executive with the presumption of a hokey television evangelist. Throw in the audacity of an ambulance-chasing lawyer and the cowardice of a drive-by sniper. Stir in a pinch of a pimp's morality, and finish it off with the drug peddler's code of ethics—and what do you have?

A first-century tax collector.

According to the Jews, these guys ranked barely above plankton on the food chain. Caesar permitted these Jewish citizens to tax almost anything—your boat, the fish you caught, your house, your crops. As long as Caesar got his due, they could keep the rest.

Matthew was a public tax collector. Private tax collectors hired other people to do the dirty work. Public publicans, like Matthew, just pulled their stretch limos into the poor side of town and set up shop. As crooked as corkscrews.

His given name was Levi, a priestly name (Mark 2:14; Luke 5:27–28). Did his parents aspire for him to enter the priesthood? If so, he was a flop in the family circle.

You can bet he was shunned. The neighborhood cookouts? Never invited. High-school reunions? Somehow his name was left off the list. The guy was avoided like streptococcus A. Everybody kept his distance from Matthew.

Everyone except Jesus. "'Come, be my disciple,' Jesus said to him. So Matthew got up and followed him" (Matt. 9:9 NLT).

Matthew must have been ripe. Jesus hardly had to tug. Within a punctuation mark, Matthew's shady friends and Jesus' green followers are swapping e-mail addresses. "Then Levi gave a big dinner for Jesus at his house. Many tax collectors and other people were eating there, too" (Luke 5:29 NCV).

What do you suppose led up to that party? Let's try to imagine. I can see Matthew going back to his office and packing up. He removes the Quisling of the Year Award from the wall and boxes up the Shady Business School certificate. His coworkers start asking questions.

"What's up, Matt? Headed on a cruise?"

"Hey, Matthew, the Missus kick you out?"

Matthew doesn't know what to say. He mumbles something about a job change. But as he reaches the door, he pauses. Holding his box full of office supplies, he looks back. They're giving him hangdog looks—kind of sad, puzzled.

He feels a lump in his throat. Oh, these guys aren't much. Parents warn their kids about this sort. Salty language. Mardi Gras morals. They keep the phone number of the bookie on speed dial. The bouncer at the gentlemen's club sends them birthday cards. But a friend is a friend. Yet what can he do? Invite them to meet Jesus? Yeah, right. They like preachers the way sheep like butchers. Tell them to tune in to the religious channel on TV? Then they'd think cotton-candy hair is a requirement for following Christ. What if he snuck little Torah tracts in their desks? Nah, they don't read.

So, not knowing what else to do, he shrugs his shoulders and gives them a nod. "These stupid allergies," he says, rubbing the mist from one eye.

Later that day the same thing happens. He goes to the bar to settle up his account. The décor is blue-collar chic: a seedy, smoky place with a Budweiser chandelier over the pool table and a jukebox in the corner. Not the country club, but for Matthew, it's his home on the way home. And when he tells the owner he's moving on, the bartender responds, "Whoa, Matt. What's comin' down?"

Matthew mumbles an excuse about a transfer but leaves with an empty feeling in his gut.

Later on he meets up with Jesus at a diner and shares his problem. "It's my buddies—you know, the guys at the office. And the fellows at the bar."

"What about them?" Jesus asks.

"Well, we kinda run together, you know. I'm gonna miss 'em. Take Josh for instance—as slick as a can of Quaker State, but he visits orphans on Sunday. And Bruno at the gym? Can crunch you like a roach, but I've never had a better friend. He's posted bail for me three times."

Jesus motions for him to go on. "What's the problem?"

"Well, I'm gonna miss those guys. I mean, I've got nothing against Peter and James and John, Jesus . . . but they're Sunday morning, and I'm Saturday night. I've got my own circle, ya know?"

Jesus starts to smile and shake his head. "Matthew, Matthew, you think I came to quarantine you? Following me doesn't mean forgetting your friends. Just the opposite. I want to meet them."

"Are you serious?"

"Is the high priest a Jew?"

"But, Jesus, these guys . . . half of them are on parole. Josh hasn't worn socks since his Bar Mitzvah . . ."

"I'm not talking about a religious service, Matthew. Let me ask you— what do you like to do? Bowl? Play Monopoly? How's your golf game?"

Matthew's eyes brighten. "You ought to see me cook. I get on steaks like a whale on Jonah."

"Perfect." Jesus smiles. "Then throw a little going-away party. A hang-up-the-clipboard bash. Get the gang together."

Matthew's all over it. Calling the caterer, his housekeeper, his secretary. "Get the word out, Thelma. Drinks and dinner at my house tonight. Tell the guys to come and bring a date."

And so Jesus ends up at Matthew's house, a classy split-level with a view of the Sea of Galilee. Parked out front is everything from BMWs to Harleys to limos. And the crowd inside tells you this is anything but a clergy conference.

Earrings on the guys and tattoos on the girls. Moussified hair. Music that rumbles teeth roots. And buzzing around in the middle of the group is Matthew, making more connections than an electrician. He hooks up Peter with the tax collector bass club and Martha with the kitchen staff. Simon the Zealot meets a high-school debate partner. And Jesus? Beaming. What could be better? Sinners and saints in the same room, and no one's trying to determine who is which. But an hour or so into the evening the door opens, and an icy breeze blows in. "The Pharisees and the men who taught the law for the Pharisees began to complain to Jesus' followers, 'Why do you eat and drink with tax collectors and sinners?'" (Luke 5:30 NCV).

Enter the religious police and their thin-lipped piety. Big black books under arms. Cheerful as Siberian prison guards. Clerical collars so tight that veins bulge. They like to grill too. But not steaks.

Matthew is the first to feel the heat. "Some religious fellow you are," one says, practically pulling an eyebrow muscle. "Look at the people you hang out with."

Matthew doesn't know whether to get mad or get out. Before he has time to choose, Jesus intervenes, explaining that Matthew is right where he needs to be. "Healthy people don't need a doctor—sick people do. I have come to call sinners to turn from their sins, not to spend my time with those who think they are already good enough" (vv. 31–32 NLT).

Quite a story. Matthew goes from double-dealer to disciple. He throws a party that makes the religious right uptight, but Christ proud. The good guys look good, and the bad guys hit the road. Some story indeed.

What do we do with it?

That depends on which side of the tax collector's table you find yourself. You and I are Matthew. Don't look at me that way. There's enough hustler in the best of us to qualify for Matthew's table. Maybe you've never taken taxes, but you've taken liberty with the truth, taken credit that wasn't yours, taken advantage of the weak. You and me? Matthew.

If you're still at the table, you receive an invitation. "Follow me." So what if you've got a rube reputation? So did Matthew. You may end up writing your own gospel.

If you've left the table, you receive a clarification. You don't have to be weird to follow Jesus. You don't have to stop liking your friends to follow him. Just the opposite. A few introductions would be nice. Do you know how to grill a steak? . . .

A woman in a small Arkansas community was a single mom with a frail baby. Her neighbor would stop by every few days and keep the child so she could shop. After some weeks her neighbor shared more than time; she shared her faith, and the woman did what Matthew did. She followed Christ.

The friends of the young mother objected. "Do you know what those people teach?" they contested.

"Here is what I know," she told them. "They held my baby."[8]

I think Jesus likes that kind of answer, don't you?

—*Next Door Savior*

The kindness of Jesus. We are quick to think of his power, his passion, and his devotion. But those near him knew and know God comes cloaked in kindness. Kind enough to care about a faux pas. Kind enough to have lunch with a crook. Kind enough to bless a suffering sister.

"Love is kind," writes Paul.

Nehemiah agrees: "You are God, ready to pardon, gracious and merciful, slow to anger, abundant in kindness" (Neh. 9:17 NKJV).

David agrees, "Your lovingkindness is better than life" (Ps. 63:3 NASB).

Paul speaks of "the kindness and love of God our Savior" (Titus 3:4 NIV). He is exuberant as he announces: "Now God has us where he wants us, with all the time in this world and the next to shower grace and kindness upon us in Christ Jesus. Saving is all his idea, and all his work. All we do is trust him enough to let him do it" (Eph. 2:7–8 MSG).

But Jesus' invitation offers the sweetest proof of the kindness of heaven:

Come to Me, all you who labor and are heavy laden, and I will give you rest. Take My yoke upon you and learn from Me, for I am gentle and lowly in heart, and you will find rest for your souls. For My yoke is easy and My burden is light. (Matt. 11:28–30 NKJV)

Farmers in ancient Israel used to train an inexperienced ox by yoking it to an experienced one with a wooden harness. The straps around the older animal were tightly drawn. He carried the load. But the yoke around the younger animal was loose. He walked alongside the more mature ox, but his burden was light. In this verse Jesus is saying, "I walk alongside you. We are yoked together. But I pull the weight and carry the burden."

I wonder, how many burdens is Jesus carrying for us that we know nothing about? We're aware of some. He carries our sin. He carries our shame. He carries our eternal debt. But are there others? Has he lifted fears before we felt them? Has he carried our confusion so we wouldn't have to? Those times when we have been surprised by our own sense of peace? Could it be that Jesus has lifted our anxiety onto his shoulders and placed a yoke of kindness on ours?

And how often do we thank him for his kindness? Not often enough. But does our ingratitude restrict his kindness? No. "Because he is kind even to people who are ungrateful and full of sin" (Luke 6:35 NCV).

In the original language, the word for *kindness* carries an added idea the English word does not. Chiefly it refers to an act of grace. But it also refers to a deed or person who is "useful, serviceable, adapted to its purpose."[9] *Kindness* was even employed to describe food that was tasty as well as healthy. Sounds odd to our ears. "Hey, honey, what a great meal. The salad is especially *kind* tonight."

But the usage makes sense. Isn't kindness good *and* good for you? Pleasant *and* practical? Kindness not only says good morning, kindness makes the coffee. Again, doesn't Jesus fit this description? He not only attended the wedding, he rescued it. He not only healed the woman, he honored her. He did more than call Zacchaeus by name; he entered his house.

Hasn't he acted similarly with you? Hasn't he helped you out of a few jams? Hasn't he come into your house? And has there ever been a time when he was too busy to listen to your story? The Bible says, "Whoever is wise will observe these things, and they will understand the lovingkindness of the LORD" (Ps. 107:43 NKJV). Hasn't God been kind—pleasantly useful—to you? And since God has been so kind to you (you know what I am about to say), can't you be kind to others?

—A Love Worth Giving

*W*hy did Jesus go to the wedding? The answer? It's found in the second verse of John 2 . . . "Jesus and his followers were also invited to the wedding" (NCV).

When the bride and groom were putting the guest list together,

Jesus' name was included. And when Jesus showed up with a half-dozen friends, the invitation wasn't rescinded. Whoever was hosting this party was happy to have Jesus present.

"Be sure and put Jesus' name on the list," he might have said. "He really lightens up a party."

Jesus wasn't invited because he was a celebrity. He wasn't one yet. The invitation wasn't motivated by his miracles. He'd yet to perform any. Why did they invite him?

I suppose they liked him. Big deal? I think so. I think it's significant that common folk in a little town enjoyed being with Jesus. I think it's noteworthy that the Almighty didn't act high and mighty. The Holy One wasn't holier-than-thou. The One who knew it all wasn't a know-it-all. The One who made the stars didn't keep his head in them. The One who owns all the stuff of earth never strutted it.

Never. He could have. Oh, how he could have!

He could have been a name dropper: *Did I ever tell you of the time Moses and I went up on the mountain?*

He could have been a showoff: *Hey, want me to beam you into the twentieth century?*

He could have been a smart aleck: *I know what you're thinking. Want me to prove it?*

He could have been highbrow and uppity: *I've got some property on Jupiter . . .*

Jesus could have been all of these, but he wasn't. His purpose was not to show off but to show up. He went to great pains to be as human as the guy down the street. He didn't need to study, but he still went to the synagogue. He had no need for income, but he still worked in the workshop. He had known the fellowship of angels and heard the harps of heaven, yet he still went to parties thrown by tax collectors. And upon his shoulders rested the challenge of redeeming creation, but he still took time to walk ninety miles from Jericho to Cana to go to a wedding.

As a result, people liked him. Oh, there were those who chaffed at his claims. They called him a blasphemer, but they never called him a braggart. They accused him of heresy, but never arrogance. He was branded as a radical, but never called unapproachable.

There is no hint that he ever used his heavenly status for personal gain. Ever. You just don't get the impression that his neighbors grew sick of his haughtiness and asked, "Well, who do you think made you God?"

His faith made him likable, not detestable. Would that ours would do the same!

Where did we get the notion that a good Christian is a solemn Christian? Who started the rumor that the sign of a disciple is a long face? How did we create this idea that the truly gifted are the heavy-hearted?

May I state an opinion that may raise an eyebrow? May I tell you why I think Jesus went to the wedding? I think he went to the wedding to— now hold on, hear me out, let me say it before you heat the tar and pluck the feathers—I think Jesus went to the wedding to have fun.

Think about it. It's been a tough season. Forty days in the desert. No food or water. A standoff with the devil. A week breaking in some greenhorn Galileans. A job change. He's left home. It hasn't been easy. A break would be welcome. Good meal with some good wine and some good friends . . . well, it sounds pretty nice.

So off they go.

His purpose wasn't to turn the water to wine. That was a favor for his friends.

His purpose wasn't to show his power. The wedding host didn't even know what Jesus did.

His purpose wasn't to preach. There is no record of a sermon.

Really leaves only one reason. Fun. Jesus went to the wedding because he liked the people, he liked the food, and heaven forbid, he may have even wanted to swirl the bride around the dance floor a time or two. (After all, he's planning a big wedding himself. Maybe he wanted the practice?)

So, forgive me, Deacon Drydust and Sister Somberheart. I'm sorry to rain on your dirge, but Jesus was a likable fellow. And his disciples should be the same. I'm not talking debauchery, drunkenness, and adultery. I'm not endorsing compromise, coarseness, or obscenity. I am simply crusading for the freedom to enjoy a good joke, enliven a dull party, and appreciate a fun evening.

Maybe these thoughts catch you by surprise. They do me. It's been awhile since I pegged Jesus as a party lover. But he was. His foes accused him of eating too much, drinking too much, and hanging out with the wrong people! (See Matt. 11:19.) I must confess: it's been a while since I've been accused of having too much fun. How about you?

We used to be good at it. What has happened to us? What happened to clean joy and loud laughter? Is it our neckties that choke us? Is it our diplomas that dignify us? Is it the pew that stiffens us?

Couldn't we learn to be children again?

Bring out the marbles—(so what if the shoes get scuffed?).

Bring out the bat and glove—(so what if the muscles ache?).

Bring out the taffy—(so what if it sticks to your teeth?).

Be a child again. Flirt. Giggle. Dip your cookie in your milk. Take a nap. Say you're sorry if you hurt someone. Chase a butterfly. Be a child again.

Loosen up. Don't you have some people to hug, rocks to skip, or lips to kiss? Someone needs to laugh at Bugs Bunny; might as well be you. Someday you're going to learn to paint; might as well be now. Someday you're going to retire; why not today?

Not retire from your job, just retire from your attitude. Honestly, has complaining ever made the day better? Has grumbling ever paid the bills? Has worrying about tomorrow ever changed it?

Let someone else run the world for a while.

Jesus took time for a party . . . shouldn't we?

—*When God Whispers Your Name*

4

Example

*W*hat if, for one day, Jesus were to become you? What if, for twenty-four hours, Jesus wakes up in your bed, walks in your shoes, lives in your house, assumes your schedule? Your boss becomes his boss, your mother becomes his mother, your pains become his pains? With one exception, nothing about your life changes. Your health doesn't change. Your circumstances don't change. Your schedule isn't altered. Your problems aren't solved. Only one change occurs.

What if, for one day and one night, Jesus lives your life with his heart? Your heart gets the day off, and your life is led by the heart of Christ. His priorities govern your actions. His passions drive your decisions. His love directs your behavior.

What would you be like? Would people notice a change? Your family—would they see something new? Your coworkers—would they sense a difference? What about the less fortunate? Would you treat them the same? And your friends? Would they detect more joy? How about your enemies? Would they receive more mercy from Christ's heart than from yours?

And you? How would you feel? What alterations would this transplant have on your stress level? Your mood swings? Your temper? Would you sleep better? Would you see sunsets differently? Death differently? Taxes differently? Any chance you'd need fewer aspirin or sedatives? How about your reaction to traffic delays? (Ouch, that touched a nerve.) Would you still dread what you are dreading? Better yet, would you still do what you are doing?

Would you still do what you had planned to do for the next twenty-four hours? Pause and think about your schedule. Obligations. Engagements. Outings. Appointments. With Jesus taking over your heart, would anything change?

Keep working on this for a moment. Adjust the lens of your imagination until you have a clear picture of Jesus leading your life, then snap the shutter and frame the image. What you see is what God wants. He wants you to "think and act like Christ Jesus" (Phil. 2:5 NCV).

God's plan for you is nothing short of a new heart. If you were a car, God would want control of your engine. If you were a computer, God would claim the software and the hard drive. If you were an airplane, he'd take his seat in the cockpit. But you are a person, so God wants to change your heart.

"You were taught to be made new in your hearts, to become a new person. That new person is made to be like God—made to be truly good and holy" (Eph. 4:23–24 NCV).

God wants you to be just like Jesus. He wants you to have a heart like his.

—Just Like Jesus

I have a sketch of Jesus laughing. It hangs on the wall across from my desk.

It's quite a drawing. His head is back. His mouth is open. His eyes are sparkling. He isn't just grinning. He isn't just chuckling. He's roaring. He hasn't heard or seen one like that in quite a while. He's having trouble catching his breath.

It was given to me by an Episcopal priest who carries cigars in his pocket and collects portraits of Jesus smiling. "I give them to anyone who might be inclined to take God too seriously," he explained as he handed me the gift.

He pegged me well.

I'm not one who easily envisions a smiling God. A weeping God, yes. An angry God, OK. A mighty God, you bet. But a chuckling God? It seems too . . . too . . . too unlike what God should do—and be. Which just shows how much I know—or don't know—about God.

What do I think he was doing when he stretched the neck of the giraffe? An exercise in engineering? What do I think he had in mind when he told the ostrich where to put his head? Spelunking? What do I think he was doing when he designed the mating call of an ape? Or the eight legs of the octopus? And what do I envision on his face when he saw Adam's first glance at Eve? A yawn?

Hardly.

As my vision improves and I'm able to read without my stained glasses, I'm seeing that a sense of humor is perhaps the only way God has put up with us for so long.

Is that him with a smile as Moses does a double take at the burning bush that speaks?

Is he smiling again as Jonah lands on the beach, dripping gastric juices and smelling like whale breath?

Is that a twinkle in his eye as he watches the disciples feed thousands with one boy's lunch?

Do you think that his face is deadpan as he speaks about the man with a two-by-four in his eye who points out a speck in a friend's eye?

Can you honestly imagine Jesus bouncing children on his knee with a somber face?

No, I think that Jesus smiled. I think that he smiled a bit at people and a lot with people. . . .

When I think about the prayers God has answered for me in spite of the life I've lived, I think he must be smiling still.

So I think I'll keep his picture on the wall.

—In the Eye of the Storm

*J*esus' relationship with God went far deeper than a daily appointment. Our Savior was always aware of his Father's presence. Listen to his words:

> The Son can do nothing on his own, but only what he sees the Father doing; for whatever the Father does, the Son does likewise. (John 5:19 NRSV)
>> I can do nothing on my own. As I hear, I judge. (John 5:30 NRSV)
>> I am in the Father and the Father is in me. (John 14:11 NRSV)

Clearly, Jesus didn't act unless he saw his Father act. He didn't judge until he heard his Father judge. No act or deed occurred without his Father's guidance. His words have the ring of a translator.

There were a few occasions in Brazil when I served as a translator for an English speaker. He stood before the audience, complete with the message. I stood at his side, equipped with the language. My job was to convey his story to the listeners. I did my best to allow his words to come through me. I was not at liberty to embellish or subtract. When the speaker gestured, I gestured. As his volume increased, so did mine. When he got quiet, I did too.

When he walked this earth, Jesus was "translating" God all the time. When God got louder, Jesus got louder. When God gestured, Jesus gestured. He was so in sync with the Father that he could declare, "I am in the Father and the Father is in me" (John 14:11 NRSV). It was as if he heard a voice others were missing.

I witnessed something similar to this on an airplane once. I kept hearing outbursts of laughter. The flight was turbulent and bumpy, hardly a reason for humor. But some fellow behind me was cracking up. No one else, just him. Finally I turned to see what was so funny. He was wearing headphones and apparently listening to a comedian. Because he could hear what I couldn't, he acted differently than I did.

The same was true with Jesus. Because he could hear what others couldn't, he acted differently than they did. Remember when everyone was troubled about the man born blind? Jesus wasn't. Somehow he knew that the blindness would reveal God's power (John 9:3). Remember when everyone was distraught about Lazarus's illness? Jesus wasn't. Rather than hurry to his friend's bedside, he said, "This sickness will not end in death. It is for the glory of God, to bring glory to the Son of God" (John 11:4 NCV). It was as if Jesus could hear what no one else could. How could a relationship be more intimate? Jesus had unbroken communion with his Father.

Do you suppose the Father desires the same for us? Absolutely. Paul said that we have been "predestined to be conformed to the image of his Son" (Rom. 8:29 NRSV). Let me remind you: God loves you just the way you are, but he refuses to leave you that way. He wants you to be just like Jesus. God desires the same abiding intimacy with you that he had with his Son.

—Just Like Jesus

*C*hristians battle anxiety. Jesus battled anxiety, for heaven's sake! In the Garden of Gethsemane he prayed three times that he wouldn't have to drink of the cup (Matt. 26:36–44). His heart pumped with such ferocity that capillaries broke and rivulets of crimson streaked down his face (Luke 22:44). He was anxious.

But he didn't stay anxious. He entrusted his fears to his heavenly Father and completed his earthly mission with faith. He will help us do likewise.

—Anxious for Nothing

People are prone to pecking orders. We love the high horse. The boy over the girl or girl over boy. The affluent over the destitute. The educated over the dropout. The old-timer over the newcomer. The Jew over the Gentile.

An impassable gulf yawned between Jews and Gentiles in the days of the early church. A Jew could not drink milk drawn by Gentiles or eat their food. Jews could not aid a Gentile mother in her hour of need. Jewish physicians could not attend to non-Jewish patients.[1] No Jew would have anything to do with a Gentile. They were unclean.

Unless that Jew, of course, was Jesus. Suspicions of a new order began to surface because of his curious conversation with the Canaanite woman. Her daughter was dying, and her prayer was urgent. Yet her ancestry was Gentile. "I was sent only to help God's lost sheep—the people of Israel," Jesus told her. "That's true, Lord," she replied, "but even dogs are allowed to eat the scraps that fall beneath their masters' table" (Matt. 15:24, 27 NLT).

Jesus healed the woman's daughter and made his position clear. He was more concerned about bringing everyone in than shutting certain people out.

—Outlive Your Life

The greatest example of . . . humility is none other than Jesus Christ. Who had more reason to boast than he? Yet he never did. He walked on water but never strutted on the beach. He turned a basket into a buffet but never demanded applause. A liberator and a prophet came to visit him, but he never dropped names in his sermon. He could have. "Just the other day I was conferring with Moses and Elijah." But Jesus never thumped his chest. He refused even to take credit. "I can do nothing on my own" (John 5:30 NRSV). He was utterly reliant upon the Father and the Holy Spirit. "All by myself"? Jesus never spoke such words. If he didn't, how dare we?

We can rise too high but can never stoop too low. What gift are you giving that he did not first give? What truth are you teaching that he didn't first teach? You love. But who loved you first? You serve. But who served the most? What are you doing for God that he could not do alone? How kind of him to use us. How wise of us to remember.

—Outlive Your Life

*O*h, the peculiar puzzle of prayer.

We aren't the first to struggle. The sign-up sheet for Prayer 101 contains some familiar names: the apostles John, James, Andrew, and Peter. When one of Jesus' disciples requested, "Lord, teach us to pray" (Luke 11:1 NIV), none of the others objected. No one walked away saying, "Hey, I have prayer figured out." The first followers of Jesus needed prayer guidance.

In fact, the only tutorial they ever requested was on prayer. They could have asked for instructions on many topics: bread multiplying, speech making, storm stilling. Jesus raised people from the dead. But a "How to Vacate the Cemetery" seminar? His followers never called for one. But they did want him to do this: "Lord, teach us to pray."

Might their interest have had something to do with the jaw-dropping, eye-popping promises Jesus attached to prayer? "Ask and it will be given to you" (Matt. 7:7 NIV). "If you believe, you will get anything you ask for in prayer" (Matt. 21:22 NCV). Jesus never attached such power to other endeavors. *"Plan* and it will be given to you." "You will get anything you *work* for." Those words are not in the Bible. But these are—"If you remain in me and follow my teachings, you can ask anything you want, and it will be given to you" (John 15:7 NCV).

Jesus gave stunning prayer promises.

And he set a compelling prayer example. Jesus prayed before he ate. He prayed for children. He prayed for the sick. He prayed with thanks. He prayed with tears. He had made the planets and shaped the stars, yet he prayed. He is the Lord of angels and Commander of heavenly hosts, yet he prayed. He is coequal with God, the exact representation of the Holy One, and yet he devoted himself to prayer. He prayed in the desert, cemetery, and garden. "He went out and departed to a solitary place; and there He prayed" (Mark 1:35 NKJV).

This dialogue must have been common among his friends:

"Has anyone seen Jesus?"

"Oh, you know. He's up to the same thing."

"Praying *again?*

"Yep. He's been gone since sunrise."

Jesus would even disappear for an entire night of prayer. I'm thinking of one occasion in particular. He'd just experienced one of the most stressful days of his ministry. The day began with the news of the death of his relative John the Baptist. Jesus sought to retreat with his disciples, yet a throng of thousands followed him. Though grief-stricken, he spent the day teaching and healing people. When it was discovered that the host of people had no food to eat, Jesus multiplied bread out of a basket and fed the entire multitude. In the span of a few hours, he battled sorrow, stress, demands, and needs. He deserved a good night's rest. Yet when evening finally came, he told the crowd to leave and the disciples to board their boat, and "he went up into the hills by himself to pray" (Mark 6:46 NLT).

Apparently it was the correct choice. A storm exploded over the Sea of Galilee, leaving the disciples "in trouble far away from land, for a strong wind had risen, and they were fighting heavy waves. About three o'clock in the morning Jesus came toward them, walking on the water" (Matt. 14:24–25 NLT). Jesus ascended the mountain depleted. He reappeared invigorated. When he reached the water, he never broke his stride. You'd have thought the water was a park lawn and the storm a spring breeze.

Do you think the disciples made the prayer–power connection? "Lord, teach us to pray *like that.* Teach us to find strength in prayer. To banish fear in prayer. To defy storms in prayer. To come off the mountain of prayer with the authority of a prince."

What about you? The disciples faced angry waves and a watery grave. You face angry clients, a turbulent economy, raging seas of stress and sorrow.

"Lord," we still request, "teach us to pray."

—Before Amen

*E*ver feel like you're racing downhill on a runaway bike and you don't remember how to brake? Ever feel the wheels of your life racing faster and faster as you speed past the people you love? Could you use a reminder on how to slow it all down?

If so, read what Jesus did during the last Sabbath of his life. Start in the Gospel of Matthew. Didn't find anything? Try Mark. Read what Mark recorded about the way Jesus spent the Sabbath. Nothing there either? Strange. What about Luke? What does Luke say? Not a reference to the day? Not a word about it? Well, try John. Surely John mentions the Sabbath. He doesn't? No reference? Hmmmm. Looks like Jesus was quiet that day.

"Wait a minute. That's it?"

That's it.

"You mean with one week left to live, Jesus observed the Sabbath?" As far as we can tell.

"You mean with all those apostles to train and people to teach, he took a day to rest and worship?" Apparently so.

"You're telling me that Jesus thought worship was more important than work?" That's exactly what I'm telling you.

For such is the purpose of the Sabbath. And such was the practice of Jesus. "On the Sabbath day he went to the synagogue, *as he always did, and stood up to read.*"[2] Should we do any less?

If Jesus found time in the midst of a racing agenda to stop the rush and sit in the silence, do you think we could too?

—*And the Angels Were Silent*

*J*esus . . . knew the frenzy of life. People back-to-backed his calendar with demands. But he also knew how to step away from the game.

When the sun was setting, all those who had any that were sick with various diseases brought them to Him; and He laid His hands on every one of them and healed them. And demons also came out of many, crying out and saying, "You are the Christ, the Son of God!" And He, rebuking them, did not allow them to speak, for they knew that He was the Christ. Now when it was day, He departed and went into a deserted place. And the crowd sought Him and came to Him, and tried to keep Him from leaving them; but He said to them, "I must preach the kingdom of God to the other cities also, because for this purpose I have been sent." And He was preaching in the synagogues of Galilee. (Luke 4:40–44 NKJV)

These words document Jesus's entry into the public arena. Having withstood the devil's wilderness temptation and his hometown's harsh rejection, Jesus journeyed to Capernaum, where the citizens gave him a tickertape reception. Think John Kennedy at the 1960 Democratic National Convention. (Young hope has arrived.)

They were astonished at His teaching. (Luke 4:32 NKJV)

The story of what he had done spread like wildfire throughout the whole region. (v. 37 NLT)

People throughout the village brought sick family members to Jesus. No matter what their diseases were, the touch of his hand healed every one. (v. 40 NLT)

Could Christ have wanted more? Enthralled masses, just-healed believers, and thousands who would follow his lead. So Jesus . . . Rallied a movement? Organized a leadership team? Mobilized a political-action society?

No. He baffled the public-relations experts by placing the mob in the rearview mirror and ducking into a wildlife preserve, a hidden cove, a vacant building, a deserted place.

Verse 42 identifies the reason: "the crowd . . . tried to keep Him from leaving them." People brought Jesus more than sick bodies and seeking souls. They brought him agendas. Itineraries. Unsolicited advice. The herd of humanity wanted to set Jesus's course. "Heed us," they said. "We'll direct your steps."

They say the same to you. Look over your shoulder, my friend. The crowd is one step back. They don't consult your strengths or know your S.T.O.R.Y. Still, they seem to know more about your life than you do. Where you should work. Whom you should marry. What you should study. They will lead your life if you allow them.

Jesus didn't.

More than once he exercised crowd control. "When Jesus saw the crowd around him, he told his followers to go to the other side of the lake" (Matt. 8:18 NCV).

When the crowd ridiculed his power to raise a girl from the dead, he evicted them from the premises. "After the crowd had been thrown out of the house, Jesus went into the girl's room and took hold of her hand, and she stood up" (Matt. 9:25 NCV).

After a day of teaching, "Jesus left the crowd and went into the house" (Matt. 13:36 NCV).

Though surrounded by possibly twenty thousand fans, he turned away from them: "After Jesus had sent the crowds away" (Matt. 15:39 CEV).

Christ repeatedly escaped the noise of the crowd in order to hear the voice of God. After his forty-day pause in the wilderness, the people of Capernaum "tried to keep Him from leaving them; but He said to them, 'I must preach the kingdom of God to the other cities also, because for this purpose I have been sent'" (Luke 4:42–43 NKJV).

He resisted the undertow of the people by anchoring to the rock of his purpose: employing his uniqueness (to "preach . . . to the other cities also") to make a big deal out of God ("the kingdom of God") everywhere he could. And aren't you glad he did? Suppose he had heeded the crowd and set up camp in Capernaum, reasoning, "I thought the whole world was my target and the cross my destiny. But the entire town tells me to stay in Capernaum. Could all these people be wrong?" Yes, they could! In defiance of the crowd, Jesus turned his back on the Capernaum pastorate and followed the will of God. Doing so meant leaving some sick people unhealed and some confused people untaught. He said no to good things so he could say yes to the right thing: his unique call.

Not an easy choice for anyone. . . .

The devil implants taximeters in our brains. We hear the relentless tick, tick, tick telling us to hurry, hurry, hurry, time is money . . . resulting in this roaring blur called the human race.

But Jesus stands against the tide, countering the crescendo with these words: "Come to Me, all you who labor and are heavy laden, and I will give you rest" (Matt. 11:28 NKJV). Follow the example of Jesus, who "often withdrew into the wilderness and prayed" (Luke 5:16 NKJV).

—Cure for the Common Life

*O*ne of the most astounding assessments of Christ is this summary: "He had done nothing wrong, and he had never lied" (Isa. 53:9 NCV). Jesus was staunchly honest. His every word accurate, his every sentence true. No cheating on tests. No altering the accounts. Not once did Jesus stretch the truth. Not once did he shade the truth. Not once did he avoid the truth. He simply told the truth. No deceit was found in his mouth.

And if God has his way with us, none will be found in ours. He longs for us to be just like Jesus. His plan, if you remember, is to shape us along the lines of his Son (Rom. 8:28). He seeks not to decrease or minimize our deception but to eliminate our deception. God is blunt about dishonesty: "No one who is dishonest will live in my house" (Ps. 101:7 NCV).

Our Master has a strict honor code. From Genesis to Revelation, the theme is the same: God loves the truth and hates deceit.

—*Just Like Jesus*

*H*ad golf existed in the New Testament era, I'm sure the writers would have spoken of mulligans and foot wedges, but it didn't, so they wrote about running. The word *race* is from the Greek *agon*, from which we get the word *agony*. The Christian's race is not a jog but rather a demanding and grueling, sometimes agonizing race. It takes a massive effort to finish strong.

Likely you've noticed that many don't? Surely you've observed there are many on the side of the trail? They used to be running. There was a time when they kept the pace. But then weariness set in. They didn't think the run would be this tough. Or they were discouraged by a bump and daunted by a fellow runner. Whatever the reason, they don't run anymore. They may be Christians. They may come to church. They may put a buck in the plate and warm a pew, but their hearts aren't in the race. They retired before their time. Unless something changes, their best work will have been their first work, and they will finish with a whimper.

By contrast, Jesus' best work was his final work, and his strongest step was his last step. Our Master is the classic example of one who endured. The writer of Hebrews goes on to say that Jesus "held on while wicked people were doing evil things to him" (Heb. 12:3 NCV). The Bible says Jesus "held on," implying that Jesus could have "let go." The runner could have given up, sat down, gone home. He could have quit the race. But he didn't. "He held on while wicked people were doing evil things to him."

Have you ever thought about the evil things done to Christ? Can you think of times when Jesus could have given up? How about his time of temptation? You and I know what it is like to endure a moment of temptation or an hour of temptation, even a day of temptation. But *forty* days? That was what Jesus faced: "The Spirit led Jesus into the desert where the devil tempted Jesus for forty days" (Luke 4:1–2 NCV).

We imagine the wilderness temptation as three isolated events scattered over a forty-day period. Would that it had been. In reality, Jesus' time of testing was nonstop; "the devil tempted Jesus for forty days." Satan got on Jesus like a shirt and refused to leave. Every step, whispering in his ear. Every turn of the path, sowing doubt. Was Jesus affected by the devil? Apparently so. Luke doesn't say that Satan *tried* to tempt Jesus. The verse doesn't read, the devil *attempted* to tempt Jesus. No, the passage is clear: "the devil *tempted* Jesus." Jesus was *tempted*, he was *tested*. Tempted to change sides? Tempted to go home? Tempted to settle for a kingdom on earth? I don't know, but I know he was tempted. A war raged within. Stress stormed without. And since he was tempted, he could have quit the race. But he didn't. He kept on running.

Temptation didn't stop him, nor did accusations. Can you imagine what it would be like to run in a race and be criticized by the bystanders? . . .

That's what happened to Jesus. His own family called him a lunatic.

His neighbors treated him even worse. When Jesus returned to his hometown, they tried to throw him off a cliff (Luke 4:29). But Jesus didn't quit running. Temptations didn't deter him. Accusations didn't defeat him. Nor did shame dishearten him.

I invite you to think carefully about the supreme test Jesus faced in the race. Hebrews 12:2 offers this intriguing statement: "[Jesus] accepted the shame as if it were nothing" (NCV).

Shame is a feeling of disgrace, embarrassment, humiliation. Forgive me for stirring the memory, but don't you have a shameful moment in your history? Can you imagine the horror you would feel if everyone knew about it? What if a videotape of that event were played before your family and friends? How would you feel?

That was exactly what Jesus felt. *Why?* you ask. *He never did anything worthy of shame.* No, but we did. And since on the cross God made him become sin (2 Cor. 5:21), Jesus was covered with shame. He was shamed before his family. Stripped naked before his own mother and loved ones. Shamed before his fellow men. Forced to carry a cross until the weight caused him to stumble. Shamed before his church. The pastors and elders of his day mocked him, calling him names. Shamed before the city of Jerusalem. Condemned to die a criminal's death. Parents likely pointed to him from a distance and told their children, "That's what they do to evil men."

But the shame before men didn't compare with the shame Jesus felt before his Father. Our individual shame seems too much to bear. Can you imagine bearing the collective shame of all humanity? One wave of shame after another was dumped on Jesus. Though he never cheated, he was convicted as a cheat. Though he never stole, heaven regarded him as a thief. Though he never lied, he was considered a liar. Though he never lusted, he bore the shame of an adulterer. Though he always believed, he endured the disgrace of an infidel.

Such words stir one urgent question: How? How did he endure such disgrace? What gave Jesus the strength to endure the shame of the entire world? We need an answer, don't we? Like Jesus we are tempted. Like Jesus we are accused. Like Jesus we are ashamed. But unlike Jesus, we give up. We give out. We sit down. How can we keep running as Jesus did? How can our hearts have the endurance Jesus had?

By focusing where Jesus focused: on "the joy that God put before him" (Heb. 12:2 NCV).

—Just Like Jesus

*C*an you think of a greater gift than to be like Jesus? Christ felt no guilt; God wants to banish yours. Jesus had no bad habits; God wants to remove yours. Jesus had no fear of death; God wants you to be fearless. Jesus had kindness for the diseased and mercy for the rebellious and courage for the challenged. God wants you to have the same.

He loves you just the way you are, but he refuses to leave you that way. He wants you to be just like Jesus.

—Just Like Jesus

5

Teacher

*C*hrist: the One and Only Ruler . . . claims to be the One and Only Revealer. "No one really knows the Son except the Father, and no one really knows the Father except the Son" (Matt. 11:27 NLT).

Jesus enjoys an intimacy with God, a mutuality the Father shares with no one else.

Married couples know something of this. They finish each other's sentences, anticipate each other's actions. Some even begin to look like each other (a possibility that deeply troubles my wife).

Denalyn and I have been married more than twenty-five years. We no longer converse; we communicate in code. She walks into the kitchen while I'm making a sandwich.

"Denalyn?" I ask.

"No, I don't want one."

I'll open the fridge and stare for a few moments. "Denalyn?"

She'll look at my sandwich preparations and answer, "Mayo on the top shelf. Pickles on the door."

She knows what I'll say before I say it. Consequently, she can speak on my behalf with highest credibility. If she says, "Max would prefer a different color" or "Max would approve this idea," listen to her. She knows what she's talking about. She qualifies as my proxy like no one else.

How much more does Jesus qualify as God's! Jesus "who exists at the very heart of the Father, has made him plain as day" (John 1:18 MSG).

When Jesus says, "In My Father's house are many mansions" (John 14:2 NKJV), count on it. He knows. He has walked them.

When he says, "You are worth more than many sparrows" (Matt. 10:31 NIV), trust him. Jesus knows. He knows the value of every creature.

When Christ declares, "Your Father knows what you need before you ask him" (Matt. 6:8 NAB), believe it. After all, "He was in the beginning with God" (John 1:2 NAB).

Jesus claims to be, not a top theologian, an accomplished theologian, or even the Supreme Theologian, but rather the Only Theologian. "No one really knows the Father except the Son." He does not say, "No one really knows the Father like the Son" or "in the fashion of the Son." But rather, "No one really knows the Father except the Son."

Heaven's door has one key, and Jesus holds it. Think of it this way. You're a fifth grader studying astronomy. The day you read about the first mission to the moon, you and your classmates pepper the teacher with space-travel questions.

"What does moondust feel like?"

"Can you swallow when there's no gravity?"

"What about going to the bathroom?"

The teacher does the best she can but prefaces most replies with "I would guess . . ." or "I think . . ." or "Perhaps . . ."

How could she know? She's never been there. But the next day she brings a guest who has. Neil Armstrong enters the room. Yes, the "one small step for man, one giant leap for mankind" Neil Armstrong.

"Now ask your questions," the teacher invites. And Astronaut Armstrong answers each with certainty. He knows the moon; he's walked on it. No speculation or hesitation—he speaks with conviction.

So did Jesus. "He was teaching them as one who had authority" (Matt. 7:29 ESV). Jesus knows the dimensions of God's throne room, the fragrance of its incense, the favorite songs of the unceasing choir. He has a unique, one-of-a-kind, unrivaled knowledge of God and wants to share his knowledge with you. "No one really knows the Father except the Son and those to whom the Son chooses to reveal him" (Matt. 11:27 NLT).

Jesus doesn't boast in his knowledge; he shares it. He doesn't gloat; he gives. He doesn't revel; he reveals. He reveals to us the secrets of eternity.

And he shares them, not just with the top brass or purebred, but with the hungry and needy. In the very next line, Jesus invites: "Come to me, all of you who are weary and carry heavy burdens, and I will give you rest. Take my yoke upon you. Let me teach you, because I am humble and gentle at heart, and you will find rest for your souls" (vv. 28–29 NLT).

Do yourself a favor. Find the brightest highlighter manufactured and the darkest ink produced. Underscore, underline, and accept his invitation: "Let me teach you . . ."

—3:16: The Numbers of Hope

*M*ake it your aim to cling to Christ. Abide in him. Is he not true, honorable, right, pure, lovely, admirable, excellent, and worthy of praise? Is this not the invitation of his message in the vineyard?

> Abide in Me, and I in you. As the branch cannot bear fruit of itself unless it abides in the vine, so neither can you unless you abide in Me. I am the vine, you are the branches; he who abides in Me and I in him, he bears much fruit, for apart from Me you can do nothing. If anyone does not abide in Me, he is thrown away as a branch and dries up; and they gather them, and cast them into the fire and they are burned. If you abide in Me, and My words abide in you, ask whatever you wish, and it will be done for you. My Father is glorified by this, that you bear much fruit, and so prove to be My disciples. Just as the Father has loved Me, I

have also loved you; abide in My love. If you keep My commandments, you will abide in My love; just as I have kept My Father's commandments and abide in His love. (John 15:4–10 NASB)

Jesus' allegory is simple. God is like a vine keeper. He lives and loves to coax the best out of his vines. He pampers, prunes, blesses, and cuts. His aim is singular: "What can I do to prompt produce?" God is a capable orchardist who carefully superintends the vineyard.

And Jesus plays the role of the vine. We nongardeners might confuse the vine and the branch. To see the vine, lower your gaze from the stringy, winding branches to the thick base below. The vine is the root and trunk of the plant. It cables nutrients from the soil to the branches. Jesus makes the stunning claim, "I am the real root of life." If anything good comes into our lives, he is the conduit.

And who are we? We are the branches. We bear fruit: "love, joy, peace, patience, kindness, goodness, faithfulness" (Gal. 5:22 NASB). We meditate on what is "true, and honorable, and right, and pure, and lovely, and admirable . . . excellent and worthy of praise" (Phil. 4:8 NLT). Our gentleness is evident to all. We bask in the "peace of God, which transcends all understanding" (Phil. 4:7 NIV).

And as we cling to Christ, God is honored. "My Father is glorified by this, that you bear much fruit, and so prove to be My disciples" (John 15:8 NASB).

The Father tends. Jesus nourishes. We receive, and grapes appear. Passersby, stunned at the overflowing baskets of love, grace, and peace, can't help but ask, "Who runs this vineyard?" And God is honored. For this reason fruit bearing matters to God.

And it matters to you! You grow weary of unrest. You're ready to be done with sleepless nights. You long to be "anxious for nothing." You long for the fruit of the Spirit. But how do you bear this fruit? Try harder? No, hang tighter. Our assignment is not fruitfulness but faithfulness. The secret to fruit bearing and anxiety-free living is less about doing and more about abiding. . . .

We Christians tend to miss this. We banter about pledges to "change the world," "make a difference for Christ," "lead people to the Lord." Yet these are by-products of the Christ-focused life. Our goal is not to bear fruit. Our goal is to stay attached.

—Anxious for Nothing

*C*ould you use some courage? Are you backing down more than you are standing up? If so, let the Master lead you up the mountain again. Let him remind you why you should "fear not." Listen to the time Jesus scattered the butterflies out of the stomachs of his nervous disciples and see if his words help you.[1]

We need to remember that the disciples were common men given a compelling task. Before they were the stained-glassed saints in the windows of cathedrals, they were somebody's next-door neighbors trying to make a living and raise a family. They weren't cut from theological cloth or raised on supernatural milk. But they were an ounce more devoted than they were afraid and, as a result, did some extraordinary things.

They would have done nothing, however, had they not learned to face their fears. Jesus knew that. That is why he spoke his words of courage.

The disciples are being sent out on their own. For a limited time they will go into the cities and do what Jesus has done—but without Jesus. Jesus assembles them to give them the final instructions. Perhaps the disciples look nervous, for they have reason to be nervous. What Jesus tells them would raise the pulse rate of the stoutest heart.

First Jesus tells them not to take any extra money or extra clothing on their journey.

"No money?"

Then he assures them that they are being sent out "like sheep among wolves."

"Uh, what do you mean, Jesus?"

His answer is not reassuring. He tells them they will be taken before the authorities (uh-oh), flogged (ouch), and arrested (groan).

And it gets worse before it gets better.

Jesus goes on to describe the impact their mission will have on people: "Brother will betray brother to death, and a father his child; children will rebel against their parents and have them put to death. All men will hate you because of me, but he who stands firm to the end will be saved."[2]

Some eyes duck. Some eyes widen. Someone swallows. Feet shift. A brow is wiped. And though no one says it, you know someone is thinking, "Is it too late to get out of this?"

That's the setting for Jesus' paragraph on courage. Three times in five verses[3] he says, "Do not be afraid." Read the words and see his call and cause for courage. See the reason you should sleep well tonight:

> "So do not be afraid of them. There is nothing concealed that will not
> be disclosed, or hidden that will not be made known."[4]

On the surface, those words would seem like a reason for panic rather than a source of peace. Who of us would like to have our secret thoughts made public? Who would want our private sins published? Who would get excited over the idea that every wrong deed we've ever done? . . .

The answer is found in Romans 2:16. Let out a sigh of relief as you underline the last three words of the verse: "This will take place on the day when God will judge men's secrets *through Jesus Christ*" (NIV, emphasis mine).

Did you see it? Jesus is the screen through which God looks when he judges our sins. . . .

You are guaranteed that your sins will be filtered through, hidden in, and screened out by the sacrifice of Jesus. When God looks at you, he doesn't see you; he sees the One who surrounds you. That means that failure is not a concern for you. Your victory is secure. How could you not be courageous?

—The Applause of Heaven

Jesus, in his first message, declared his passion for the poor. Early in his ministry he returned to his hometown of Nazareth to deliver an inaugural address of sorts. He entered the same synagogue where he had worshipped as a young man and looked into the faces of the villagers. They were simple folk: stonecutters, carpenters, and craftsmen. They survived on minimal wages and lived beneath the shadow of Roman oppression. There wasn't much good news in Nazareth.

But this day was special. Jesus was in town. The hometown boy who had made the big time. They asked him to read Scripture, and he accepted. "And He was handed the book of the prophet Isaiah. And when He had opened the book, He found the place where it was written . . ." (Luke 4:17 NKJV).

This is the only such moment in all the Gospels. Jesus quoted Scripture many times. But the Son of God, selecting and reading Scripture? This is it. On the singular occasion we know of, which verse did he choose? He shuffled the scroll toward the end of the text and read, "The Spirit of the LORD is upon Me, because He has anointed Me to preach the gospel to the poor; He has sent Me to heal the brokenhearted" (Luke 4:18, quoting Isaiah 61:1 NKJV).

Jesus lifted his eyes from the parchment and quoted the rest of the words. The crowd, who cherished the words as much as he did, mouthed the lines along with him: "To proclaim liberty to the captives and recovery of sight to the blind, to set at liberty those who are oppressed; to proclaim the acceptable year of the LORD" (Luke 4:18–19 NKJV).

Jesus had a target audience. The poor. The brokenhearted. Captives. The blind and oppressed.

His to-do list? Help for the body and soul, strength for the physical and the spiritual, therapy for the temporal and eternal. "This is my mission statement," Jesus declared. The Nazareth Manifesto.

Preach the gospel to the poor.
Heal the brokenhearted.
Proclaim liberty to the captives.
Proclaim recovery of sight to the blind.
Set at liberty those who are oppressed.
And proclaim the acceptable year of the Lord.

"Acceptable year of the LORD" describes, perhaps more than any other words, Jesus' radical commitment to the poor.

—Outlive Your Life

*G*od is not the God of confusion, and wherever he sees sincere seekers with confused hearts, you can bet your sweet December that he will do whatever it takes to help them see his will. That's what he was doing on the road to Emmaus.

Everybody else was online, and they were on foot. They saw the death of Jesus as the death of the movement, and they packed their bags and headed home. And that is where they were going when Jesus appeared to them. . . .

The disciples disregarded the Word of God. . . . Rather than consult the Scriptures, they listened to their fears. Jesus corrects this by appearing to them and conducting a Bible study. We'd expect something a bit more dramatic from one who had just defeated death—turn a tree into a dog or suspend the disciples a few feet in the air. But Jesus sees no need to do more than reacquaint his followers with Scripture.

> "You are foolish and slow to believe everything the prophets said. They said that the Christ must suffer these things before he enters his glory." Then starting with what Moses and the prophets had said about him, Jesus began to explain everything that had been written about himself in the Scriptures. (Luke 24:25–27 NCV)

Through the words of the prophets, he used Scripture to reveal his will. Doesn't he do the same today? Open the Word of God and you'll find his will.

> "This is the will of the Father . . . that of all He has given Me I should lose nothing, but should raise it up." (John 6:39 NKJV)

> It is God's will that you be born again, that you be born not "of the will of the flesh, nor of the will of man, but of God." (John 1:13 NKJV)

> It is not God's will that one little one perish. (Matt. 18:14)

> "This is the will of my Father, that every one who sees the Son and believes in him should have eternal life, and I will raise him up at the last day." (John 6:40 RSV)

It is his will that the world be saved. Knowing that, then, my task is to align myself with his will. Anytime I find myself choosing between two roads I must ask, "Which road will contribute more to the kingdom of God?"

—The Great House of God

*N*icodemus comes at night. His colleagues can't know of the meeting. They wouldn't understand. But Nicodemus can't wait until they do. As the shadows darken the city, he steps out, slips unseen through the cobbled, winding streets. He passes servants lighting lamps in the courtyards and takes a path that ends at the door of a simple house. Jesus and his followers are staying here, he's been told. Nicodemus knocks.

The noisy room silences as he enters. The men are wharf workers and tax collectors, unaccustomed to the highbrow world of a scholar. They shift in their seats. Jesus motions for the guest to sit. Nicodemus does and initiates the most famous conversation in the Bible: "Rabbi, we know that You are a teacher come from God; for no one can do these signs that You do unless God is with him" (John 3:2 NKJV).

Nicodemus begins with what he "knows." *I've done my homework*, he implies. *Your work impresses me.* We listen for a kindred salutation from Jesus: "And I've heard of you, Nicodemus." We expect, and Nicodemus expected, some hospitable chitchat.

None comes. Jesus makes no mention of Nicodemus's VIP status, good intentions, or academic credentials, not because they don't exist, but because, in Jesus's algorithm, they don't matter. He simply issues this proclamation: "Unless one is born again, he cannot see the kingdom of God" (v. 3 NKJV).

Behold the Continental Divide of Scripture, the international date line of faith. Nicodemus stands on one side, Jesus on the other, and Christ pulls no punches about their differences.

Nicodemus inhabits a land of good efforts, sincere gestures, and hard work. Give God your best, his philosophy says, and God does the rest.

Jesus' response? Your best won't do. Your works don't work. Your finest efforts don't mean squat. Unless you are born again, you can't even see what God is up to.

Nicodemus hesitates on behalf of us all. Born again? "How can a man be born when he is old?" (v. 4 NKJV). You must be kidding. Put life in reverse? Rewind the tape? Start all over? We can't be born again.

Oh, but wouldn't we like to? A do-over. A try-again. A reload. Broken hearts and missed opportunities bob in our wake. A mulligan would be nice. Who wouldn't cherish a second shot? But who can pull it off? Nicodemus scratches his chin and chuckles. "Yeah, a graybeard like me gets a maternity-ward recall."

Jesus doesn't crack a smile. "Most assuredly, I say to you, un less one is born of water and the Spirit, he cannot enter the kingdom of God" (v. 5 NKJV). About this time a gust of wind blows a few leaves through the still-open door. Jesus picks one off the floor and holds it up. God's power works like that wind, Jesus explains. Newborn hearts are born of heaven. You can't wish, earn, or create one. New birth? Inconceivable. God handles the task, start to finish.

Nicodemus looks around the room at the followers. Their blank expressions betray equal bewilderment.

Old Nick has no hook upon which to hang such thoughts. He speaks self-fix. But Jesus speaks—indeed introduces—a different language. Not works born of men and women, but a work done by God.

—3:16: The Numbers of Hope

It may surprise you that Jesus made preparedness the theme of his last sermon. It did me. I would have preached on love or family or the importance of church. Jesus didn't. Jesus preached on what many today consider to be old-fashioned. He preached on being ready for heaven and staying out of hell.

It's his message when he tells of the wise and the foolish servants.[5] The wise one was ready for the return of the master; the foolish one was not.

It's his message when he tells about the ten bridesmaids. Five were wise and five were foolish[6]. The wise ones were ready when the groom came and the foolish ones were at the corner store looking for more oil.

It's his message when he tells of the three servants and the bags of gold[7]. Two servants put the money to work and made more money for the master. The third hid his in a hole. The first two were ready and rewarded when the master returned. The third was unprepared and punished.

Be ready. It's a first-step, nonnegotiable . . . principle.

That is the theme of Jesus' last sermon, "So always be ready, because you don't know the day your Lord will come."[8] He didn't tell when the day of the Lord would be, but he did describe what the day would be like. It's a day no one will miss.

Every person who has ever lived will be present at that final gathering. Every heart that has ever beat. Every mouth that has ever spoken. On that day you will be surrounded by a sea of people. Rich, poor. Famous, unknown. Kings, bums. Brilliant, demented. All will be present. And all will be looking in one direction. All will be looking at him. Every human being.

"The Son of Man will come again in his great glory."[9]

You won't look at anyone else. No side glances to see what others are wearing. No whispers about new jewelry or comments about who is present. At this, the greatest gathering in history, you will have eyes for only one—the Son of Man. Wrapped in splendor. Shot through with radiance. Imploded with light and magnetic in power.

Jesus describes this day with certainty.

He leaves no room for doubt. He doesn't say he may return, or might return, but that he *will* return. By the way, one-twentieth of your New Testament speaks about his return. There are over three hundred references to his second coming. Twenty-three of the twenty-seven New Testament books speak of it. And they speak of it with confidence.

"You also must be ready, because the Son of Man will come at a time you don't expect him."[10]

". . . Jesus, who has been taken from you into heaven, will come back in the same way you have seen him go into heaven."[11]

". . . he will come a second time, not to offer himself for sin, but to bring salvation to those who are waiting for him."[12]

". . . the day of the Lord will come like a thief in the night."[13]

His return is certain.

His return is final.

Upon his return "he will separate them into two groups as a shepherd separates the sheep from the goats. The Son of Man will put the sheep on his right and the goats on his left."[14]

The word *separate* is a sad word. To separate a mother from a daughter, a father from a son, a husband from a wife. To separate people on earth is sorrowful, but to think of it being done for eternity is horrible.

Especially when one group is destined for heaven and the other group is going to hell.

We don't like to talk about hell, do we? In intellectual circles the topic of hell is regarded as primitive and foolish. It's not logical. "A loving God wouldn't send people to hell." So we dismiss it.

But to dismiss it is to dismiss a core teaching of Jesus. The doctrine of hell is not one developed by Paul, Peter, or John. It is taught by Jesus himself. . . .

It's interesting that Jesus' first and last sermons have the same message. In his first sermon, the Sermon on the Mount, Jesus calls you and me to choose between the rock and the sand,[15] the wide gate and the narrow gate, the wide road and the narrow road, the big crowd and the small crowd, the certainty of hell and the joy of heaven.[16] In his last sermon he calls us to do the same. He calls us to be ready.

—*And the Angels Were Silent*

"*For* God so loved the world that he gave his one and only son, that whoever believes in him shall not perish but have eternal life" (NIV).

Whoever unfurls 3:16 as a banner for the ages. *Whoever* unrolls the welcome mat of heaven to humanity. *Whoever* invites the world to God.

Jesus could have so easily narrowed the scope, changing whoever into whatever. "Whatever Jew believes" or "Whatever woman follows me." But he used no qualifier. The pronoun is wonderfully indefinite. After all, who isn't a *whoever?*

The word sledgehammers racial fences and dynamites social classes. It bypasses gender borders and surpasses ancient traditions. *Whoever* makes it clear: God exports his grace worldwide. For those who attempt to restrict it, Jesus has a word: *Whoever.*

> *Whoever* acknowledges me before men, I will also acknowledge him before my Father in heaven. (Matt. 10:32 NIV)

> *Whoever* finds his life will lose it, and whoever loses his life for my sake will find it. (Matt. 10:39 ESV)

> *Whoever* does God's will is my brother and sister and mother. (Mark 3:35 NIV)

> *Whoever* believes and is baptized will be saved, but whoever does not believe will be condemned. (Mark 16:16 NIV)

> *Whoever* believes in the Son has eternal life, but whoever rejects the Son will not see life, for God's wrath remains on him. (John 3:36 NIV)

> *Whoever* drinks the water I give him will never thirst. (John 4:14 NIV)

Whoever comes to me I will never drive away. (John 6:37 NIV)

Whoever lives and believes in me will never die. (John 11:26 NIV)

Whoever is thirsty, let him come; and whoever wishes, let him take the free gift of the water of life. (Rev. 22:17 NIV)

Titus 2:11 assures us that "the grace of God . . . has appeared to all men." Paul contends that Jesus Christ sacrificed himself "to win freedom for all mankind" (1 Tim. 2:6 NEB). Peter affirms that "it is not his [God's] will for any to be lost, but for all to come to repentance" (2 Pet. 3:9 NEB). God's gospel has a "whoever" policy.

We need to know this. The downturns of life can create such a sad state of affairs that we wonder if God still wants us. Surely Lazarus the beggar wondered. Jesus tells us this about him:

There was a rich man who was dressed in purple and fine linen and lived in luxury every day. At his gate was laid a beggar named Lazarus, covered with sores and longing to eat what fell from the rich man's table. Even the dogs came and licked his sores. (Luke 16:19–21 NIV)

The two men indwell opposite sides of the city tracks. The rich man lives in posh luxury and wears the finest clothing. The language suggests he uses fabric worth its weight in gold.[17] He eats exotic food, enjoys a spacious house with botanical gardens. He's the New Testament version of a Monaco billionaire.

Lazarus is a homeless street sleeper. Dogs lick the sores that cavern his skin. He languishes outside the mansion, hoping for scraps. Infected. Rejected. No possessions. No family. An exception to God's "whoever" policy, right?

Wrong.

In sudden drama, the curtain of death falls on act 1, and eternal destiny is revealed in act 2.

> The time came when the beggar died and the angels carried him to Abraham's side. The rich man also died and was buried. In hell, where he was in torment, he looked up and saw Abraham far away, with Lazarus by his side. (vv. 22–23)

Just-poor Lazarus now needs nothing. The now-poor rich man needs everything. He loses the lap of luxury, and Lazarus discovers the lap of Abraham.

Lazaruses still populate our planet. You may be one. Not begging for bread, but struggling to buy some. Not sleeping on streets, but on the floor perhaps? In your car sometimes? On a couch often? Does God have a place for people in your place?

Of all the messages this account conveys, don't miss this one: God takes you however he finds you. No need to clean up or climb up. Just look up. . . .

If heaven's banquet table has nameplates, one bears your name.

We lose much in life—sobriety, solvency, and sanity. We lose jobs and chances, and we lose at love. We lose youth and its vigor, idealism and its dreams. We lose much, but we never lose our place on God's "whoever" list.

Whoever—God's wonderful word of welcome.

—3:16: The Numbers of Hope

6

Healer

*W*e don't know her name, but we know her situation. Her world was midnight black. Grope-in-the-dark-and-hope-for-help black. Read these two verses and see what I mean:

A large crowd followed Jesus and pushed very close around him. Among them was a woman who had been bleeding for twelve years. She had suffered very much from many doctors and had spent all the money she had, but instead of improving, she was getting worse. (Mark 5:24–26 NCV)

She was a bruised reed: "bleeding for twelve years," "suffered very much," "spent all the money she had," and "getting worse."

A chronic menstrual disorder. A perpetual issue of blood. Such a condition would be difficult for any woman of any era. But for a Jewess, nothing could be worse. No part of her life was left unaffected.

Sexually . . . she could not touch her husband.
Maternally . . . she could not bear children.
Domestically . . . anything she touched was considered unclean. No washing dishes. No sweeping floors.

Spiritually . . . she was not allowed to enter the temple.

She was physically exhausted and socially ostracized.

She had sought help "under the care of many doctors" (v. 26 NIV). The Talmud gives no fewer than eleven cures for such a condition. No doubt she had tried them all. Some were legitimate treatments. Others, such as carrying the ashes of an ostrich egg in a linen cloth, were hollow superstitions.

She "had spent all she had" (v. 26 NIV). To dump financial strain on top of the physical strain is to add insult to injury. A friend battling cancer told me that the hounding of the creditors who demand payments for ongoing medical treatment is just as devastating as the pain.

"Instead of getting better she grew worse" (v. 26 NIV). She was a bruised reed. She awoke daily in a body that no one wanted. She is down to her last prayer. And on the day we encounter her, she's about to pray it.

By the time she gets to Jesus, he is surrounded by people. He's on his way to help the daughter of Jairus, the most important man in the community. What are the odds that he will interrupt an urgent mission with a high official to help the likes of her? Very few. But what are the odds that she will survive if she doesn't take a chance? Fewer still. So she takes a chance.

"If I can just touch his clothes," she thinks, "I will be healed" (v. 28 NCV).

Risky decision. To touch him, she will have to touch the people. If one of them recognizes her . . . hello rebuke, good-bye cure. But what choice does she have? She has no money, no clout, no friends, no solutions. All she has is a crazy hunch that Jesus can help and a high hope that he will.

Maybe that's all you have: a crazy hunch and a high hope. You have nothing to give. But you are hurting. And all you have to offer him is your hurt.

Maybe that has kept you from coming to God. Oh, you've taken a step or two in his direction. But then you saw the other people around him. They seemed so clean, so neat, so trim and fit in their faith. And when you saw them, they blocked your view of him. So you stepped back.

If that describes you, note carefully, only one person was commended that day for having faith. It wasn't a wealthy giver. It wasn't a loyal follower. It wasn't an acclaimed teacher. It was a shame-struck, penniless outcast who clutched onto her hunch that he could and her hope that he would.

Which, by the way, isn't a bad definition of faith: *a conviction that he can and a hope that he will.* Sounds similar to the definition of faith given by the Bible. "Without faith no one can please God. Anyone who comes to God must believe that he is real and that he rewards those who truly want to find him" (Heb. 11:6 NCV). . . .

A healthy lady never would have appreciated the power of a touch of the hem of his robe. But this woman was sick . . . and when her dilemma met his dedication, a miracle occurred. Her part in the healing was very small. All she did was extend her arm through the crowd.

"If only I can touch him."

What's important is not the form of the effort but the fact of the effort. The fact is, she did something. She refused to settle for sickness another day and resolved to make a move.

Healing begins when we do something. Healing begins when we reach out. Healing starts when we take a step.

God's help is near and always available, but it is only given to those who seek it. Nothing results from apathy. The great work in this story is the mighty healing that occurred. But the great truth is that the healing began with her touch. And with that small, courageous gesture, she experienced Jesus' tender power.

—He Still Moves Stones

*J*esus encounters the man near a large pool north of the temple in Jerusalem. It's 360 feet long, 130 feet wide, and 75 feet deep. A colonnade with five porches overlooks the body of water. It's a monument of wealth and prosperity, but its residents are people of sickness and disease.

It's called Bethesda. It could be called Central Park, Metropolitan Hospital, or even Joe's Bar and Grill. It could be the homeless huddled beneath a downtown overpass. It could be Calvary Baptist. It could be any collection of hurting people.

An underwater spring caused the pool to bubble occasionally. The people believed the bubbles were caused by the dipping of angels' wings. They also believed that the first person to touch the water after the angel did would be healed. Did healing occur? I don't know. But I do know crowds of invalids came to give it a try.

Picture a battleground strewn with wounded bodies, and you see Bethesda. Imagine a nursing home overcrowded and understaffed, and you see the pool. Call to mind the orphans in Bangladesh or the abandoned in New Delhi, and you will see what people saw when they passed Bethesda. As they passed, what did they hear? An endless wave of groans. What did they witness? A field of faceless need. What did they do? Most walked past, ignoring the people.

But not Jesus. He is in Jerusalem for a feast. He is alone. He's not there to teach the disciples or to draw a crowd. The people need him—so he's there.

Can you picture it? Jesus walking among the suffering.

What is he thinking? When an infected hand touches his ankle, what does he do? When a blind child stumbles in Jesus' path, does he reach down to catch the child? When a wrinkled hand extends for alms, how does Jesus respond?

Whether the watering hole is Bethesda or Bill's Bar . . . how does God feel when people hurt?

It's worth the telling of the story if all we do is watch him walk. It's worth it just to know he even came. He didn't have to, you know. Surely there are more sanitary crowds in Jerusalem. Surely there are more enjoyable activities. After all, this is the Passover feast. It's an exciting time in the holy city. People have come from miles around to meet God in the temple.

Little do they know that God is with the sick.

Little do they know that God is walking slowly, stepping carefully between the beggars and the blind.

Little do they know that the strong young carpenter who surveys the ragged landscape of pain is God.

"When they suffered, he suffered also" Isaiah wrote (Isa. 63:9 NCV). On this day Jesus must have suffered much.

On this day Jesus must have sighed often as he walked along the poolside of Bethesda . . . and he sighs when he comes to you and me. . . .

We, like the invalid, are paralyzed. We, like the invalid, are trapped. We, like the invalid, are stuck; we have no solution for our predicament.

That's you and me lying on the ground. That's us wounded and weary. When it comes to healing our spiritual condition, we don't have a chance. We might as well be told to pole-vault the moon. We don't have what it takes to be healed. Our only hope is that God will do for us what he did for the man at Bethesda—that he will step out of the temple and step into our ward of hurt and helplessness.

Which is exactly what he has done. . . . I want you to look at the brief but revealing dialogue between the paralytic and the Savior. Before Jesus heals him, he asks him a question: "Do you want to be well?" "Sir, there is no one to help me get into the pool when the water starts moving. While I am coming to the water, someone else always gets in before me" (John 5:6–7 NCV).

Is the fellow complaining? Is he feeling sorry for himself? Or is he just stating the facts? Who knows. But before we think about it too much, look what happens next.

"'Stand up. Pick up your mat and walk.'"

"And immediately the man was well; he picked up his mat and began to walk."

I wish we would do that; I wish we would take Jesus at his word. I wish, like heaven, that we would learn that when he says something, it happens. What is this peculiar paralysis that confines us? What is this stubborn unwillingness to be healed? When Jesus tells us to stand, let's stand.

When he says we're forgiven, let's unload the guilt.
When he says we're valuable, let's believe him.
When he says we're eternal, let's bury our fear.
When he says we're provided for, let's stop worrying.
When he says, "Stand up," let's do it.

—He Still Moves Stones

*J*esus met an invalid. The man couldn't walk. He couldn't stand. His limbs were bent and his body twisted. A waist-high world walked past as he sat and watched.

Perhaps he was palsied, his body ridden with disease since birth. While other children had jumped and run, he had labored to bring a spoon to his mouth. As his brothers and sisters spoke and sang, his words slurred and slipped. Maybe he had never known what it was to be whole.

Or maybe he had known. Maybe he had once been healthy. Was there a time when he was known for his ability, not his disability? Was there an era when he could outrun anyone? Was there a time when he was the strongest in the shop? Was there a day when every kid in the village wanted to be like him?

Then came the fall—a tumble down a canyon, perhaps a stumble down some stairs. The pain in his skull was unbearable, but the numbness in his legs and arms was far worse. His feet hung like ornaments on the ends of his legs. His hands dangled like empty sleeves from his sides. He could see his limbs, but he couldn't feel them.

Whether he was born paralyzed or became paralyzed—the end result was the same: total dependence on others. Someone had to wash his face and bathe his body. He couldn't blow his nose or go on a walk. When he ran, it was in his dreams, and his dreams would always awaken to a body that couldn't roll over and couldn't go back to sleep for all the hurt the night dream had brought.

"What he needs is a new body," any man in half his mind would say. What he needs is a God in heaven to restore what tragedy has robbed: arms that swing, hands that grip, and feet that dance.

When people looked at him, they didn't see the man; they saw a body in need of a miracle. That's not what Jesus saw, but that's what the people saw. And that's certainly what his friends saw. So they did what any of us would do for a friend. They tried to get him some help.

Word was out that a carpenter-turned-teacher-turned-wonderworker was in town. And as the word got out, the people came. They came from every hole and hovel in Israel. They came like soldiers returning from battle—bandaged, crippled, sightless. The old with prune faces and toothless mouths. The young with deaf babies and broken hearts. Fathers with sons who couldn't speak. Wives with wombs that wouldn't bear fruit. The world, it seemed, had come to see if he was real or right or both.

By the time his friends arrived at the place, the house was full. People jammed the doorways. Kids sat in the windows. Others peeked over shoulders. How would this small band of friends ever attract Jesus' attention? They had to make a choice: do we go in or give up?

What would have happened had the friends given up? What if they had shrugged their shoulders and mumbled something about the crowd being big and dinner getting cold and turned and left? After all, they had done a good deed in coming this far. Who could fault them for turning back? You can only do so much for somebody. But these friends hadn't done enough.

One said that he had an idea. The four huddled over the paralytic and listened to the plan to climb to the top of the house, cut through the roof, and lower their friend down with their sashes.

It was risky—they could fall. It was dangerous—he could fall. It was unorthodox—de-roofing is antisocial. It was intrusive—Jesus was busy. But it was their only chance to see Jesus. So they climbed to the roof.

Faith does those things. Faith does the unexpected. And faith gets God's attention. Look what Mark says: "When Jesus saw the faith of these people, he said to the paralyzed man, 'Young man, your sins are forgiven'" (Mark 2:5 NCV).

Finally, someone took him at his word! Four men had enough hope in him and love for their friend that they took a chance. The stretcher above was a sign from above—somebody believes! Someone was willing to risk embarrassment and injury for just a few moments with the Galilean. . . .

Jesus was moved by the scene of faith. So he applauds—if not with his hands, at least with his heart. And not only does he applaud, he blesses. And we witness a divine loveburst.

The friends want him to heal their friend. But Jesus won't settle for a simple healing of the body—he wants to heal the soul. He leapfrogs the physical and deals with the spiritual. To heal the body is temporal; to heal the soul is eternal.

The request of the friends is valid—but timid. The expectations of the crowd are high—but not high enough. They expect Jesus to say, "I heal you." Instead he says, "I forgive you."

They expect him to treat the body, for that is what they see.

He chooses to treat not only the body, but also the spiritual, for that is what he sees.

They want Jesus to give the man a new body so he can walk. Jesus gives grace so the man can live.

Remarkable. Sometimes God is so touched by what he sees that he gives us what we need and not simply that for which we ask.

—He Still Moves Stones

Jesus left there and went along the Sea of Galilee. Then he went up on a mountainside and sat down. Great crowds came to him, bringing the lame, the blind, the crippled, the mute and many others, and laid them at his feet; and he healed them. The people were amazed when they saw the mute speaking, the crippled made well, the lame walking and the blind seeing. And they praised the God of Israel. Jesus called his disciples to him and said, "I have compassion for these people; they have already been with me three days and have nothing to eat. I do not want to send them away hungry, or they may collapse on the way."[1]

This is not the day that Jesus fed the five thousand men; it is the day he fed the four thousand. Although the events have much in common, they are different in several respects:

- When Jesus fed the five thousand, he was with Jews. When he fed the four thousand (plus women and children), he was in Decapolis, a Gentile region.
- When Jesus fed the five thousand, he taught and healed them. When he was with the four thousand, there is no record that he taught—only that he healed.
- When Jesus was with the five thousand, he was with them for one afternoon. When he was with the four thousand, he was with them for three days.

And for three days he did a most remarkable thing: he healed them.

"The lame, the blind, the crippled, the mute and many others" came to him, Matthew wrote, "and he healed them."

Many times I wish that the New Testament writers had been a bit more descriptive. This is one of those times. "And he healed them" is too short a phrase to describe what must have been an astonishing sight.

Let your imagination go. Can you see the scene?

Can you see the blind husband seeing his wife for the first time? His eyes gazing into her tear-filled ones like she was the queen of the morning?

Envision the man who had never walked, now walking! Don't you know that he didn't want to sit down? Don't you know that he ran and jumped and did a dance with the kids?

And what about the mute who could speak? Can you picture him sitting by the fire late into the night and talking? Saying and singing everything and anything that he had ever wanted to say and sing.

And the deaf woman who could now hear. What was it like when she heard her child call her "Mamma" for the first time?

For three days it went on. Person after person. Mat after mat. Crutch after crutch. Smile after smile. No record is given of Jesus preaching or teaching or instructing or challenging. He just healed.

"The people," Matthew wrote, "were amazed when they saw the mute speaking, the crippled made well, the lame walking and the blind seeing." Four thousand amazed people, each telling a story grander than the other. In the midst of them all is Jesus. Not complaining. Not postponing. Not demanding. Just enjoying every minute.

Then Matthew, still the great economizer of words, gave us another phrase on which I wish he would have elaborated:

"They praised the God of Israel."

I wonder how they did that. I feel more certain of what they didn't do than of what they did do. I feel confident that they didn't form a praise committee. I feel confident that they didn't make any robes. I feel confident that they didn't sit in rows and stare at the back of each other's heads.

I doubt seriously if they wrote a creed on how they were to praise this God they had never before worshiped. I can't picture them getting into an argument over technicalities. I doubt if they felt it had to be done indoors.

And I know they didn't wait until the Sabbath to do it.

In all probability, they just did it. Each one—in his or her own way, with his or her own heart—just praised Jesus. Perhaps some people came and fell at Jesus' feet. Perhaps some shouted his name. Maybe a few just went up on the hillside, looked into the sky, and smiled.

I can picture a mom and dad standing speechless before the Healer as they hold their newly healed baby.

I can envision a leper staring in awe at the One who took away his terror.

I can imagine throngs of people pushing and shoving. Wanting to get close. Not to request anything or demand anything, but just to say "thank you."

Perhaps some tried to pay Jesus, but what payment would have been sufficient?

Perhaps some tried to return his gift with another, but what could a person give that would express the gratitude?

All the people could do was exactly what Matthew said they did. "They praised the God of Israel."

However they did it, they did it. And Jesus was touched, so touched that he insisted they stay for a meal before they left.

Without using the word *worship*, this passage defines it.

Worship is when you're aware that what you've been given is far greater than what you can give. Worship is the awareness that were it not for his touch, you'd still be hobbling and hurting, bitter and broken. Worship is the half-glazed expression on the parched face of a desert pilgrim as he discovers that the oasis is not a mirage.

Worship is the "thank you" that refuses to be silenced.

We have tried to make a science out of worship. We can't do that. We can't do that any more than we can "sell love" or "negotiate peace."

Worship is a voluntary act of gratitude offered by the saved to the Savior, by the healed to the Healer, and by the delivered to the Deliverer. And if you and I can go days without feeling an urge to say "thank you" to the One who saved, healed, and delivered us, then we'd do well to remember what he did.

—*In the Eye of the Storm*

*J*ohn introduces him to us with these words. "As [Jesus] passed by, He saw a man blind from birth" (John 9:1 NASB). This man has never seen a sunrise. Can't tell purple from pink. The disciples fault the family tree. "Rabbi, who sinned, this man or his parents, that he would be born blind?" (v. 2).

Neither, the God-man replies. Trace this condition back to heaven. The reason the man was born sightless? So "the works of God might be displayed in him" (v. 3).

Talk about a thankless role. Selected to suffer. Some sing to God's glory. Others teach to God's glory. Who wants to be blind for God's glory? Which is tougher—the condition or discovering it was God's idea?

The cure proves to be as surprising as the cause. "[Jesus] spat on the ground, and made clay of the spittle, and applied the clay to his eyes" (v. 6).

The world abounds with paintings of the God-man: in the arms of Mary, in the Garden of Gethsemane, in the Upper Room, in the darkened tomb. Jesus touching. Jesus weeping, laughing, teaching . . . but I've never seen a painting of Jesus spitting.

Christ smacking his lips a time or two, gathering a mouth of saliva, working up a blob of drool, and letting it go. Down in the dirt. (Kids, next time your mother tells you not to spit, show her this passage.) Then he squats, stirs up a puddle of . . . I don't know, what would you call it?

Holy putty? Spit therapy? Saliva solution? Whatever the name, he places a fingerful in his palm, and then, as calmly as a painter spackles a hole in the wall, Jesus streaks mud-miracle on the blind man's eyes. "Go, wash in the pool of Siloam" (v. 7).

The beggar feels his way to the pool, splashes water on his mud-streaked face, and rubs away the clay. The result is the first chapter of Genesis, just for him. Light where there was darkness. Virgin eyes focus, fuzzy figures become human beings, and John receives the Understatement of the Bible Award when he writes: "He . . . came back seeing" (v. 7).

Come on, John! Running short of verbs? How about "he *raced* back seeing"? "He *danced* back seeing"? "He *roared* back whooping and hollering and kissing everything he could, for the first time, see"? The guy had to be thrilled.

We would love to leave him that way, but if this man's life were a cafeteria line, he would have just stepped from the sirloin to the boiled Brussels sprouts. Look at the reaction of the neighbors: "'Is not this the one who used to sit and beg?' Others were saying, 'This is he,' still others were saying, 'No, but he is like him.' He kept saying, 'I am the one'" (vv. 8–9).

These folks don't celebrate; they debate! They have watched this man grope and trip since he was a kid (v. 20). You'd think they would rejoice. But they don't. . . .

"Jesus heard that they had thrown him out, and went and found him" (v. 35 MSG). In case the stable birth wasn't enough. If three decades of earth walking and miracle working are insufficient. If there be any doubt regarding God's full-bore devotion, he does things like this. He tracks down a troubled pauper.

The beggar lifts his eyes to look into the face of the One who started all this. Is he going to criticize Christ? Complain to Christ? You couldn't blame him for doing both. After all, he didn't volunteer for the disease or the deliverance. But he does neither. No, "he worshiped Him" (v. 38 NASB). Don't you know he knelt? Don't you think he wept? And how could he keep from wrapping his arms around the waist of the One who gave him sight? He worshiped him.

And when you see him, you will too.

—Next Door Savior

*G*ratitude is the firstborn child of grace, the appropriate response of the blessed. So appropriate, in fact, that its absence surprises Jesus. We know this because of ten men he healed.

"It happened that as he made his way toward Jerusalem, he crossed over the border between Samaria and Galilee. As he entered a village, ten men, all lepers, met him. They kept their distance but raised their voices, calling out, 'Jesus, Master, have mercy on us!'" (Luke 17:11–13 MSG).

Lepers. A huddle of half-draped faces and bent bodies. Who could discern where one form stopped and the other began, they leaned on each other so? Yet upon whom else could they lean?

Their appearance repulsed people: lumps on the cheeks, nose, lips, and forehead. Ulcerated vocal cords rendered their voices a raspy wheeze. Hairless eyebrows turned eyes into hollow stares. Muscles atrophied and tendons contracted until hands looked like claws. People avoided lepers.

But Christ had compassion on them. So when people stepped back from the ten lepers, the Master stepped forward. "'Go, show yourselves to the priests.' They went, and while still on their way, became clean" (17:14).

Wouldn't you love to have witnessed the miracle? No therapy. No treatment. No medicine. Just one prayer to one man and Pow! Complete healing. Gnarled hands straightening. Open sores closing. Energy pulsating through veins. Ten hoods thrown back and twenty crutches dropped. A mass of misery becomes a leaping, jumping, celebrating chorus of health.

Can you imagine how the lepers felt? If you're in Christ, you can. What he did for the lepers physically, he has done for you spiritually. . . .

He closes the open sores of our hearts and straightens the gnarled limbs of our inner beings. He swaps sin rags for righteous robes. He still heals. And he still looks for gratitude.

—Great Day Every Day

*A*re you waiting for Jesus to heal you? Take hope from Jesus' response to the blind men.[2]

"Have mercy on us, O Lord," they cried.

"Jesus stood still." He stopped dead in his tracks. Everyone else kept going. Jesus froze. Something caught his attention. Something interrupted his journey. We can see him raising his hand to stop the people, lifting a finger to his lips for them to be quiet. "Sh." What was it? What did Jesus hear?

A prayer. An unembellished appeal for help, floating across the path on the winds of faith and landing against his ear. Jesus heard the words and stopped.

He still does. And he still asks, "What do you want me to do for you?"

The duo in Jericho told him. "Lord, that our eyes may be opened," they said.

And you?

Lord, heal this heart condition.

Remove this arthritis.

Restore my hearing.

Jesus' heart went out to the blind men. He "had compassion and touched their eyes." The Greek term means "he felt for them deep down inside his stomach."[3] Jesus moved in where others had stepped away. He healed them.

He will heal you, my friend. I pray he heals you instantly. He may choose to heal you gradually. But this much is sure: Jesus will heal us all ultimately. Wheelchairs, ointments, treatments, and bandages are confiscated at the gateway to heaven. God's children will once again be whole.

—Before Amen

7

Provider

The wedding was moving. The guests were celebrating . . . but the wine was gone. Back then, wine was to a wedding what cake is to a wedding today. Can you imagine a wedding without cake? They couldn't imagine a wedding without wine. To offer wine was to show respect to your guests. Not to offer wine at a wedding was an insult.

What Mary faced was a social problem. A foul-up. A snafu. A calamity on the common scale. No need to call 911, but no way to sweep the embarrassment under the rug, either.

When you think about it, most of the problems we face are of the same caliber. Seldom do we have to deal with dilemmas of national scale or world conflict. Seldom do our crises rock the Richter scale. Usually the waves we ride are made by pebbles, not boulders. We're late for a meeting. We leave something at the office. A coworker forgets a report. Mail gets lost. Traffic gets snarled. The waves rocking our lives are not life threatening yet. But they can be. A poor response to a simple problem can light a fuse. What begins as a snowflake can snowball into an avalanche unless proper care is taken.

For that reason you might want to note how Mary reacted. Her solution poses a practical plan for untangling life's knots. "They have no more wine," she told Jesus (John 2:3 NCV). That's it. That's all she said.

She didn't go ballistic. She simply assessed the problem and gave it to Christ.

"A problem well stated is a problem half solved," John Dewey said. Mary would have liked that, for that's what she did. She defined the problem.

She could have exploded: "Why didn't you plan better? There's not enough wine! Whose fault is this anyway? You guys never do anything right. If anything is to be done right around here I have to do it myself!"

Or she could have imploded: "This is my fault. I failed. I'm to blame. I deserve it. If only I'd majored in culinary art. I'm a failure in life. Go ahead; do the world a favor. Tie me up and march me to the gallows. I deserve it."

It's so easy to focus on everything but the solution. Mary didn't do that. She simply looked at the knot, assessed it, and took it to the right person. "I've got one here I can't untie, Jesus."

"When all the wine was gone, Jesus' mother said to him, 'They have no more wine'" (John 2:3 NCV).

Please note, she took the problem to Jesus before she took it to anyone else. A friend told me about a tense deacons' meeting he attended. Apparently there was more agitation than agreement, and after a lengthy discussion, someone suggested, "Why don't we pray about it?" to which another questioned, "Has it come to that?"

What causes us to think of prayer as the last option rather than the first? I can think of two reasons: feelings of independence and feelings of insignificance.

Sometimes we're independent. We begin to think we are big enough to solve our own problems. . . .

Other times we don't feel independent; we feel insignificant. We think, "Sure, Mary can take her problems to Jesus. She's his mother. He doesn't want to hear my problems. Besides, he's got famine and the Mafia to deal with. I don't want to trouble him with my messes."

If that is your thought, may I share with you a favorite verse of mine? (Of course I can, I'm writing the book!) I like it so much I wrote it on the first page of my Bible.

"Because he delights in me, he saved me" (Ps. 18:19 NCV).

And you thought he saved you because of your decency. You thought he saved you because of your good works or good attitude or good looks. Sorry. If that were the case, your salvation would be lost when your voice went south or your works got weak. There are many reasons God saves you: to bring glory to himself, to appease his justice, to demonstrate his sovereignty. But one of the sweetest reasons God saved you is because he is fond of you. He likes having you around. He thinks you are the best thing to come down the pike in quite awhile. "As a man rejoices over his new wife, so your God will rejoice over you" (Isa. 62:5 NCV).

If God had a refrigerator, your picture would be on it. If he had a wallet, your photo would be in it. He sends you flowers every spring and a sunrise every morning. Whenever you want to talk, he'll listen. He can live anywhere in the universe, and he chose your heart. And the Christmas gift he sent you in Bethlehem? Face it, friend. He's crazy about you.

The last thing you should worry about is being a nuisance to God. All you need to concentrate on is doing what he tells you to do. Note the sequence of events in the next verse: "Jesus said to the servants, 'Fill the jars with water.' So they filled the jars to the top. Then he said to them, 'Now take some out and give it to the master of the feast.' So they took the water to the master. When he tasted it, the water had become wine" (John 2:7–9 NCV).

Did you see the sequence? First the jars were filled with water. Then Jesus instructed the servants to take the water (not the wine) to the master.

Now, if I'm a servant, I don't want to do that. How is that going to solve the problem? And what is the master going to say when I give him a cup of water? But these servants either had enough naiveté or trust to do what Jesus said, and so the problem was solved. Note, the water became wine after they had obeyed, not before.

What if the servants had refused? What if they had said, "No way"? Or, to bring the point closer to home, what if *you* refuse? What if you identify the problem, take it to Jesus, and then refuse to do what he says?

That's possible. After all, God is asking you to take some pretty gutsy steps. Money is tight, but he still asks you to give. You've been offended, but he asks you to forgive your offender. Someone else blew the assignment, but he still asks you to be patient. You can't see God's face, but he still asks you to pray.

Not commands for the faint of faith. But then again, he wouldn't ask you to do it if he thought you couldn't. So go ahead. Next time you face a common calamity, follow the example of Mary at the wineless wedding:

Identify the problem. (You'll half-solve it.)

Present it to Jesus. (He's happy to help.)

Do what he says. (No matter how crazy.)

—A Gentle Thunder

*W*hy did Jesus change the water to wine? To impress the crowd? No, they didn't even know he did it. To get the wedding master's attention? No, he thought the groom was being generous. Why did Jesus do it? What motivated his first miracle?

His friends were embarrassed. What bothered them bothered him. If it hurts the child, it hurts the father.

So go ahead. Tell God what hurts. Talk to him. He won't turn you away. He won't think it's silly. "For our high priest is *able to understand* our weaknesses. When he lived on earth, he was tempted in every way that we are, but he did not sin. Let us, then, feel very sure that we can come before God's throne where there is grace" (Heb. 4:15–16 NCV, emphasis added).

Does God care about the little things in our lives? You better believe it. If it matters to you, it matters to him.

—He Still Moves Stones

*W*hen [Jesus] finished teaching, he said to Simon [Peter], "Push out into deep water and let your nets out for a catch."

Simon said, "Master, we've been fishing hard all night and haven't caught even a minnow. But if you say so, I'll let out the nets." (Luke 5:4–5 MSG)

Root-canal patients display more excitement. Who can blame Peter? His shoulders ache. His nets are packed away. A midmorning fishing expedition has no appeal. Still, he complies. "I will do as You say and let down the nets" (v. 5 NASB). Hardly hopping up and down. (Nice to know that obedience needn't always wear goose bumps.)

In the light of day, in full sight of the crowd, the fishermen dip their oars and hoist the sail. Somewhere in the midst of the lake, Jesus gives the signal for them to drop their nets, and "it was no sooner said than done—a huge haul of fish, straining the nets past capacity. They waved to their partners in the other boat to come help them. They filled both boats, nearly swamping them with the catch" (vv. 6–7 MSG).

Peter and his cohorts stand knee high in gills. The catch and the message of their lifetimes surround them. What is the message? Some say it's take Jesus to work and get rich! The presence of Christ guarantees more sales, bigger bonuses, longer weekends, and early retirement. With Jesus in your boat, you'll go from Galilean fishing to Caribbean sailing.

But if this passage promises prosperity, Peter missed it. The catch didn't catch his eye. Jesus did. Though surrounded by scales of silver, Peter didn't see dollar signs. He saw Jesus. Not Jesus, the carpenter. Not Jesus, the teacher. Not Jesus, the healer. Peter saw Jesus, the Lord: mighty enough to control the sea and kind enough to do so from a fisherman's boat. "Simon Peter, when he saw it, fell to his knees before Jesus. 'Master, leave. I'm a sinner and can't handle this holiness. Leave me to myself'" (v. 8 MSG).

What a scene. Christ amid the common grind, standing shoulder to shoulder with cranky workers. Directing fishermen how to fish; showing net casters where to throw. Suppose you were to do what Peter did. Take Christ to work with you. Invite him to superintend your nine-to-five. He showed Peter where to cast nets. Won't he show you where to transfer funds, file the documents, or take the students on a field trip? . . .

Everything changes when you give Jesus your boat.

—Cure for the Common Life

*J*esus had taken them on a retreat. His heart was heavied by the news of the murder of John the Baptist, so he told his disciples, "Come aside by yourselves to a deserted place and rest a while" (Mark 6:31 NKJV).

But then came the hungry crowd. Droves of people—fifteen, maybe twenty, thousand individuals—followed them. A multitude of misery and sickness who brought nothing but needs. Jesus treated the people with kindness. The disciples didn't share his compassion. "That evening the disciples came to him and said, 'This is a remote place, and it's already getting late. Send the crowds away so they can go to the villages and buy food for themselves'" (Matt. 14:15 NLT).

Whoops, somebody was a bit testy. The followers typically prefaced their comments with the respectful Lord. Not this time. Anxiety makes tyrants out of us. They issued a command, not a request: "Send them home so they can buy food for themselves." Do they think we have the keys to Fort Knox? The disciples didn't have the resources for such a mob.

Their disrespect didn't perturb Jesus; he simply issued them an assignment: "They do not need to go away. You give them something to eat" (v. 16). I'm imagining a few shoulder shrugs and rolled eyes, the disciples huddling and tallying their supplies. Peter likely led the discussion with a bark: "Let's count the bread: one, two, three, four, five. I have five loaves. Andrew, you check me on this." He does: "One, two, three, four, five . . ."

Peter set aside the bread and inquired about the fish. Same routine, lower number. "Fish? Let me see. One, two, three . . . Change that. I counted one fish twice. Looks like the grand total of fish is two!"

The aggregate was declared. "We have here only five loaves and two fish" (v. 17). The descriptor only stands out. As if to say, "Our resources are hopelessly puny. There is nothing left but this wimpy lunch." The fuel needle was on empty; the clock was on the last hour; the pantry was down to crumbs. Philip added a personal audit: "Eight months' wages would not buy enough bread for each one to have a bite!" (John 6:7 NIV). The exclamation point was an exasperation point. "Your assignment is too great!"

How do you suppose Jesus felt about the basket inventory? Any chance he might have wanted them to include the rest of the possibilities? Involve all the options? Do you think he was hoping someone might count to eight?

"Well, let's see. We have five loaves, two fish, and . . . Jesus!" Jesus Christ. The same Jesus who told us:

Ask and it will be given to you; seek and you will find; knock and the door will be opened to you. (Luke 11:9 NIV)

If you remain in me and my words remain in you, ask whatever you wish, and it will be given you. (John 15:7 NIV)

Whatever you ask for in prayer, believe that you have received it, and it will be yours. (Mark 11:24 NIV)

Standing next to the disciples was the solution to their problems . . . but they didn't go to him. They stopped their count at seven and worried.

What about you? Are you counting to seven, or to eight?

—Fearless

$\mathcal{W}$hat do you do when you run out of gas? You don't exhaust your petroleum perhaps, but all of us run out of something. You need kindness, but the gauge is on empty. You need hope, but the needle is in the red. You want five gallons of solutions but can only muster a few drops. When you run out of steam before you run out of day, what do you do? Stare at the gauge? Blame your upbringing? Deny the problem?

No. Pity won't start the car. Complaints don't fuel an engine. Denial doesn't bump the needle. In the case of an empty tank, we've learned: get the car to a gas pump ASAP. In the case of the empty marriage, life, or heart, however, we tend to make the mistake the disciples made.

They haven't run out of gas but out of food. Five thousand men and their families surround Jesus. They are getting hungry, and the disciples are getting antsy. "When it was late in the day, his followers came to him and said, 'No one lives in this place, and it is already very late'" (Mark 6:35 NCV).

His followers came to him. The five words imply an adjourned meeting. A committee had been formed, convened, and dismissed, all in the absence of Jesus. The disciples didn't consult their leader; they just described the problems and then told him what to do.

Problem number one: location. "No one lives in this place."

Problem number two: time. "It is already very late."

Problem number three: budget. In a parallel passage, Philip, the deacon in charge of finance, produces a just-printed pie chart. "Someone would have to work almost a year to buy enough bread for each person to have only a little piece" (John 6:7 NCV).

Do you detect an attitude behind those phrases? "No one lives in this place." (Who picked this venue?) "It's already very late." (Whoever preached forgot to watch the clock.) "We would all have to work a month." (Why didn't these people bring their own food?) The disciples' frustration borders on downright irreverence. Rather than *ask* Jesus what to do, they *tell* Jesus what to do. "Send the people away so they can go to the countryside and towns around here to buy themselves something to eat" (Mark 6:36 NCV). The disciples tell Jesus to tell the people to get lost.

Not one of their finer moments. Shouldn't they have known better? This is not the first problem they've seen Jesus face or fix. . . .

Veteran disciples have seen Jesus in action. The whole country has seen Jesus in action. He has earned a national reputation for doing the impossible. But do the disciples ask Jesus for his opinion? Does anyone in the committee meeting think about asking the miracle man what to do? Does John or Peter or James raise a hand and say, "Hey, I've got an idea. Let's go talk to the one who stilled the storm and raised the dead. Maybe he has a suggestion"?

Please note: the mistake of the disciples is not that they calculated the problem but that they calculated without Christ. In giving Jesus no chance, they gave their day no chance. They reserved a table for twelve at the Restaurant of the Rotten Day.

How unnecessary! If your father were Bill Gates and your computer broke, where would you turn? If Stradivari were your dad and your violin string snapped, to whom would you go? If your father is God and you have a problem on your hands, what do you do?

Scripture tells us what to do:

Is your problem too large? "God . . . is able . . . to accomplish infinitely more than we might ask or think" (Ephesians 3:20 NLT).

Is your need too great? "God is able to provide you with every blessing in abundance" (2 Corinthians 9:8 RSV).

Is your temptation too severe? "[God] is able to help us when we are being tested" (Hebrews 2:18 NLT).

Are your sins too numerous? "He is able, once and forever, to save those who come to God through him" (Hebrews 7:25 NLT).

Is your future too frightening? "God . . . is able to keep you from falling away and will bring you with great joy into his glorious presence without a single fault" (Jude 24 NLT).

Is your enemy too strong? "[God] is able even to subdue all things to Himself" (Philippians 3:21 NKJV).

Make these verses a part of your daily diet. God is able to accomplish, provide, help, save, keep, subdue . . . He is able to do what you can't. He already has a plan. Regarding the hungry crowd, "Jesus already knew what he planned to do" (John 6:6 NCV). God's not bewildered. Go to him. . . .

Look how the story ends:

Andrew . . . said, "There's a little boy here who has five barley loaves and two fish. But that's a drop in the bucket for a crowd like this. . . ."

Then Jesus took the bread and, having given thanks, gave it to those who were seated. He did the same with the fish. All ate as much as they wanted. When the people had eaten their fill, he said to his disciples, "Gather the leftovers so nothing is wasted." They went to work and filled twelve large baskets with leftovers from the five barley loaves.

The people realized that God was at work among them. (John 6:8–14 MSG)

The boy surfaces as the hero of the story. All he does is give his lunch to Jesus. He leaves the problem in the hands of the one with the oversight to do something about it. . . .

God is able to do what you can't. So give your problem to Jesus. Don't make the mistake of the disciples. They analyzed, organized, evaluated, and calculated—all without Jesus. The result? They became anxious and bossy.

Go first to Christ. You're going to run out of gas. We all do. Next time the needle sits on the wrong side of empty, remember: the one who fed the crowds is a prayer away.

—Great Day Every Day

I think it is our weakness that reveals how great God is. He [said], "When you are weak, my power is made perfect in you" (2 Cor. 12:9 NCV). The feeding of the five thousand is an ideal example. The scene answers the question, What does God do when his children are weak?

If God ever needed an excuse to give up on people, he has one here. Surely God is going to banish these followers until they learn to believe.

Is that what he does? You decide. "Then Jesus took the loaves of bread, thanked God for them, and gave them to the people who were sitting there. He did the same with the fish, giving as much as the people wanted" (John 6:11).

When the disciples didn't pray, Jesus prayed. When the disciples didn't see God, Jesus sought God. When the disciples were weak, Jesus was strong. When the disciples had no faith, Jesus had faith. He thanked God.

For what? The crowds? The pandemonium? The weariness? The faithless disciples? No, he thanked God for the basket of bread. He ignored the clouds and found the ray and thanked God for it.

Look what he does next. "Jesus divided the bread and gave it to his followers, who gave it to the people" (Matt. 14:19).

Rather than punish the disciples, he employs them. There they go, passing out the bread they didn't request, enjoying the answer to the prayer they didn't even pray. If Jesus would have acted according to the faith of his disciples, the multitudes would have gone unfed. But he didn't, and he doesn't. God is true to us even when we forget him.

God's blessings are dispensed according to the riches of his grace, not according to the depth of our faith. "If we are not faithful, he will still be faithful, because he cannot be false to himself" (2 Tim. 2:13).

Why is that important to know? So you won't get cynical. Look around you. Aren't there more mouths than bread? Aren't there more wounds than physicians? Aren't there more who need the truth than those who tell it? Aren't there more churches asleep than churches afire?

So what do we do? Throw up our hands and walk away? Tell the world we can't help them? That's what the disciples wanted to do. Should we just give up on the church? . . .

No, we don't give up. We look up. We trust. We believe. And our optimism is not hollow. Christ has proven worthy. He has shown that he never fails, though there is nothing but failure in us. . . .

God is faithful even when his children are not.

That's what makes God, God.

—A Gentle Thunder

*W*here do you find water for the soul? Jesus gave an answer one October day in Jerusalem. People had packed the streets for the annual reenactment of the rock-giving-water miracle of Moses. In honor of their nomadic ancestors, they slept in tents. In tribute to the desert stream, they poured out water. Each morning a priest filled a golden pitcher with water from the Gihon spring and carried it down a people-lined path to the temple. Announced by trumpets, the priest encircled the altar with a libation of liquid. He did this every day, once a day, for seven days. Then on the last day, the great day, the priest gave the altar a Jericho loop—seven circles—dousing it with seven vessels of water. It may have been at this very moment that the rustic rabbi from the northlands commanded the people's attention. "On the last day, that great day of the feast, Jesus stood and cried out, saying, 'If anyone thirsts, let him come to Me and drink. He who believes in Me, as the Scripture has said, out of his heart will flow rivers of living water'" (John 7:37–38 NKJV).

Finely frocked priests turned. Surprised people looked. Wide-eyed children and toothless grandparents paused. They knew this man. Some had heard him preach in the Hebrew hills; others, in the city streets. Two and a half years had passed since he'd emerged from the Jordan waters. The crowd had seen this carpenter before.

But had they seen him this intense? He "stood and shouted" (NLT). The traditional rabbinic teaching posture was sitting and speaking. But Jesus stood up and shouted out. The blind man shouted, appealing for sight (Mark 10:46–47); the sinking Peter shouted, begging for help (Matt. 14:29–30); and the demon-possessed man shouted, pleading for mercy (Mark 5:2–7). John uses the same Greek verb to portray the volume of Jesus's voice. Forget a kind clearing of the throat. God was pounding his gavel on heaven's bench. Christ demanded attention.

He shouted because his time was short. The sand in the neck of his hourglass was down to measurable grains. In six months he'd be dragging a cross through these streets. And the people? The people thirsted. They needed water, not for their throats, but for their hearts. So Jesus invited: *Are your insides starting to shrivel? Drink me.*

What H_2O can do for your body, Jesus can do for your heart. Lubricate it. Aquify it. Soften what is crusty, flush what is rusty. How?

Like water, Jesus goes where we can't. Throw a person against a wall, his body thuds and drops. Splash water against a wall, and the liquid conforms and spreads. Its molecular makeup grants water great flexibility: one moment separating and seeping into a crack, another collecting and thundering over the Victoria Falls. Water goes where we cannot.

So does Jesus. He is a spirit and, although he forever has a body, he is not bound by a body. In fact, John parenthetically explains, "(When he said 'living water,' he was speaking of the Spirit, who would be given to everyone believing in him . . .)" (John 7:39 NLT). The Spirit of Jesus threads down the throat of your soul, flushing fears, dislodging regrets. He does for your soul what water does for your body. And, thankfully, we don't have to give him directions.

We give none to water, do we? Before swallowing, do you look at the liquid and say, "Ten drops of you go to my spleen. I need fifty on cardiovascular detail. The rest of you head north to my scalp. It's really itchy today." Water somehow knows where to go.

Jesus knows the same. Your directions are not needed, but your permission is. Like water, Jesus won't come in unless swallowed. That is, we must willingly surrender to his lordship. You can stand waist deep in the Colorado River and still die of thirst. Until you scoop and swallow, the water does your system no good. Until you gulp Christ, the same is true.

Don't you need a drink? Don't you long to flush out the fear, anxiety, and guilt? You can. Note the audience of his invitation. "If *anyone* thirsts, let him come to Me and drink" (v. 37 NKJV, emphasis mine). Are you anyone? If so, then step up to the well. You qualify for his water.

All ages are welcome. Both genders invited. No race excluded. Scoundrels. Scamps. Rascals and rubes. All welcome. You don't have to be rich to drink, religious to drink, successful to drink; you simply need to follow the instructions on what—or better, who—to drink. Him. In order for Jesus to do what water does, you must let him penetrate your heart. Deep, deep inside.

Internalize him. Ingest him. Welcome him into the inner workings of your life. Let Christ be the water of your soul.

—*Come Thirsty*

$\mathscr{T}$he desperate man sits in the corner of the church assembly. Dry mouth, moist palms. He scarcely moves. He feels out of place in a room of disciples, but where else can he go? He just violated every belief he cherishes. Hurt every person he loves. Spent a night doing what he swore he'd never do. And now, on Sunday, he sits and stares. He doesn't speak. *If these people knew what I did. . . .*

Scared, guilty, and alone.

He could be an addict, a thief, a child-beater, a wife-cheater.

He could be a she—single, pregnant, confused. He could be any number of people, for any number of people come to God's people in his condition—hopeless, hapless, helpless.

How will the congregation react? What will he find? Criticism or compassion? Rejection or acceptance? Raised eyebrows or extended hands? . . .

Did I mention the size of the congregation? Small. A dozen or so souls clustered together for strength. Did I tell you the location of the gathering? A borrowed upstairs room in Jerusalem. And the date? Sunday. The Sunday after Friday's crucifixion. The Sunday after Thursday night's betrayal.

A church of desperate disciples.

Peter cowers in the corner and covers his ears, but he can't silence the sound of his empty promise. "I'd die for you!" he had vowed (Luke 22:33 MSG). But his courage had melted in the midnight fire and fear. And now he and the other runaways wonder what place God has for them. Jesus answers the question by walking through the door. He brings bread for their souls. "Peace be with you" (John 20:19 NCV). He brings a sword for the struggle. "Receive the Holy Spirit" (v. 22).

Bread and swords. He gives both to the desperate.

Still.

—Facing Your Giants

8

Victor

*H*ell is a hideous topic. Any person who discusses it glibly or proclaims it gleefully has failed to ponder it deeply. Scripture writers dip pens in gloomy ink to describe its nature. They speak of the "blackest darkness" (Jude 13 NIV), "everlasting destruction" (2 Thess. 1:9 NIV), "weeping and gnashing of teeth" (Matt. 8:12 NIV).

A glimpse into the pit won't brighten your day, but it will enlighten your understanding of Jesus. He didn't avoid the discussion. Quite the contrary. He planted a one-word caution sign between you and hell's path: *perish.* "Whoever believes in him shall not *perish* but have eternal life" (John 3:16 NIV).

Jesus spoke of hell often. Thirteen percent of his teachings refer to eternal judgment and hell.[1] Two-thirds of his parables relate to resurrection and judgment.[2] Jesus wasn't cruel or capricious, but he was blunt. His candor stuns.

He speaks in tangible terms. "Fear Him," he warns, "who is able to destroy both soul and body in hell" (Matt. 10:28 NKJV). He quotes Hades's rich man pleading for Lazarus to "dip the tip of his finger in water and cool my tongue" (Luke 16:24 NKJV). Words such as *body, finger,* and *tongue* presuppose a physical state in which a throat longs for water and a person begs for relief—physical relief.

The apostles said that Judas Iscariot had gone "to his own place" (Acts 1:25 NASB). The Greek word for place is *topos*, which means geographical location.[3] Jesus describes heaven with the same noun: "In My Father's house are many mansions. . . . I go to prepare a place for you" (John 14:2 NKJV). Hell, like heaven, is a location, not a state of mind, not a metaphysical dimension of floating spirits, but an actual place populated by physical beings.

Woeful, this thought. God has quarantined a precinct in his vast universe as the depository of the hard-hearted. . . .

We wonder, is the punishment fair? Such a penalty seems inconsistent with a God of love—overkill. A sinner's rebellion doesn't warrant an eternity of suffering, does it? Isn't God overreacting? . . .

Accuse God of unfairness? He has wrapped caution tape on hell's porch and posted a million and one red flags outside the entrance. To descend its stairs, you'd have to cover your ears, blindfold your eyes, and, most of all, ignore the epic sacrifice of history: Christ, in God's hell on humanity's cross, crying out to the blackened sky, "My God, my God, why have you forsaken me?" (Matt. 27:46 NIV). You'll more easily capture the Pacific in a jar than describe that sacrifice in words. But a description might read like this: God, who hates sin, unleashed his wrath on his sin-filled son. Christ, who never sinned, endured the awful forsakenness of hell. The supreme surprise of hell is this: Christ went there so you won't have to. Yet hell could not contain him. He arose, not just from the dead, but from the depths. "Through death He [destroyed] him who had the power of death, that is, the devil" (Heb. 2:14 NKJV).

Christ emerged from Satan's domain with this declaration: "I have the keys of Hades and of Death" (Rev. 1:18 NKJV). He is the warden of eternity. The door he shuts, no one opens. The door he opens, no one shuts (Rev. 3:7).

Thanks to Christ, this earth can be the nearest you come to hell.

But apart from Christ, this earth is the nearest you'll come to heaven.

A friend told me about the final hours of her aunt. The woman lived her life with no fear of God or respect for his Word. She was an atheist. Even in her final days, she refused to permit anyone to speak of God or eternity. Only her Maker knows her last thoughts and eternal destiny, but her family heard her final words. Hours from death, scarcely conscious of her surroundings, she opened her eyes. Addressing a face visible only to her, she defied, "You don't know me? You don't know me?"

Was she hearing the pronouncement of Christ: "I never knew you; depart from me" (Matt. 7:23 ESV)?

Contrast her words with those of a Christ-follower. The dying man made no secret of his faith or longing for heaven. The day he succumbed to cancer, he awoke from a deep sleep and told his wife, "I'm living in two realities." Then he asked, "Am I special?" "What do you mean, special?" the wife asked. The dying man looked up, whispering, "That I should be allowed to have all this."

Facing death with fear or faith, dread or joy. "Whoever believes in him shall not perish . . ." God makes the offer. We make the choice.

—3:16: The Numbers of Hope

*J*esus has unimpeachable authority. "He sustains everything by the mighty power of his command" (Heb. 1:3 NLT). "God exalted him to the highest place and gave him the name that is above every name" (Phil. 2:9 NIV).

The Roman government tried to intimidate him. False religion tried to silence him. The devil tried to kill him. All failed. Even "death was no match for him" (Acts 2:24 MSG).

Jesus "disarmed the spiritual rulers and authorities. He shamed them publicly by his victory over them on the cross" (Col. 2:15 NLT). He was not kidding when he declared, "All authority in heaven and on earth has been given to me" (Matt. 28:18 NIV). Jesus is the command center of the galaxies. "Two sparrows cost only a penny, but not even one of them can die without your Father's knowing it" (Matt. 10:29 NCV). He occupies the Oval Office. He called a coin out of the mouth of a fish. He stopped the waves with a word. He spoke, and a tree withered. He spoke again, and a basket became a banquet. Economy. Meteorology. Botany. Food supply. "All things have been handed over to me by my Father" (Matt. 11:27 NRSV).

That includes Satan. The devil was soundly defeated by Christ on the cross. Jesus outranks him in every situation. He must obey Jesus, and he knows it. Prayers offered in the name of Jesus have "divine power to demolish strongholds" (2 Cor. 10:4 NIV). Demolish! Not damage or hamper but demolish. Prayer falls on strongholds like lit matches on a grass hut. . . .

Prayer slaps handcuffs on Satan. Prayer takes problems out of the domain of the devil and into the presence of God. Prayer confesses, "God can handle IT. Since he can, I have hope!"

When we pray in the name of Jesus, we come to God on the basis of Jesus' accomplishment. "Since we have a great high priest [Jesus] over the house of God, let us draw near with a true heart in full assurance of faith" (Heb. 10:21–22 HCSB). As our high priest, Jesus offers our prayers to God. His prayers are always heard. "Truly, truly, I say to you, if you ask the Father for anything in My name, He will give it to you" (John 16:23 NASB). . . .

The phrase "In Jesus' name" is not an empty motto or talisman. It is a declaration of truth: My cancer is not in charge; Jesus is. The economy is not in charge; Jesus is. The grumpy neighbor doesn't run the world; Jesus, you do! You, Jesus, are the Head Coach, CEO, President, King, Supreme Ruler, Absolute Monarch, High and Holy Baron, Czar, Overlord, and Rajah of all history.

—Before Amen

*N*ehemiah knew how to press the mute button on his dissenters.

Jesus did too. He responded to Satan's temptations with three terse sentences and three Bible verses. He didn't dialogue with the devil. When Peter told Christ to sidestep the cross, Jesus wouldn't entertain the thought. "Get behind Me, Satan!" (Matt. 16:23 NIV). A crowd of people ridiculed what he said about a young girl: "'The girl is not dead, only asleep.' But the people laughed at him" (Matt. 9:24 NCV). You know what Jesus did with the naysayers? He silenced them. "After the crowd had been thrown out of the house, Jesus went into the girl's room and took hold of her hand, and she stood up" (9:25 NCV). . . .

Jesus practiced selective listening. Can't we do the same?

—Facing Your Giants

*J*esus has a word or two about this brutal world: "Do not fear those who kill the body but cannot kill the soul" (Matt. 10:28 NRSV).

The disciples needed this affirmation. Jesus had just told them to expect scourging, trials, death, hatred, and persecution (vv. 17–23). Not the kind of locker room pep talk that rallies the team. To their credit none defected. Perhaps they didn't because of the fresh memory of Jesus' flexed muscles in the graveyard. Jesus had taken his disciples to "the other side into the country of the Gadarenes, [where] two men who were demon-possessed met Him as they were coming out of the tombs. They were so extremely violent that no one could pass by that way. And they cried out, saying, 'What business do we have with each other, Son of God? Have You come here to torment us before the time?'" (Matt. 8:28–29 NASB).

The most dramatic and immediate reactions to the presence of God on earth emerged from demons like these—the numberless, invisible, sexless, fiendish djinns of Satan. These two men were demon possessed and, consequently, "extremely violent." People walked wide detours around the cemetery to avoid them.

Not Jesus. He marched in as if he owned the place. The stunned demons never expected to see Jesus here in the devil's digs on the foreign side of Galilee, the region of pagans and pigs. Jews avoided such haunts. Jesus didn't.

The demons and Jesus needed no introduction. They had battled it out somewhere else, and the demons had no interest in a rematch. They didn't even put up a fight. "Have you come to punish us before our time?" (v. 29 CEV). Backpedaling. Stuttering. Translation? "We know you will put it to us in the end, but do we get double trouble in the meantime?" They crumpled like stringless puppets. Pathetic, their appeal: "Please send us into those pigs!" (v. 31 CEV).

Jesus did so. "Move," he exorcised. No shout, scream, incantation, dance, incense, or demand. Just one small word. He who sustains the worlds with a word directs demonic traffic with the same. . . .

The contest between good and evil lasted a matter of seconds. Christ is fire, and demons are rats on the ship. They scurried overboard at first heat.

This is the balance on which Jesus writes the check of courage: "Do not fear those who kill the body but cannot kill the soul" (Matt. 10:28 NKJV). You indwell the garrison of God's guardianship. "Can anything separate us from the love Christ has for us? Can troubles or problems or sufferings or hunger or nakedness or danger or violent death? . . . Nothing above us, nothing below us, nor anything else in the whole world will ever be able to separate us from the love of God that is in Christ Jesus our Lord" (Rom. 8:35, 39 NCV).

—*Fearless*

*O*ur enemy has a complex and conniving spiritual army. Dismiss any image of a red-suited Satan with pitchfork and pointy tail. The devil is a strong devil.

But, and this is the point of the passage, in God's presence, the devil is a wimp. Satan is to God what a mosquito is to an atomic bomb.

> Now a large herd of swine was feeding there near the mountains. So all the demons begged Him, saying, "Send us to the swine, that we may enter them." And at once Jesus gave them permission. Then the unclean spirits went out and entered the swine (there were about two thousand); and the herd ran violently down the steep place into the sea, and drowned in the sea. (Mark 5:11–13 NKJV)

How hell's court cowers in Christ's presence! Demons bow before him, solicit him, and obey him. They can't even lease a pig without his permission. Then how do we explain Satan's influence? . . .

Satan can disturb us, but he cannot defeat us. The head of the serpent is crushed.

I saw a literal picture of this in a prairie ditch. A petroleum company was hiring strong backs and weak minds to lay a pipeline. Since I qualified, much of a high-school summer was spent shoveling in a shoulder-high, multimile West Texas trough. A large digging machine trenched ahead of us. We followed, scooping out the excess dirt and rocks.

One afternoon the machine dislodged more than dirt. "Snake!" shouted the foreman. We popped out of that hole faster than a jack-in-the-box and looked down at the rattlesnake nest. Big momma hissed, and her little kids squirmed. Reentering the trench was not an option. One worker launched his shovel and beheaded the rattler. We stood on the higher ground and watched as she—now headless—writhed and twisted in the soft dirt below. Though defanged, the snake still spooked us.

Gee, Max, thanks for the inspirational image.

Inspirational? Maybe not. But hopeful? I think so. That scene in the West Texas summer is a parable of where we are in life. Is the devil not a snake? John calls him "that old snake who is the devil" (Rev. 20:2 NCV).

Has he not been decapitated? Not with a shovel, but with a cross. "God disarmed the evil rulers and authorities. He shamed them publicly by his victory over them on the cross of Christ" (Col. 2:15 NLT).

So how does that leave us? *Confident.* The punch line of the passage is Jesus' power over Satan. One word from Christ, and the demons are swimming with the swine, and the wild man is "clothed and in his right mind" (Mark 5:15 NRSV). Just one command! No séance needed. No hocus-pocus. No chants were heard or candles lit. Hell is an anthill against heaven's steamroller. Jesus "commands . . . evil spirits, and they obey him" (Mark 1:27 NCV). The snake in the ditch and Lucifer in the pit—both have met their match.

And, yet, both stir up dust long after their defeat. For that reason, though confident, we are still *careful.* For a toothless ol' varmint, Satan sure has some bite! He spooks our work, disrupts our activities, and leaves us thinking twice about where we step. Which we need to do. "Be self-controlled and alert. Your enemy the devil prowls around like a roaring lion looking for someone to devour" (1 Pet. 5:8 NIV). Alertness is needed. Panic is not. The serpent still wiggles and intimidates, but he has no poison. He is defeated, and he knows it! "He knows his time is short" (Rev. 12:12 CEV).

"Greater is He who is in you than he who is in the world" (1 John 4:4 NASB). Believe it. Trust the work of your Savior. "Resist the devil and he will flee from you" (James 4:7 NASB). In the meantime, the best he can do is squirm.

—Next Door Savior

*J*esus faced temptation for forty nights. Please note, he didn't face temptation for one day out of forty. Jesus was "in the wilderness for forty days, being tempted by the devil" (Luke 4:1–2 NASB). The battle wasn't limited to three questions. Jesus spent a month and ten days slugging it out with Satan. . . .

Jesus was "tempted by the devil" (v. 2). Satan's words, if for but a moment, gave him pause. He may not have eaten the bread, but he stopped long enough in front of the bakery to smell it. Christ knows the wilderness. More than you might imagine. After all, going there was his idea.

Don't blame this episode on Satan. He didn't come to the desert looking for Jesus. Jesus went to the badlands looking for him. "The Spirit led Jesus into the desert *to be tempted* by the devil" (Matt. 4:1 NCV, emphasis mine). Heaven orchestrated this date. How do we explain this? The list of surprising places grows again. If Jesus in the womb and the Jordan waters doesn't stun you, Jesus in the wilderness will. Why did Jesus go to the desert?

Does the word *rematch* mean anything to you? For the second time in history an unfallen mind will be challenged by the fallen angel. The Second Adam has come to succeed where the first Adam failed. Jesus, however, faces a test far more severe. Adam was tested in a garden; Christ is in a stark wasteland. Adam faced Satan on a full stomach; Christ is in the midst of a fast. Adam had a companion: Eve. Christ has no one. Adam was challenged to remain sinless in a sinless world. Christ, on the other hand, is challenged to remain sinless in a sin-ridden world.

Stripped of any aid or excuses, Christ dares the devil to climb into the ring. "You've been haunting my children since the beginning. See what you can do with me." And Satan does. For forty days the two go toe-to-toe. The Son of heaven is tempted but never wavers, struck but never struck down. He succeeds where Adam failed. This victory, according to Paul, is a huge victory for us all. "Here it is in a nutshell: Just as one person did it wrong and got us in all this trouble with sin and death, another person did it right and got us out of it" (Rom. 5:18 MSG). . . .

Listen, you and I are no match for Satan. Jesus knows this. So he donned our jersey. Better still, he put on our flesh. He was "tempted in every way, just as we are—yet was without sin" (Heb. 4:15 NIV). And because he did, we pass with flying colors.

God gives you Jesus' wilderness grade. Believe that. If you don't, the desert days will give you a one-two punch. The right hook is the struggle. The left jab is the shame for not prevailing against it. Trust his work.

And trust his Word. Don't trust your emotions. Don't trust your opinions. Don't even trust your friends. In the wilderness heed only the voice of God.

Again, Jesus is our model. Remember how Satan teased him? "If you are the Son of God . . ." (Luke 4:3, 9 NCV). Why would Satan say this? Because he knew what Christ had heard at the baptism. "This is My beloved Son, in whom I am well-pleased" (Matt. 3:17 NASB).

"Are you really God's Son?" Satan is asking. Then comes the dare— "Prove it!" Prove it by doing something:

"Tell this stone to become bread" (Luke 4:3 NASB).

"If You worship before me, it shall all be Yours" (v. 7).

"Throw Yourself down from here" (v. 9).

What subtle seduction! Satan doesn't denounce God; he simply raises doubts about God. Is his work enough? Earthly works—like bread changing or temple jumping—are given equal billing with heavenly works. He attempts to shift, ever so gradually, our source of confidence away from God's promise and toward our performance.

Jesus doesn't bite the bait. No heavenly sign is requested. He doesn't solicit a lightning bolt; he simply quotes the Bible. Three temptations. Three declarations.

"It is written . . ." (v. 4 NCV).

"It is written . . ." (v. 8 NCV).

"It is said . . ." (v. 12 NASB).

Jesus' survival weapon of choice is Scripture. If the Bible was enough for his wilderness, shouldn't it be enough for ours? Don't miss the point here. Everything you and I need for desert survival is in the Book. We simply need to heed it. . . .

Hang in there. Your time in the desert will pass. Jesus' did. "The devil left Him; and behold, angels came and began to minister to Him" (Matt. 4:11 NASB).

—Next Door Savior

A sinless Savior was covered with sin.

The Author of Life was placed in the cave of death. Satan's victory appeared sure. Finally the devil had scored on the right end of the court. And not only had he scored; he'd slam-dunked the MVP and left him lying on the floor. The devil had blown it with everyone from Sarah to Peter, but this time he'd done it right. The whole world had seen it. The victory dance had already begun.

But all of a sudden there was a light in the tomb and a rumbling of the rock; then Friday's tragedy emerged as Sunday's Savior, and even Satan knew he'd been had. He'd been a tool in the hand of the Gardener. All the time he thought he was defeating heaven, he was helping heaven. God wanted to prove his power over sin and death, and that's exactly what he did. And guess who helped him do it? Once again Satan's layup becomes a foul-up. Only this time, he didn't give heaven some points, he gave heaven the championship game.

Jesus emerged as the victor, and Satan was left looking like a . . . well, I'll let you figure that out. Take the first letter of each of the ways God uses the devil and see if you can find Satan's true identity.

Refine the faithful.

Awaken the sleeping.

Teach the church.

—The Great House of God

We held our breath as he disappeared into the tunnel. There were five of us. Five energetic boys. School was out for the summer so we have turned our attention to the vacant lot next to our house. The flat, West Texas land was a perfect summer playground.

On this particular day it seemed that the attention of the entire world was focused on that tunnel We had dug a ditch about three feet wide and four feet deep that ran halfway across the lot To give it the appearance of a tunnel we covered it with several plants of scavenged plywood and a thick layer of dirt. We camouflaged the entrance and exit with a few tumbleweeds and mesquite bushes, and—presto!—we had an underground tunnel. It was ready to entertain and entire neighborhood of ruffians as they fought off Indians, escaped from slavery, and invaded Normandy.

Today was the day we would test the tunnel. Was it strong enough? Wide enough? Would it collapse? Was it deep enough? Was it too long? The only way to find out was to send a volunteer through the tunnel first. (Memory mail fail me here, but I think it was my brother who agreed to test the tunnel.)

It was a tense moment. The five of us stood solemnly in our T-shirts and jeans. We gave him last words of encouragement. We patted him on the back. (We admired his self-sacrifice.) We stood quietly as he decisively got down on hands and knees and scurried into the hole. We held our breath as we watched the soles of his high-top sneakers disappear into the darkness.

No one spoke as we waited. The only movement was the pounding of our young hearts. Our eyes stayed fixed on the tunnel exit.

Finally, after we had each died a thousand deaths, my brother's sandy-blond hair emerged from the other end. I can remember his triumphant fist leading the way as he scrambled out, yelling, "There's nothing to it! Don't worry!" And who could argue with the testimony of seeing him alive and well, jumping up and down at the tunnel's exit? We all went in!

There is something about a living testimony that gives us courage. Once we see someone else emerge from life's dark tunnels we realize that we, too, can overcome.

Could this be why Jesus is called our pioneer? Is this one of the reasons that he consented to enter the horrid chambers of death? It must be. His words, though persuasive, were not enough. His promises, though truth, didn't quite allay the fear of the people. His actions, *even* the act of calling Lazarus from the tomb, didn't convince the crowds that death was nothing to fear. No. In the eyes of humanity, death was still the black veil that separated them from joy. There was no victory over this hooded foe. Its putrid odor invaded the nostril of every human, convincing them that life was only meant to end abruptly and senselessly.

It was left to the Son of God to disclose the true nature of this force. It was on the cross that the showdown occurred. Christ called for Satan's cards. Weary of seeing humanity fooled by a coverup, he entered the tunnel of death to prove that there was indeed an exit. And, as the world darkened, creation held her breath.

Satan threw his best punch, but it wasn't enough Even the darkness of hell's tunnel was no match for God's Son. Even the chambers of Hades couldn't stop this raider. Legions of screaming demons held nothing over the Lion of Judah.

Christ emerged from death's tunnel, lifted a triumphant fist toward the sky, and freed all from the fear of death.

"Death has been swallowed up in victory!"

—On the Anvil

*R*emember, you are a coheir with Christ. Every attribute of Jesus is at your disposal. Was Jesus victorious? Did he overcome sin and death? Yes! Will you be victorious? Can you overcome sin and death? Yes! The question is not, will you overcome? It is, *when* will you over-come? Life will always bring challenges. But God will always give strength to face them.

—Glory Days

9

Life

*J*esus offers *zoe*, the Greek word for "life as God has it."[1] Whereas *bios*, its sibling term, is life extensive, *zoe* is life intensive. Jesus talks less about life's duration and more about its quality, vitality, energy, and fulfillment. What the new mate, sports car, or unexpected check could never do, Christ says, "I can." You'll love how he achieves it. He reconnects your soul with God. . . .

"Because Jesus was raised from the dead, we've been given a brand-new life and have everything to live for, including a future in heaven—and the future starts now!" (1 Pet. 1:3–4 MSG).

Others offer life, but no one offers to do what Jesus does—to reconnect us to his power. But how can we know? How do we know that Jesus knows what he's talking about? The ultimate answer, according to his flagship followers, is the vacated tomb. Did you notice the words you just read? "Because Jesus *was raised from the dead*, we've been given a brand-new life." In the final sum, it was the disrupted grave that convinced the maiden Christians to cast their lots with Christ. "He was seen by Peter and then by the twelve apostles. After that, Jesus was seen by more than five hundred of the believers at the same time" (1 Cor. 15:5–6 NCV).

Can Jesus actually replace death with life? He did a convincing job with his own. We can trust him because he has been there. . . .

He's been to the grave. Not as a visitor, but as a corpse. Buried amidst the cadavers. Numbered among the dead. Heart silent and lungs vacant. Body wrapped and grave sealed. The cemetery. He's been buried there.

You haven't yet. But you will be. And since you will, don't you need someone who knows the way out?

> God . . . has given us new birth into a living hope through the resurrection of Jesus Christ from the dead. . . . He destroyed death, and through the Good News he showed us the way to have life that cannot be destroyed. (1 Pet. 1:3 NIV; 2 Tim. 1:10 NCV)
>
> —*3:16: The Numbers of Hope*

The canyon of death.

It is a desolate canyon. The dry ground is cracked and lifeless. A blistering sun heats the wind that moans eerily and stings mercilessly. Tears burn and words come slowly as visitors to the canyon are forced to stare into the ravine. The bottom of the crevice is invisible, the other side unreachable. You can't help but wonder what is hidden in the darkness. And you can't help but long to leave.

Have you been there? Have you been called to stand at the thin line that separates the living from the dead? Have you lain awake at night listening to machines pumping air in and out of your lungs? Have you watched sickness corrode and atrophy the body of a friend? Have you lingered behind at the cemetery long after the others have left, gazing in disbelief at the metal casket that contains the body that contained the soul of the one you can't believe is gone? . . .

It is possible that I'm addressing someone who is walking the canyon wall. Someone you love dearly has been called into the unknown and you are alone. Alone with your fears and alone with your doubts. If this is the case, please read the rest of this piece very carefully. Look carefully at the scene described in John 11.

In this scene there are two people: Martha and Jesus. And for all practical purposes they are the only two people in the universe.

Her words were full of despair. "If you had been here . . ." She stares into the Master's face with confused eyes. She'd been strong long enough; now it hurt too badly. Lazarus was dead. Her brother was gone. And the one man who could have made a difference didn't. He hadn't even made it for the burial. Something about death makes us accuse God of betrayal. "If God were here there would be no death!" we claim.

You see, if God is God anywhere, he has to be God in the face of death. Pop psychology can deal with depression. Pep talks can deal with pessimism. Prosperity can handle hunger. But only God can deal with our ultimate dilemma—death. And only the God of the Bible has dared to stand on the canyon's edge and offer an answer. He has to be God in the face of death. If not, he is not God anywhere.

Jesus wasn't angry at Martha. Perhaps it was his patience that caused her to change her tone from frustration to earnestness. "Even now God will give you whatever you ask."

Jesus then made one of those claims that place him either on the throne or in the asylum: "Your brother will rise again."

Martha misunderstood. (Who wouldn't have?) "I know he will rise again in the resurrection at the last day."

That wasn't what Jesus meant. Don't miss the context of the next words. Imagine the setting: Jesus has intruded on the enemy's turf; he's standing in Satan's territory, Death Canyon. His stomach turns as he smells the sulfuric stench of the ex-angel, and he winces as he hears the oppressed wails of those trapped in the prison. Satan has been here. He has violated one of God's creations.

With his foot planted on the serpent's head, Jesus speaks loudly enough that his words echo off the canyon walls.

"I am the resurrection and the life. He who believes in me will live, even though he dies; and whoever lives and believes in me will never die" (John 11:25 NIV).

It is a hinge point in history. A chink has been found in death's armor. The keys to the halls of hell have been claimed. The buzzards scatter and the scorpions scurry as Life confronts death—and wins! The wind stops. A cloud blocks the sun and a bird chirps in the distance while a humiliated snake slithers between the rocks and disappears into the ground.

The stage has been set for a confrontation at Calvary.

But Jesus isn't through with Martha. With eyes locked on hers he asks the greatest question found in Scripture, a question meant as much for you and me as for Martha.

"Do you believe this?"

Wham! There it is. The bottom line. The dimension that separates Jesus from a thousand gurus and prophets who have come down the pike. The question that drives any responsible listener to absolute obedience to or total rejection of the Christian faith.

"Do you believe this?"

Let the question sink into your heart for a minute. Do you believe that a young, penniless itinerant is larger than your death? Do you truly believe that death is nothing more than an entrance ramp to a new highway?

"Do you believe this?"

Jesus didn't pose this query as a topic for discussion in Sunday schools. It was never intended to be dealt with while basking in the stained glass sunlight or while seated on padded pews.

No. This is a canyon question. A question which makes sense only during an all-night vigil or in the stillness of smoke-filled waiting rooms. A question that makes sense when all of our props, crutches, and costumes are taken away. For then we must face ourselves as we really are: rudderless humans tailspinning toward disaster. And we are forced to see him for what he claims to be: our only hope.

As much out of desperation as inspiration, Martha said yes. As she studied the tan face of that Galilean carpenter, something told her she'd probably never get closer to the truth than she was right now. So she gave him her hand and let him lead her away from the canyon wall.

"I am the resurrection and the life. . . . Do you believe this?"

—God Came Near

*J*airus is the leader of the synagogue. That may not mean much to you and me, but in the days of Christ the leader of the synagogue was the most important man in the community. The synagogue was the center of religion, education, leadership, and social activity. The leader of the synagogue was the senior religious leader, the highest-ranking professor, the mayor, and the best-known citizen all in one.

Jairus has it all. Job security. A guaranteed welcome at the coffee shop. A pension plan. Golf every Thursday and an annual all-expenses-paid trip to the national convention.

Who could ask for more? Yet Jairus does. He *has* to ask for more. In fact, he would trade the whole package of perks and privileges for just one assurance—that his daughter will live.

The Jairus we see in this story is not the clear-sighted, black-frocked, nicely groomed civic leader. He is instead a blind man begging for a gift. He fell at Jesus' feet, "saying again and again, 'My daughter is dying. Please come and put your hands on her so she will be healed and will live'" (Mark 5:23 NIV).

He doesn't barter with Jesus. ("You do me a favor, and I'll see you are taken care of for life.") He doesn't negotiate with Jesus. ("The guys in Jerusalem are getting pretty testy about your antics. Tell you what, you handle this problem of mine, and I'll make a few calls . . .") He doesn't make excuses. ("Normally, I'm not this desperate, Jesus, but I've got a small problem.")

He just pleads.

There are times in life when everything you have to offer is nothing compared to what you are asking to receive. Jairus is at such a point. What could a man offer in exchange for his child's life? So there are no games. No haggling. No masquerades. The situation is starkly simple: Jairus is blind to the future and Jesus knows the future. So Jairus asks for his help.

And Jesus, who loves the honest heart, goes to give it.

And God, who knows what it is like to lose a child, empowers his son.

But before Jesus and Jairus get very far, they are interrupted by emissaries from his house.

"Your daughter is dead. There is no need to bother the teacher anymore" (v. 35).

Get ready. Hang on to your hat. Here's where the story gets moving. Jesus goes from being led to leading, from being convinced by Jairus to *convincing* Jairus. From being admired to being laughed at, from helping out the people to casting out the people.

Here is where Jesus takes control.

"But Jesus paid no attention to what they said . . ." (v. 36).

I love that line! It describes the critical principle for seeing the unseen: ignore what people say. Block them out. Turn them off. Close your ears. And, if you have to, walk away.

Ignore the ones who say it's too late to start over.

Disregard those who say you'll never amount to anything.

Turn a deaf ear toward those who say that you aren't smart enough, fast enough, tall enough, or big enough—ignore them.

Faith sometimes begins by stuffing your ears with cotton.

Jesus turns immediately to Jairus and pleads: "Don't be afraid; just believe" (v. 36).

Jesus compels Jairus to see the unseen. When Jesus says, "Just believe . . . ," he is imploring, "Don't limit your possibilities to the visible. Don't listen only for the audible. Don't be controlled by the logical. Believe there is more to life than meets the eye!"

"Trust me," Jesus is pleading. "Don't be afraid; just trust." . . .

Jesus is asking Jairus to see the unseen. To make a choice. Either to live by the facts or to see by faith. When tragedy strikes we, too, are left to choose what we see. We can see either the hurt or the Healer.

The choice is ours.

Jairus made his choice. He opted for faith and Jesus . . . and faith *in* Jesus led him to his daughter.

At the house Jesus and Jairus encounter a group of mourners. Jesus is troubled by their wailing. It bothers him that they express such anxiety over death. "Why are you crying and making so much noise? The child is not dead, only asleep" (v. 39).

That's not a rhetorical question. It's an honest one. From his perspective, the girl is not dead—she is only asleep. From God's viewpoint, death is not permanent. It is a necessary step for passing from this world to the next. It's not an end; it's a beginning.

. . . From God's viewpoint, death is not to be dreaded; it is to be welcomed.

And when he sees people crying and mourning over death, he wants to know, "Why are you crying?" (v. 39).

When we see death, we see disaster. When Jesus sees death, he sees deliverance.

—*He Still Moves Stones*

*T*wo crowds. One entering the city and one leaving. They couldn't be more diverse. The group arriving buzzes with laughter and conversation.

They follow Jesus. The group leaving the city is solemn—a herd of sadness hypnotized by the requiem of death. Above them rides the reason for their grief—a cold body on a wicker stretcher.

The woman at the back of the procession is the mother. She has walked this trail before. It seems like just yesterday she buried the body of her husband. Her son walked with her then. Now she walks alone, quarantined in her sadness. She is the victim of this funeral.

She is the one with no arm around her shoulder. She is the one who will sleep in the empty house tonight. She is the one who will make dinner for one and conversation with none. She is the one most violated. The thief stole her most treasured diamond—companionship.

The followers of Jesus stop and step aside as the procession shadows by. The blanket of mourning muffles the laughter of the disciples. No one speaks. What could they say? They feel the same despair felt by the bystanders at any funeral. "Someday that will be me."

No one intervenes. What could they do? Their only choice is to stand and stare as the mourners shuffle past.

Jesus, however, knows what to say and what to do. When he sees the mother, his heart begins to break . . . and his lips begin to tighten. He glares at the angel of death that hovers over the body of the boy. "Not this time, Satan. This boy is mine."

At that moment the mother walks in front of him. Jesus speaks to her. "Don't cry." She stops and looks into this stranger's face. If she wasn't shocked by his presumption, you can bet some of the witnesses were.

Don't cry? Don't cry? What kind of request is that?

A request only God can make.

Jesus steps toward the bier and touches it. The pallbearers stop marching. The mourners cease moaning. As Jesus stares at the boy, the crowd is silent.

The demon had been perched spiderlike over the body. He was enjoying the parade. He was the warden. The people were the prisoners. He was marching the condemned to execution. They were watching from behind invisible bars, imprisoned by their impermanence. He had relished the fear in the faces. He had giggled at their despair.

Then he hears the voice. That voice . . . he knows the owner. His back arches and he hisses instinctively.

He turns. He doesn't see what others see. He doesn't see the face of a Nazarene. He doesn't hear the voice of a man. He sees the wrath of God. He hears the command of a King.

"Get out of here."

He doesn't have to be told twice.

Jesus turns his attention to the dead boy. "Young man," his voice is calm, "come back to life again."

The living stand motionless as the dead comes to life. Wooden fingers move. Gray-pale cheeks blush. The dead man sits up.

Luke's description of what happens next is captivating.

"Jesus gave him back to his mother."[2]

How would you feel at a moment like this? What would you do? A stranger tells you not to weep as you look at your dead son. One who refuses to mourn in the midst of sorrow calls the devil's bluff, then shocks you with a call into the cavern of death. Suddenly what had been taken is returned. What had been stolen is retrieved. What you had given up, you are given back.

Jesus must have smiled as the two embraced. Stunned, the crowd breaks into cheers and applause. They hug each other and slap Jesus on the back. Someone proclaims the undeniable, "God has come to help his people."[3]

Jesus gave the woman much more than her son. He gave her a secret—a whisper that was overheard by us. "That," he says, pointing at the cot, "that is fantasy. This," he grins, putting an arm around the boy, "this is reality."

—*Six Hours One Friday*

$\mathcal{A}$s youngsters, we neighborhood kids would play street football. The minute we got home from school, we'd drop the books and hit the pavement. The kid across the street had a dad with a great arm and a strong addiction to football. As soon as he'd pull in the drive way from work we'd start yelling for him to come and play ball. He couldn't resist. Out of fairness he'd always ask, "Which team is losing?" Then he would join that team, which often seemed to be mine.

His appearance in the huddle changed the whole ball game. He was confident, strong, and most of all, he had a plan. We'd circle around him, and he'd look at us and say, "Okay boys, here is what we are going to do." The other side was groaning before we left the huddle. You see, we not only had a new plan, we had a new leader.

He brought new life to our team. God does precisely the same. We didn't need a new play; we needed a new plan. We didn't need to trade positions; we needed a new player. That player is Jesus Christ, God's first-born Son.

"Though we were spiritually dead because of the things we did against God, he gave us new life with Christ" (Eph. 2:5 NCV). God's solution is not to preserve the dead—but to raise the dead. "Therefore, if anyone is in Christ, he is a new creation; the old has gone; the new has come!" (2 Cor. 5:17 NIV).

What Jesus did with Lazarus, he is willing to do with us. Which is good to know, for what Martha said about Lazarus can be said about us, "But, Lord, it has been four days since he died. There will be a bad smell" (John 11:39 NCV). Martha was speaking for us all. The human race is dead, and there is a bad smell. We have been dead and buried a long time. We don't need someone to fix us up; we need someone to raise us up. In the muck and mire of what we call life, there is death, and we have been in it so long we've grown accustomed to the stink. But Christ hasn't.

And Christ can't stand the thought of his kids rotting in the cemetery. So he comes in and calls us out. We are the corpse, and he is the corpse-caller. We are the dead, and he is the dead-raiser. Our task is not to get up but to admit we are dead. The only ones who remain in the grave are the ones who don't think they are there.

The stone has been moved. "Lazarus!" he yells. "Larry! Sue! Horatio! Come out!" he calls.

—In the Grip of Grace

*D*eath. The bully on the block of life. He catches you in the alley. He taunts you in the playground. He badgers you on the way home: "You, too, will die someday."

You see him as he escorts the procession of hearse-led cars. He's in the waiting room as you walk out of the double doors of the intensive care unit. He's near as you stare at the pictures of the bloated bellies of the starving in Zimbabwe. And he'll be watching your expression as you slow your car past the crunched metal and the blanketed bodies on the highway.

"Your time is coming," he jabs.

Oh, we try to prove him wrong. We jog. We diet. We pump iron. We play golf. We try to escape it, knowing all along that we will only, at best, postpone it.

"Everyone has a number," he reminds.

And every number will be called.

He'll make your stomach tighten. He'll leave you wide eyed and flat footed. He'll fence you in with fear. He'll steal the joy of your youth and the peace of your final years. And if he achieves what he sets out to do, he'll make you so afraid of dying that you never learn to live.

That is why you should never face him alone. The bully is too big for you to fight by yourself. That's why you need a big brother.

Read these words and take heart. "Since the children have flesh and blood (that's you and me), he too shared in their humanity (that's Jesus, our big brother) so that by his death he might destroy him who holds the power of death—that is, the devil—and free those who all their lives were held in slavery by their fear of death. For surely it is not angels he helps, but Abraham's descendants (that's us)."[4]

Jesus unmasked death and exposed him for who he really is—a ninety-eight-pound weakling dressed up in a Charles Atlas suit. Jesus had no patience for this impostor. He couldn't sit still while death pulled the veil over life.

In fact, if you ever want to know how to conduct yourself at a funeral, don't look to Jesus for an example. He interrupted each one he ever attended.

A lifeguard can't sit still while someone is drowning. A teacher can't resist helping when a student is confused. And Jesus couldn't watch a funeral and do nothing.

—Six Hours One Friday

*Y*ou are leaving the church building. The funeral is over.

The burial is next. Ahead of you walk six men who carry the coffin that carries the body of your son. Your only son.

You're numb from the sorrow. Stunned. You lost your husband, and now you've lost your son. Now you have no family. If you had any more tears, you'd weep. If you had any more faith, you'd pray. But both are in short supply, so you do neither. You just stare at the back of the wooden box.

Suddenly it stops. The pallbearers have stopped. You stop.

A man has stepped in front of the casket. You don't know him. You've never seen him. He wasn't at the funeral. He's dressed in a corduroy coat and jeans. You have no idea what he is doing. But before you can object, he steps up to you and says, "Don't cry."

Don't cry? Don't cry! This is a funeral. My son is dead. Don't cry? Who are you to tell me not to cry? Those are your thoughts, but they never become your words. Because before you can speak, he acts.

He turns back to the coffin, places his hand on it, and says in a loud voice, "Young man, I tell you, get up!"

"Now just a minute," one of the pallbearers objects. But the sentence is interrupted by a sudden movement in the casket. The men look at one another and lower it quickly to the ground. It's a good thing they do, because as soon as it touches the sidewalk the lid slowly opens . . .

Sound like something out of a science fiction novel? It's not. It's right out of the Gospel of Luke. "He went up and touched the coffin, and the people who were carrying it stopped. Jesus said, 'Young man, I tell you, get up!' And the son sat up and began to talk" (Luke 7:14–15 NCV).

Be careful now. Don't read that last line too fast. Try it again. Slowly.

"The son sat up and began to talk."

Incredible sentence, don't you think? At the risk of overdoing it, let's read it one more time. This time say each word aloud. "The son sat up and began to talk."

Good job. (Did everyone around you look up?) Can we do it again? This time read it aloud again, but very s-l-o-w-l-y. Pause between each word.

"The . . . son . . . sat . . . up . . . and . . . began . . . to . . . talk."

Now the question. What's odd about that verse?

You got it. Dead people don't sit up! Dead people don't talk! Dead people don't leave their coffins!

Unless Jesus shows up. Because when Jesus shows up, you never know what might happen.

Jairus can tell you. His daughter was already dead. The mourners were already in the house. The funeral had begun. The people thought the best Jesus could do was offer some kind words about Jairus's girl. Jesus had some words all right. Not about the girl, but for the girl. "My child, stand up!" (Luke 8:54 NCV).

The next thing the father knew, she was eating, Jesus was laughing, and the hired mourners were sent home early.

Martha can tell you. She'd hoped Jesus would show up to heal Lazarus. He didn't. Then she'd hoped he'd show up to bury Lazarus. He didn't. By the time he made it to Bethany, Lazarus was four-days buried and Martha was wondering what kind of friend Jesus was. She hears he's at the edge of town so she storms out to meet him. "Lord, if you had been here," she confronts, "my brother would not have died" (John 11:21 NCV).

There is hurt in those words. Hurt and disappointment. The one man who could have made a difference didn't, and Martha wants to know why.

Maybe you do too. Maybe you've done what Martha did. Someone you love ventures near the edge of life, and you turn to Jesus for help. You, like Martha, turn to the only one who can pull a person from the ledge of death. You ask Jesus to give a hand.

Martha must have thought, *Surely he will come. Didn't he aid the paralytic? Didn't he help the leper? Didn't he give sight to the blind? And they hardly knew Jesus. Lazarus is his friend. We're like family. Doesn't Jesus come for the weekend? Doesn't he eat at our table? When he hears that Lazarus is sick, he'll be here in a heartbeat.*

But he didn't come. Lazarus got worse. She watched out the window. Jesus didn't show. Her brother drifted in and out of consciousness. "He'll be here soon, Lazarus," she promised. "Hang on."

But the knock at the door never came. Jesus never appeared. Not to help. Not to heal. Not to bury. And now, four days later, he finally shows up. The funeral is over. The body is buried, and the grave is sealed.

And Martha is hurt.

Her words have been echoed in a thousand cemeteries. "If you had been here, my brother would not have died."

If you were doing your part, God, my husband would have survived.

If you'd done what was right, Lord, my baby would have lived.

If only you'd have heard my prayer, God, my arms wouldn't be empty.

The grave unearths our view of God.

When we face death, our definition of God is challenged. Which, in turn, challenges our faith. Which leads me to ask a grave question. Why is it that we interpret the presence of death as the absence of God? Why do we think that if the body is not healed then God is not near? Is healing the only way God demonstrates his presence?

Sometimes we think so. And as a result, when God doesn't answer our prayers for healing, we get angry. Resentful. Blame replaces belief. "If you had been here, doing your part, God, then this death would not have happened."

It's distressing that this view of God has no place for death. . . .

Jesus couldn't bear to sit and watch the bereaved be fooled.

Please understand, he didn't raise the dead for the sake of the dead. He raised the dead for the sake of the living.

"Lazarus, come out!" (v. 43).

Martha was silent as Jesus commanded. The mourners were quiet. No one stirred as Jesus stood face to face with the rock-hewn tomb and demanded that it release his friend.

No one stirred, that is, except for Lazarus. Deep within the tomb, he moved. His stilled heart began to beat again. Wrapped eyes popped open. Wooden fingers lifted. And a mummied man in a tomb sat up. And want to know what happened next?

Let John tell you. "The dead man came out, his hands and feet wrapped with pieces of cloth, and a cloth around his face" (v. 44). . . .

Question: What's wrong with this picture?

Answer: Dead men don't walk out of tombs.

Question: What kind of God is this?

Answer: The God who holds the keys to life and death.

The kind of God who rolls back the sleeve of the trickster and reveals death for the parlor trick it is.

The kind of God you want present at your funeral.

He'll do it again, you know. He's promised he would. And he's shown that he can.

"The Lord himself will come down from heaven with a loud command" (1 Thess. 4:16 NCV).

The same voice that awoke the boy near Nain, that stirred the still daughter of Jairus, that awakened the corpse of Lazarus—the same voice will speak again. The earth and the sea will give up their dead. There will be no more death.

Jesus made sure of that.

—He Still Moves Stones

10

Forgiver

The Samaritan woman. By the time Jesus met her, she was on a first-century version of a downward spiral. Five ex-husbands and half a dozen kids, each looking like a different daddy. Decades of loose living had left her tattooed and tabooed and living with a boyfriend who thought a wedding was a waste of time.

Gossipers wagged their tongues about her. How else can we explain her midday appearance at the water well? Other women filled their buckets at sunrise, but this woman opted for noon, preferring, I suppose, the heat of the sun over the heat of their scorn.

Were it not for the appearance of a Stranger, her story would have been lost in the Samaritan sands. But he entered her life with a promise of endless water and quenched thirst. He wasn't put off by her past. Just the opposite. He offered to make music out of her garbage. She accepted his offer. We know because of what happened next.

Many Samaritans from the village believed in Jesus because the woman had said, "He told me everything I ever did!" When they came out to see him, they begged him to stay in their village. So he stayed for two days, long enough for many more to hear his message and believe. Then they said to the woman, "Now we believe, not just because of what you told us, but because we have heard him ourselves. Now we know that he is indeed the Savior of the world." (John 4:39–42 NLT)

The woman on the margin became the woman with the message. No one else gave her a chance. Jesus gave her the chance of a lifetime. He came for people like her.

—*Glory Days*

*T*he voices yanked her out of bed.

"Get up, you harlot."

"What kind of woman do you think you are?"

Priests slammed open the bedroom door, threw back the window curtains, and pulled off the covers. Before she felt the warmth of the morning sun, she felt the heat of their scorn.

"Shame on you."

"Pathetic."

"Disgusting."

She scarcely had time to cover her body before they marched her through the narrow streets. Dogs yelped. Roosters ran. Women leaned out their windows. Mothers snatched children off the path. Merchants peered out the doors of their shops. Jerusalem became a jury and rendered its verdict with glares and crossed arms.

And as if the bedroom raid and parade of shame were inadequate, the men thrust her into the middle of a morning Bible class.

Early the next morning [Jesus] was back again at the Temple. A crowd soon gathered, and he sat down and taught them. As he was speaking, the teachers of religious law and Pharisees brought a woman they had caught in the act of adultery. They put her in front of the crowd.

"Teacher," they said to Jesus, "this woman was caught in the very act of adultery. The law of Moses says to stone her. What do you say?" (John 8:2–5 NLT)

Stunned students stood on one side of her. Pious plaintiffs on the other. They had their questions and convictions; she had her dangling negligee and smeared lipstick. "This woman was caught in the very act of adultery," her accusers crowed. Caught in the very act. In the moment. In the arms. In the passion. Caught in the very act by the Jerusalem Council on Decency and Conduct. "The law of Moses says to stone her. What do you say?"

The woman had no exit. Deny the accusation? She had been caught. Plead for mercy? From whom? From God? His spokesmen were squeezing stones and snarling their lips. No one would speak for her.

But someone would stoop for her.

Jesus "stooped down and wrote in the dust" (v. 6 NLT). We would expect him to stand up, step forward, or even ascend a stair and speak. But instead he leaned over. He descended lower than anyone else—beneath the priests, the people, even beneath the woman. The accusers looked down on her. To see Jesus, they had to look down even farther.

He's prone to stoop. He stooped to wash feet, to embrace children. Stooped to pull Peter out of the sea, to pray in the garden. He stooped before the Roman whipping post. Stooped to carry the cross. Grace is a God who stoops. Here he stooped to write in the sand.

Remember the first occasion his fingers touched dirt? He scooped soil and formed Adam. As he touched the sun-baked soil beside the woman, Jesus may have been reliving the creation moment, reminding himself from whence we came. Earthly humans are prone to do earthy things. Maybe Jesus wrote in the soil for his own benefit.

Or for hers? To divert gaping eyes from the scantily clad, just-caught woman who stood in the center of the circle?

The posse grew impatient with the silent, stooping Jesus. "They kept demanding an answer, so he stood up" (v. 7 NLT).

He lifted himself erect until his shoulders were straight and his head was high. He stood, not to preach, for his words would be few. Not for long, for he would soon stoop again. Not to instruct his followers; he didn't address them. He stood on behalf of the woman. He placed himself between her and the lynch mob and said, "'All right, stone her. But let those who have never sinned throw the first stones!' Then he stooped down again and wrote in the dust" (vv. 7–8 NLT).

Name-callers shut their mouths. Rocks fell to the ground. Jesus resumed his scribbling. "When the accusers heard this, they slipped away one by one, beginning with the oldest, until only Jesus was left in the middle of the crowd with the woman" (v. 9 NLT).

Jesus wasn't finished. He stood one final time and asked the woman, "Where are your accusers?" (v. 10 NLT).

My, my, my. What a question—not just for her but for us. Voices of condemnation awaken us as well.

"You aren't good enough."

"You'll never improve."

"You failed—again."

The voices in our world.

And the voices in our heads! Who is this morality patrolman who issues a citation at every stumble? Who reminds us of every mistake? Does he ever shut up?

No. Because Satan never shuts up. The apostle John called him the Accuser: "This great dragon—the ancient serpent called the Devil, or Satan, the one deceiving the whole world—was thrown down to the earth with all his angels. Then I heard a loud voice shouting across the heavens, '. . . For the Accuser has been thrown down to earth—the one who accused our brothers and sisters before our God day and night'" (Rev. 12:9–10 NLT).

Day after day, hour after hour. Relentless, tireless. The Accuser makes a career out of accusing. Unlike the conviction of the Holy Spirit, Satan's condemnation brings no repentance or resolve, just regret. He has one aim: "to steal, and to kill, and to destroy" (John 10:10 NKJV). Steal your peace, kill your dreams, and destroy your future. He has deputized a horde of silver-tongued demons to help him. He enlists people to peddle his poison. Friends dredge up your past. Preachers proclaim all guilt and no grace. And parents, oh, your parents. They own a travel agency that specializes in guilt trips. They distribute it twenty-four hours a day. Long into adulthood you still hear their voices: "Why can't you grow up?" "When are you going to make me proud?"

Condemnation—the preferred commodity of Satan. He will repeat the adulterous woman scenario as often as you permit him to do so, marching you through the city streets and dragging your name through the mud. He pushes you into the center of the crowd and megaphones your sin:

This person was caught in the act of
Immorality . . . stupidity . . . dishonesty . . . irresponsibility.

But he will not have the last word. Jesus has acted on your behalf.

He stooped. Low enough to sleep in a manger, work in a carpentry shop, sleep in a fishing boat. Low enough to rub shoulders with crooks and lepers. Low enough to be spat upon, slapped, nailed, and speared. Low. Low enough to be buried.

And then he stood. Up from the slab of death. Upright in Joseph's tomb and right in Satan's face. Tall. High. He stood up for the woman and silenced her accusers, and he does the same for you. He stands up. . . .

"Where are your accusers? Didn't even one of them condemn you?" "No, Lord," she said. And Jesus said, "Neither do I. Go and sin no more." (John 8:10–11 NLT)

Within a few moments the courtyard was empty. Jesus, the woman, her critics—they all left. But let's linger. Look at the rocks on the ground, abandoned and unused. And look at the scribbling in the sand. It's the only sermon Jesus ever wrote. While we don't know the words, I'm wondering if they read like this:

Grace happens here.

—Grace

*W*hen grace happens, generosity happens. Unsquashable, eye-popping bigheartedness happens.

It certainly happened to Zacchaeus. If the New Testament has a con artist, this is the man. He never met a person he couldn't swindle or saw a dollar he couldn't hustle. He was a "chief tax collector" (Luke 19:2 NKJV). First-century tax collectors fleeced anything that walked. The Roman government allowed them to keep all they could take. Zacchaeus took a lot. "He was rich" (v. 2). Two-seat roadster rich. Alligator shoes rich. Tailored suit and manicured nails rich. Filthy rich.

And guilty rich? He wouldn't be the first shyster to feel regrets. And he wouldn't be the first to wonder if Jesus could help him shake them. Maybe that's how he ended up in the tree. When Jesus traveled through Jericho, half the town showed up to take a look. Zacchaeus was among them. Citizens of Jericho weren't about to let short-in-stature, long-on-enemies Zacchaeus elbow his way to the front of the crowd. He was left hopping up and down behind the wall of people, hoping to get a glimpse.

That's when he spotted the sycamore, shimmied up, and scurried out. He was happy to go out on a limb to get a good look at Christ. He never imagined that Christ would take a good look at him. But Jesus did. "Zacchaeus, come down immediately. I must stay at your house today" (v. 5 NIV).

The pint-sized petty thief looked to one side, then the other, in case another Zacchaeus was in the tree. Turns out, Jesus was talking to him. To him! Of all the homes in town, Jesus selected Zack's. Financed with illegal money, avoided by neighbors, yet on that day it was graced by the presence of Jesus.

Zacchaeus was never quite the same. "Look, Lord! Here and now I give half of my possessions to the poor, and if I have cheated anybody out of anything, I will pay back four times the amount" (v. 8 NIV).

Grace walked in the front door, and selfishness scampered out the back. It changed his heart.

Is grace changing yours?

—Grace

Therefore, the Kingdom of Heaven can be compared to a king who decided to bring his accounts up to date with servants who had borrowed money from him. In the process, one of his debtors was brought in who owed him millions of dollars. He couldn't pay, so his master ordered that he be sold—along with his wife, his children, and everything he owned—to pay the debt. (Matthew 18:23–25 NLT)

Such an immense debt. More literal translations say the servant owed 10,000 talents. One talent equaled 6,000 denarii. One denarius equaled one day's wage (Matthew 20:2). One talent, then, would equate to 6,000 days' worth of work. Ten thousand talents would represent 60 million days or 240,000 years of labor. A person earning $100 a day would owe $6 billion.

Whoa! What an astronomical sum. Jesus employs hyperbole, right? He's exaggerating to make a point. Or is he? One person would never owe such an amount to another. But might Jesus be referring to the debt we owe to God?

Let's calculate our indebtedness to him. How often do you sin, hmm, in an hour? To sin is to "fall short" (Romans 3:23 NIV). Worry is falling short on faith. Impatience is falling short on kindness. The critical spirit falls short on love. How often do you come up short with God? For the sake of discussion, let's say ten times an hour and tally the results. Ten sins an hour, times sixteen waking hours (assuming we don't sin in our sleep), times 365 days a year, times the average male life span of seventy-four years. I'm rounding the total off at 4,300,000 sins per person.

Tell me, how do you plan to pay God for your 4.3 million sin increments? Your payout is unachievable. Unreachable. You're swimming in a Pacific Ocean of debt. Jesus' point precisely. The debtor in the story? You and me. The king? God. Look at what God does.

> He [the servant] couldn't pay, so his master ordered that he be sold—along with his wife, his children, and everything he owned—to pay the debt. But the man fell down before his master and begged him, "Please be patient with me, and I will pay it all." Then his master was filled with pity for him, and he released him and forgave his debt. (Matthew 18:25–27 NLT)

God pardons the zillion sins of selfish humanity. Forgives sixty million sin-filled days. "Out of sheer generosity he put us in right standing with himself. A pure gift. He got us out of the mess we're in and restored us to where he always wanted us to be. And he did it by means of Jesus Christ" (Romans 3:24 MSG).

—Great Day Every Day

*T*he sun was in the water before Peter noticed it—a wavy circle of gold on the surface of the sea. A fisherman is usually the first to spot the sun rising over the crest of the hills. It means his night of labor is finally over.

But not for this fisherman. Though the light reflected on the lake, the darkness lingered in Peter's heart. The wind chilled, but he didn't feel it. His friends slept soundly, but he didn't care. The nets at his feet were empty, the sea had been a miser, but Peter wasn't thinking about that.

His thoughts were far from the Sea of Galilee. His mind was in Jerusalem, reliving an anguished night. As the boat rocked, his memories raced:

the clanking of the Roman guard,

the flash of a sword and the duck of a head,

a touch for Malchus, a rebuke for Peter,

soldiers leading Jesus away.

"What was I thinking?" Peter mumbled to himself as he stared at the bottom of the boat. *Why did I run?*

Peter had run; he had turned his back on his dearest friend and run. We don't know where. Peter may not have known where. He found a hole, a hut, an abandoned shed—he found a place to hide and he hid.

He had bragged, "Everyone else may stumble . . . but I will not" (Matt. 26:33 NCV). Yet he did. Peter did what he swore he wouldn't do. He had tumbled face first into the pit of his own fears. And there he sat. All he could hear was his hollow promise. *Everyone else may stumble . . . but I will not. Everyone else . . . I will not. I will not. I will not.* A war raged within the fisherman.

At that moment the instinct to survive collided with his allegiance to Christ, and for just a moment allegiance won. Peter stood and stepped out of hiding and followed the noise till he saw the torch-lit jury in the courtyard of Caiaphas.

He stopped near a fire and warmed his hands. The fire sparked with irony. The night had been cold. The fire was hot. But Peter was neither. He was lukewarm.

"Peter followed at a distance," Luke described (22:54 NIV).

He was loyal . . . from a distance. That night he went close enough to see, but not close enough to be seen. The problem was, Peter was seen. Other people near the fire recognized him. "You were with him," they had challenged. "You were with the Nazarene." Three times people said it, and each time Peter denied it. And each time Jesus heard it.

Please understand that the main character in this drama of denial is not Peter, but Jesus. Jesus, who knows the hearts of all people, knew the denial of his friend. Three times the salt of Peter's betrayal stung the wounds of the Messiah.

How do I know Jesus knew? Because of what he did. Then "the Lord turned and looked straight at Peter" (Luke 22:61 NIV). When the rooster crowed, Jesus turned. His eyes searched for Peter and they found him. At that moment there were no soldiers, no accusers, no priests. At that predawn moment in Jerusalem there were only two people—Jesus and Peter.

Peter would never forget that look. Though Jesus' face was already bloody and bruised, his eyes were firm and focused. They were a scalpel, laying bare Peter's heart. Though the look had lasted only a moment, it lasted forever.

And now, days later on the Sea of Galilee, the look still seared. It wasn't the resurrection that occupied his thoughts. It wasn't the empty tomb. It wasn't the defeat of death. It was the eyes of Jesus seeing his failure. Peter knew them well. He'd seen them before. In fact he'd seen them on this very lake.

This wasn't the first night that Peter had spent on the Sea of Galilee. After all, he was a fisherman. He, like the others, worked at night. He knew the fish would feed near the surface during the cool of the night and return to the deep during the day. No, this wasn't the first night Peter had spent on the Sea of Galilee. Nor was it the first night he had caught nothing. . . .

He had turned his back on the sea to follow the Messiah. He had left the boats thinking he'd never return. But now he's back. Full circle. Same sea. Same boat. Maybe even the same spot.

But this isn't the same Peter. Three years of living with the Messiah have changed him. He's seen too much. Too many walking crippled, vacated graves, too many hours hearing his words. He's not the same Peter. It's the same Galilee, but a different fisherman.

Why did he return? What brought him back to Galilee after the crucifixion? Despair? Some think so—I don't. Hope dies hard for a man who has known Jesus. I think that's what Peter has. That's what brought him back. Hope. A bizarre hope that on the sea where he knew him first, he would know him again.

So Peter is in the boat, on the lake. Once again he's fished all night. Once again the sea has surrendered nothing.

His thoughts are interrupted by a shout from the shore. "Catch any fish?" Peter and John look up. Probably a villager. "No!" they yell. "Try the other side!" the voice yells back. John looks at Peter. What harm? So out sails the net. Peter wraps the rope around his wrist to wait.

But there is no wait. The rope pulls taut and the net catches. Peter sets his weight against the side of the boat and begins to bring in the net; reaching down, pulling up, reaching down, pulling up. He's so intense with the task, he misses the message.

John doesn't. The moment is déjà vu. This has happened before. The long night. The empty net. The call to cast again. Fish flapping on the floor of the boat. Wait a minute. He lifts his eyes to the man on the shore. "It's him," he whispers.

Then louder, "It's Jesus."

Then shouting, "It's the Lord, Peter. It's the Lord!"

Peter turns and looks. Jesus has come. Not just Jesus the teacher, but

Jesus the death-defeater, Jesus the king . . . Jesus the victor over darkness. Jesus the God of heaven and earth is on the shore . . . and he's building a fire.

Peter plunges into the water, swims to the shore, and stumbles out wet and shivering and stands in front of the friend he betrayed. Jesus has prepared a bed of coals. Both are aware of the last time Peter had stood near a fire. Peter had failed God, but God had come to him.

For one of the few times in his life, Peter is silent. What words would suffice? The moment is too holy for words. God is offering breakfast to the friend who betrayed him. And Peter is once again finding grace at Galilee.

What do you say at a moment like this?

What do you say at a moment such as this?

It's just you and God. You and God both know what you did. And neither one of you is proud of it. What do you do?

You might consider doing what Peter did. Stand in God's presence. Stand in his sight. Stand still and wait. Sometimes that's all a soul can do. Too repentant to speak, but too hopeful to leave—we just stand.

Stand amazed.

He has come back.

He invites you to try again. This time, with him.

—*He Still Moves Stones*

"*Y*ou prepare a table before me in the presence of my enemies" (Ps. 23:5 NKJV). What the shepherd did for the sheep sounds a lot like what Jesus did for Peter.

At this point in the psalm, David's mind seems to be lingering in the high country with the sheep. Having guided the flock through the valley to the alp lands for greener grass, he remembers the shepherd's added responsibility. He must prepare the pasture.

This is new land, so the shepherd must be careful. Ideally, the grazing area will be flat, a mesa or tableland. The shepherd searches for poisonous plants and ample water. He looks for signs of wolves, coyotes, and bears.

Of special concern to the shepherd is the adder, a small brown snake that lives underground. Adders are known to pop out of their holes and nip the sheep on the nose. The bite often infects and can even kill. As defense against the snake, the shepherd pours a circle of oil at the top of each adder's hole. He also applies the oil to the noses of the animals. The oil on the snake's hole lubricates the exit, preventing the snake from climbing out. The smell of the oil on the sheep's nose drives the serpent away. The shepherd, in a very real sense, has prepared the table.[1]

What if your Shepherd did for you what the shepherd did for his flock? Suppose he dealt with your enemy, the devil, and prepared for you a safe place of nourishment? What if Jesus did for you what he did for Peter? Suppose he, in the hour of your failure, invited you to a meal?

What would you say if I told you he has done exactly that? On the night before his death, Jesus prepared a table for his followers.

On the first day of the Festival of Unleavened Bread, the day the lambs for the Passover meal were killed, Jesus' disciples asked him, "Where do you want us to go and get the Passover meal ready for you?"

Then Jesus sent two of them with these instructions: "Go into the city, and a man carrying a jar of water will meet you. Follow him to the house he enters, and say to the owner of the house: 'The Teacher says, Where is the room where my disciples and I will eat the Passover meal?' Then he will show you a large, upstairs room, fixed up and furnished, where you will get everything ready for us." (Mark 14:12–15 GNT)

Look who did the "preparing" here. Jesus reserved a large room and arranged for the guide to lead the disciples. Jesus made certain the room was furnished and the food set out. What did the disciples do? They faithfully complied and were fed.

The Shepherd prepared the table.

Not only that, he dealt with the snakes. You'll remember that only one of the disciples didn't complete the meal that night. "The devil had already persuaded Judas Iscariot, the son of Simon, to turn against Jesus" (John 13:2 NCV). Judas started to eat, but Jesus didn't let him finish. On the command of Jesus, Judas left the room. "'The thing that you will do—do it quickly.' . . . Judas took the bread Jesus gave him and immediately went out. It was night" (John 13:27, 30 NCV).

There is something dynamic in this dismissal. Jesus prepared a table in the presence of the enemy. Judas was allowed to see the supper, but he wasn't allowed to stay there.

You are not welcome here. This table is for my children. You may tempt them. You may trip them. But you will never sit with them. This is how much he loves us.

And if any doubt remains, lest there be any "Peters" who wonder if there is a place at the table for them, Jesus issues a tender reminder as he passes the cup. "Every one of you drink this. This is my blood which is the new agreement that God makes with his people. This blood is poured out for many to forgive their sins" (Matt. 26:27–28 NCV).

"*Every one* of you drink this." Those who feel unworthy, drink this. Those who feel ashamed, drink this. Those who feel embarrassed, drink this.

May I share a time when I felt all three?

By the age of eighteen I was well on my way to a drinking problem. My system had become so resistant to alcohol that a six-pack of beer had little or no impact on me. At the age of twenty, God not only saved me from hell after this life, he saved me from hell during it. Only he knows where I was headed, but I have a pretty good idea.

For that reason, part of my decision to follow Christ included no more beer. So I quit. But, curiously, the thirst for beer never left. It hasn't hounded me or consumed me, but two or three times a week the thought of a good beer sure entices me. Proof to me that I have to be careful is this—nonalcoholic beers have no appeal. It's not the flavor of the drink; it's the buzz. But for more than twenty years, drinking has never been a major issue.

A couple of years ago, however, it nearly became one. I lowered my guard a bit. *One beer with barbecue won't hurt.* Then another time with Mexican food. Then a time or two with no food at all. Over a period of two months I went from no beers to maybe one or two a week. Again, for most people, no problem, but for me it could become one.

You know when I began to smell trouble? One hot Friday afternoon I was on my way to speak at our annual men's retreat. Did I say the day was hot? Brutally hot. I was thirsty. Soda wouldn't do. So I began to plot. Where could I buy a beer and not be seen by anyone I knew? With that thought, I crossed a line. What's done in secret is best not done at all. But I did it anyway. I drove to an out-of-the-way convenience store, parked, and waited until all patrons had left. I entered, bought my beer, held it close to my side, and hurried to the car.

That's when the rooster crowed.

It crowed because I was sneaking around. It crowed because I knew better. It crowed because, and this really hurt, the night before I'd scolded one of my daughters for keeping secrets from me. And now, what was I doing?

I threw the beer in the trash and asked God to forgive me. A few days later I shared my struggle with the elders and some members of the congregation and was happy to chalk up the matter to experience and move on.

But I couldn't. The shame plagued me. Of all the people to do such a thing. So many could be hurt by my stupidity. And of all the times to do such a thing. En route to minister at a retreat. What hypocrisy!

I felt like a bum. Forgiveness found its way into my head, but the elevator designed to lower it eighteen inches to my heart was out of order.

And, to make matters worse, Sunday rolled around. I found myself on the front row of the church, awaiting my turn to speak. Again, I had been honest with God, honest with the elders, honest with myself. But still, I struggled. Would God want a guy like me to preach?

The answer came in the Supper. The Lord's Supper. The same Jesus who'd prepared a meal for Peter had prepared one for me. The same Shepherd who had trumped the devil trumped him again. The same Savior who had built a fire on the shore stirred a few embers in my heart.

"*Every one* of you drink this." And so I did. It felt good to be back at the table.

—Traveling Light

*J*esus loves us too much to leave us in doubt about his grace. His "perfect love expels all fear" (1 John 4:18 NLT). If God loved with an imperfect love, we would have high cause to worry. Imperfect love keeps a list of sins and consults it often. God keeps no list of our wrongs. His love casts out fear because he casts out our sin!

Tether your heart to this promise, and tighten the knot. "If our heart condemns us, God is greater than our heart, and knows all things" (1 John 3:20 NKJV). When you feel unforgiven, evict the feelings. Emotions don't get a vote. Go back to Scripture. God's Word holds rank over self-criticism and self-doubt. As Paul told Titus, "God's readiness to give and forgive is now public. Salvation's available for everyone! . . . Tell them all this. Build up their *courage*" (Titus 2:11, 15 MSG, emphasis mine). Do you know God's grace? Then you can love boldly, live robustly. You can swing from trapeze to trapeze; his safety net will break your fall.

Nothing fosters courage like a clear grasp of grace.

And nothing fosters fear like an ignorance of mercy. May I speak candidly? If you haven't accepted God's forgiveness, you are doomed to live in fear. Nothing can deliver you from the gnawing realization that you have disregarded your Maker and disobeyed his instruction. No pill, pep talk, psychiatrist, or possession can set the sinner's heart at ease. You may deaden the fear, but you can't remove it. Only God's grace can.

Have you accepted the forgiveness of Christ? If not, do so. "If we confess our sins, He is faithful and just to forgive us our sins and to cleanse us from all unrighteousness" (1 John 1:9 NKJV). Your prayer can be as simple as this: *Dear Father, I need forgiveness. I admit that I have turned away from you. Please forgive me. I place my soul in your hands and my trust in your grace. Through Jesus I pray, amen.*

Having received God's forgiveness, live forgiven!

—Max on Life

11

Intercessor

Jesus is praying for us. This is no ho-hum warning Peter hears from the lips of Jesus. "Simon, Simon, Satan has asked to test all of you as a farmer sifts his wheat" (Luke 22:31 NCV). Loose translation? "Satan is going to slap your faith like a farmer slaps wheat on the threshing floor." You'd expect Jesus' next words to be, "So get out of town!" Or "Duck!" or "Put it in high gear before it's too late!"

But Jesus shows no panic. He is surprisingly casual. "I have prayed that you will not lose your faith! Help your brothers be stronger when you come back to me" (v. 32).

Can you hear the calmness in his voice? Forgive me, but I almost detect the accent of a steetwise, tattooed, leather-jacketed guy from Brooklyn: "Yo, Peter, Satan wanted to kill you, but you don't need to worry. I told him to go easy."

The sum of the matter is simple: Jesus has spoken, and Satan has listened. The devil may land a punch or two. He may even win a few rounds, but he never wins the fight. Why? Because Jesus takes up for you. You'll love the way this truth appears in Hebrews: "But because Jesus lives forever, he will never stop serving as priest. So he is able always to save those who come to God through him because he always lives, asking God to help them" (Heb. 7:24–25 NCV).

Here's how it reads in other translations:

"He always lives to intercede for them" (NIV).
He is always living to plead on their behalf" (NEB).
He's . . . always on the job to speak up for them" (MSG).

Paul says the same thing in Romans: "The Spirit himself speaks to God for us, even begs God for us . . ." (Rom. 8:26 NCV). And then in verse 34, "The One who died for us—who was raised to life for us!—is in the presence of God at this very moment sticking up for you" (MSG).

Jesus, at this very moment, is protecting you. . . . Don't worry. Evil must pass through Christ before it can touch you. And God will "never let you be pushed past your limit; he'll always be there to help you come through it" (1 Cor. 10:13 MSG).

"The Lord knows how to rescue godly men from trials" (2 Pet. 2:9 NIV), and he will rescue you. He will rescue us all on the day Christ comes.

We can be encouraged because Jesus is praying for us.

—*When Christ Comes*

*O*n the night before his death, Jesus made this announcement: "All of you will be made to stumble because of Me this night, for it is written: 'I will strike the Shepherd, and the sheep of the flock will be scattered.' But after I have been raised, I will go before you to Galilee" (Matt. 26:31–32 NKJV).

By this point the disciples had known Jesus for three years. They'd spent a thousand nights with him. They knew his stride, accent, and sense of humor. They'd smelled his breath, heard him snore, and watched him pick his teeth after dinner. They'd witnessed miracles we know about and countless more we don't. Bread multiplied. Lepers cleansed. They saw him turn water into Chablis and a lunch box into a buffet. They unwrapped burial clothing from a was-dead Lazarus. They watched mud fall from the eyes of a was-blind man. For three years these handpicked recruits enjoyed front-row, center-court seats to heaven's greatest display. And how would they respond?

"All of you will stumble," Jesus told them. Fall away. Turn away. Run away. Their promises would melt like wax on a summer sidewalk. Jesus' promise, however, would stay firm. "But after I have been raised, I will go before you to Galilee" (v. 32). Translation? Your fall will be great, but my grace will be greater. Stumble, I will catch you. Scatter, I will gather you. Turn from me, I will turn toward you. You'll find me waiting for you in Galilee.

The promise was lost on Peter. "Even if all are made to stumble because of You, I will never be made to stumble" (v. 33).

Not one of Peter's finer moments. "Even if all . . ." Arrogant. "I will never be made to stumble." Self-sufficient. Peter's trust was in Peter's strength. Yet Peter's strength would peter out. Jesus knew it. "Simon, Simon! Indeed, Satan has asked for you, that he may sift you as wheat. But I have prayed for you, that your faith should not fail; and when you have returned to Me, strengthen your brethren" (Luke 22:31–32 NKJV).

Satan would attack and test Peter. But Satan would never claim Peter. Why? Because Peter was strong? No, because Jesus was. "I have prayed for you." Jesus' prayers for one of his own leave Satan hamstrung. That person may stumble for a while but will not fall away completely.

Jesus prays for you as well. "Holy Father, keep them and care for them—all those you have given me—so that they will be united just as we are . . . I am praying not only for these disciples but also for all who will ever believe in me because of their testimony" (John 17:11, 20 NLT).

Will God hear the intercessory pleas of his Son? Of course he will. Like Peter, we may be sifted like wheat. Our faith will wane, our resolve waver, but we will not fall away. We are "kept by Jesus" (Jude v. 1 NIV) and "shielded by God's power" (1 Peter 1:5 NIV). And that is no small power. It is the power of a living and ever-persistent Savior.

–Grace

*O*n the last night of his life Jesus prayed a prayer that stands as a citadel for all Christians:

> I pray for these followers, but I am also praying for all those who will believe in me because of their teaching. Father, I pray that they can be one. As you are in me and I am in you, I pray that they can also be one in us. Then the world will believe that you sent me. (John 17:20–21 NCV)

How precious are these words. Jesus, knowing the end is near, prays one final time for his followers. Striking, isn't it, that he prayed not for their success, their safety, or their happiness.

He prayed for their unity. He prayed that they would love each other. As he prayed for them, he also prayed for "those who will believe because of their teaching." That means us! In his last prayer Jesus prayed that you and I be one.

–In the Grip of Grace

*O*ur prayerful Jesus.

> Awaking early to pray (Mark 1:35).
> Dismissing people to pray (Matt. 14:23).
> Ascending a mountain to pray (Luke 9:28).
> Crafting a model prayer to teach us to pray (Matt. 6:9–13).

Cleansing the temple so others could pray (Matt. 21:12–13).
Stepping into a garden to pray (Luke 22:39–46).

Jesus immersed his words and work in prayer. Powerful things happen when we do the same.

—Outlive Your Life

He turns and begins the final ascent to the garden. When he reaches the entry, he stops and turns his eyes toward his circle of friends. It will be the last time he sees them before they abandon him. He knows what they will do when the soldiers come. He knows their betrayal is only minutes away. But he doesn't accuse. He doesn't lecture. Instead, he prays. His last moments with his disciples are in prayer. And the words he speaks are as eternal as the stars that hear them.

Imagine, for a moment, yourself in this situation. Your final hour with a son about to be sent overseas. Your last moments with your dying spouse. One last visit with your parent. What do you say? What do you do? What words do you choose?

It's worth noting that Jesus chose prayer. He chose to pray for us. "I pray for these men. But I am also praying for all people who will believe in me because of the teaching of these men. Father, I pray that all people who believe in me can be one. . . . I pray that these people can also be one in us, so that the world will believe that you sent me."[1]

You need to note that in this final prayer, Jesus prayed for you. You need to underline in red and highlight in yellow his love: "I am also praying for all people who will believe in me because of the teaching." That is you. As Jesus stepped into the garden, you were in his prayers. As Jesus looked into heaven, you were in his vision. As Jesus dreamed of the day when we will be where he is, he saw you there.

His final prayer was about you. His final pain was for you. His final passion was you.

—And the Angels Were Silent

*B*ehold the power of prayer. You ask God for help, and *bam!* Fire falls to the earth. You lift your concerns to heaven, and turbulence happens! "Noises, thunderings, lightnings, and an earthquake."

Go ahead. Make the midnight knock. Stand up on behalf of those you love. And, yes, stand up on behalf of those you do not. "Pray for those who hurt you" (Matt. 5:44 NCV). The quickest way to douse the fire of anger is with a bucket of prayer. Rather than rant, rave, or seek revenge, pray. Jesus did this. While hanging on the cross, he interceded for his enemies: "Father, forgive them; they don't know what they're doing" (Luke 23:34 MSG). Jesus, even Jesus, left his enemies in God's hands.

Shouldn't we do the same? You are never more like Jesus than when you pray for others.

—Before Amen

[*J*esus] "is in the presence of God at this very moment sticking up for us" (Rom. 8:34 MSG). Let this sink in for a moment. In the presence of God, in defiance of Satan, Jesus Christ rises to your defense. He takes on the role of a priest. "Since we have a great priest over God's house, let us come near to God with a sincere heart and a sure faith, because we have been made free from a guilty conscience" (Heb. 10:21–22 NCV).

A clean conscience. A clean record. A clean heart. Free from accusation. Free from condemnation. Not just for our past mistakes but also for our future ones.

"Since he will live forever, he will always be there to remind God that he has paid for [our] sins with his blood" (Heb. 7:25 TLB). Christ offers unending intercession on your behalf.

Jesus trumps the devil's guilt with words of grace.

Though we were spiritually dead because of the things we did against God, he gave us new life with Christ. You have been saved by God's grace. And he raised us up with Christ and gave us a seat with him in the heavens. He did this for those in Christ Jesus so that for all future time he could show the very great riches of his grace by being kind to us in Christ Jesus. I mean that you have been saved by grace through believing. You did not save yourselves; it was a gift from God. It was not the result of your own efforts, so you cannot brag about it. God has made us what we are. In Christ Jesus, God made us to do good works, which God planned in advance for us to live our lives doing. (Eph. 2:5–10 NCV)

Behold the fruit of grace: saved by God, raised by God, seated with God. Gifted, equipped, and commissioned. Farewell, earthly condemnations: *Stupid. Unproductive. Slow learner. Fast-talker. Quitter. Cheapskate.* No longer. You are who he says you are: *Spiritually alive. Heavenly positioned. Connected to God. A billboard of mercy. An honored child.* This is the "aggressive forgiveness we call grace" (Rom. 5:20 MSG).

Satan is left speechless and without ammunition.

"Who can accuse the people God has chosen? No one, because God is the One who makes them right. Who can say God's people are guilty? No one, because Christ Jesus died, but he was also raised from the dead, and now he is on God's right side, appealing to God for us" (Rom. 8:33–34 NCV). The accusations of Satan sputter and fall like a deflated balloon.

Then why, pray tell, do we still hear them? Why do we, as Christians, still feel guilt?

Not all guilt is bad. God uses appropriate doses of guilt to awaken us to sin. We know guilt is God-given when it causes "indignation . . . alarm . . . longing . . . concern . . . readiness to see justice done" (2 Cor. 7:11 NIV). God's guilt brings enough regret to change us.

Satan's guilt brings enough regret to enslave us. Don't let him lock his shackles on you.

Remember, "your life is hidden with Christ in God" (Col. 3:3 NIV). When he looks at you, he sees Jesus first. In the Chinese language the word for *righteousness* is a combination of two characters, the figure of a lamb and a person. The lamb is on top, covering the person. Whenever God looks down at you, this is what he sees: the perfect Lamb of God covering you. It boils down to this choice: Do you trust your Advocate or your Accuser?

Your answer has serious implications. It did for Jean Valjean. Victor Hugo introduced us to this character in the classic Les Misérables. Valjean enters the pages as a vagabond. A just-released prisoner in midlife, wearing threadbare trousers and a tattered jacket. Nineteen years in a French prison have left him rough and fearless. He's walked for four days in the Alpine chill of nineteenth-century southeastern France, only to find that no inn will take him, no tavern will feed him. Finally he knocks on the door of a bishop's house.

Monseigneur Myriel is seventy-five years old. Like Valjean, he has lost much. The revolution took all the valuables from his family except some silverware, a soup ladle, and two candlesticks. Valjean tells his story and expects the religious man to turn him away. But the bishop is kind. He asks the visitor to sit near a fire. "You did not need to tell me who you were," he explains. "This is not my house—it is the house of Jesus Christ."[2] After some time the bishop takes the ex-convict to the table, where they dine on soup and bread, figs, and cheese with wine, using the bishop's fine silverware.

He shows Valjean to a bedroom. In spite of the comfort, the ex-prisoner can't sleep. In spite of the kindness of the bishop, he can't resist the temptation. He stuffs the silverware into his knapsack. The priest sleeps through the robbery, and Valjean runs into the night.

But he doesn't get far. The policemen catch him and march him back to the bishop's house. Valjean knows what his capture means—prison for the rest of his life. But then something wonderful happens. Before the officer can explain the crime, the bishop steps forward.

"Oh! Here you are! I'm so glad to see you. I can't believe you forgot the candlesticks! They are made of pure silver as well . . . Please take them with the forks and spoons I gave you."

Valjean is stunned. The bishop dismisses the policemen and then turns and says, "Jean Valjean, my brother, you no longer belong to evil, but to good. I have bought your soul from you. I take it back from evil thoughts and deeds and the Spirit of Hell, and I give it to God."[3]

Valjean has a choice: believe the priest or believe his past. Jean Valjean believes the priest. He becomes the mayor of a small town. He builds a factory and gives jobs to the poor. He takes pity on a dying mother and raises her daughter.

Grace changed him. Let it change you. Give no heed to Satan's voice. You "have an Advocate with the Father, Jesus Christ the righteous" (1 John 2:1 NASB). As your Advocate, he defends you and says on your behalf, "There is therefore now no condemnation to those who are in Christ Jesus" (Rom. 8:1 NRSV). Take that, Satan!

—*Grace*

[*T*here is an] often-told story of two maestros who attended a concert to hear a promising young soprano. One commented on the purity of her voice. The other responded, "Yes, but she'll sing better once her heart is broken." There are certain passions learned only by pain. And there are times when God, knowing that, allows us to endure the pain for the sake of the song.

So what does God do while we are enduring the pain? What does he do while we are in the storm? You'll love this. He prays for us. Jesus wasn't in the boat because he had gone to the hills to pray (Mark 6:46). Jesus prayed. That is remarkable. It is even more remarkable that Jesus didn't stop praying when his disciples were struggling. When he heard their cries, he remained in prayer.

Why? Two possible answers. Either he didn't care, or he believed in prayer. I think you know the correct choice.

And you know what? Jesus hasn't changed. He still prays for his disciples. "Because Jesus lives forever, he will never stop serving as priest. So he is able always to save those who come to God through him because he always lives, asking God to help them" (Heb. 7:24–25 NCV).

So where does that leave us? While Jesus is praying and we are in the storm, what are we to do? Simple. We do what the disciples did. We row. The disciples rowed most of the night. Mark says they were "struggling hard" to row the boat (Mark 6:48 NCV). The word *struggle* is elsewhere translated as "tormented." Wasn't easy. Wasn't glamorous.

Much of life is spent rowing. Getting out of bed. Fixing lunches. Turning in assignments. Changing diapers. Paying bills. Routine. Regular. More struggle than strut. More wrestling than resting.

When Denalyn and I went to Brazil, we thought the life of a missionary was one of daily charm and fascination. A Christian Indiana Jones. We learned otherwise.

You have, too? You thought marriage was going to be a lifelong date? You thought having kids was going to be like babysitting? You thought the company who hired you wanted to hear all the ideas you had in college?

Then you learned otherwise. The honeymoon ended. The IRS called, and the boss wanted you to spend the week in Muleshoe, Texas. Much of life is spent rowing.

Oh, there are moments of glamour, days of celebration. We have our share of feasts, but we also have our share of baloney sandwiches. And to have the first we must endure the second.

As things turned out, Denalyn and I had five wonderful years in Brazil. And we learned that at the right time, God comes. In the right way, he appears. So don't bail out. Don't give up! Don't lay down the oars! He is too wise to forget you, too loving to hurt you. When you can't see him, trust him. He is praying a prayer that he himself will answer.

—A Gentle Thunder

We have an Advocate with the Father, Jesus Christ the righteous.
(1 John 2:1 NKJV)

*D*o you know that you don't always have to be present in court? Sometimes your lawyer can speak for you. He understands these situations when you don't, and he speaks legalese while you stumble over the words.

You also have an advocate standing before the Father. When you are weak, he is strong. When you are timid, he speaks.

Jesus understands our every weakness. He lived in one of these tired, broken-down bodies! So he can stand in for us, appealing for us, when we just can't speak for ourselves.

We also have support from the Holy Spirit.

In the same way, the Spirit helps us in our weakness. We do not know what we ought to pray for, but the Spirit himself intercedes for us with groans that words cannot express. And he who searches our hearts knows the mind of the Spirit, because the Spirit intercedes for the saints in accordance with God's will. (Rom. 8:26–27 NIV)

Those sounds coming from your tired soul? Indecipherable? Hardly. The Holy Spirit speaks Groan-ese. Our groans are worth a thousand words.

"Uuuggghhh"—Help me, Lord. Get me out of this misery.

"Uhhhhhhhh"—I don't know what to do. The pain is too much.

"Ooohhhhhh"—Where is everyone?

God is not disappointed that we are so burdened we can't pray. He is sympathetic and picks up where we dropped off. With Jesus as your advocate and the Holy Spirit as your prayer partner, I bet you've been praying more than you think.

—Max on Life

*J*esus appeared to the followers in a flesh-and-bone body: "A spirit does not have flesh and bones as you see that I have" (Luke 24:39 NASB). His resurrected body was a real body, real enough to walk on the road to Emmaus, to be mistaken for that of a gardener, to swallow fish at breakfast.

In the same breath, Jesus' real body was really different. The Emmaus disciples didn't recognize him, and walls didn't stop him. Mark tried to describe the new look and settled for "[Jesus] appeared in another form" (Mark 16:12 NKJV). While his body was the same, it was better; it was glorified. It was a heavenly body.

And I can't find the passage that says he shed it. He ascended in it. "He was lifted up while they were looking on, and a cloud received Him out of their sight" (Acts 1:9 NASB). He will return in it. The angel told the followers, "This Jesus, who has been taken up from you into heaven, will come in just the same way as you have watched Him go into heaven" (Acts 1:11 NASB).

The God-man is still both. The hands that blessed the bread of the boy now bless the prayers of the millions. And the mouth that commissions angels is the mouth that kissed children. You know what this means? The greatest force in the cosmos understands and intercedes for you. "We have an Advocate with the Father, Jesus Christ the righteous" (1 John 2:1 NASB).

Sir John Clarke dedicated many years to Bible translation in the Belgian Congo. He had difficulty translating the word *advocate*. For two years he searched for a suitable translation. His search ended the day he visited the king of the Mulongo people. During the time with the king, an aide appeared, received his instructions, and left. The king told Clarke that the aide was his Nsenga Mukwashi, which was not a name, but a title.

The king explained that the servant represented the people to the king. Clarke immediately asked for permission to watch the man at work. He went to the edge of the village where he found him talking with three women. The husband of one of the women had died, and she was being evicted from her hut. She needed help.

"I will take you to the king," the Nsenga Mukwashi told her.

"Do not do that," she objected. "I am old and timid and would become speechless in his presence."

"There will be no need for you to speak," he assured her. "I shall speak for you."

And he did. Succinctly and clearly and passionately. Clarke noted the flash of anger in the king's eyes. The sovereign ordered his court to care for the widow and seize the culprits. The widow found justice, and Clarke found his word—*Nsenga Mukwashi*.[4]

You, too, have an advocate with the Father. When you are weak, he is strong. When you are timid, he speaks. Your next door Savior is your Nsenga Mukwashi.

> Jesus understands every weakness of ours, because he was tempted in every way that we are. But he did not sin! So whenever we are in need, we should come bravely before the throne of our merciful God. There we will be treated with undeserved kindness, and we will find help. (Heb. 4:15–16 CEV)

. . . Can I call God? Anytime. He is not too busy for me—or you. Endowed with sleepless attention and endless devotion, he listens. The fact that we can't imagine how he hears a million requests as if they were only one doesn't mean he can't or doesn't. For he can and he does.

And among the requests he hears and heeds is yours. For even though he is in heaven, he never left the neighborhood.

—Next Door Savior

12

Servant Leader

Jesus's self-assigned purpose statement reads: "For even the Son of Man did not come to be served, but to serve, and to give His life a ransom for many" (Mark 10:45 NKJV). . . .

The world needs servants. People like Jesus, who "did not come to be served, but to serve." He chose remote Nazareth over center-stage Jerusalem, his dad's carpentry shop over a marble-columned palace, and three decades of anonymity over a life of popularity.

Jesus came to serve. He selected prayer over sleep, the wilderness over the Jordan, irascible apostles over obedient angels. I'd have gone with the angels. Given the choice, I would have built my apostle team out of cherubim and seraphim or Gabriel and Michael, eyewitnesses of Red Sea rescues and Mount Carmel falling fires. I'd choose the angels.

Not Jesus. He picked the people. Peter, Andrew, John, and Matthew. When they feared the storm, he stilled it. When they had no coin for taxes, he supplied it. And when they had no wine for the wedding or food for the multitude, he made both.

He came to serve.

He let a woman in Samaria interrupt his rest, a woman in adultery interrupt his sermon, a woman with a disease interrupt his plans, and one with remorse interrupt his meal.

Though none of the apostles washed his feet, he washed theirs. Though none of the soldiers at the cross begged for mercy, he extended it. And though his followers skedaddled like scared rabbits on Thursday, he came searching for them on Easter Sunday. The resurrected King ascended to heaven only after he'd spent forty days with his friends—teaching them, encouraging them . . . serving them.

Why? It's what he came to do. He came to serve. . . .

He stripped himself of heaven's robe, layered himself in epidermis and hair, hunched down in our world, and spoke our language in the hope that he could lead this bunch of turkeys back home again. "He set aside the privileges of deity and took on the status of a slave, became human! Having become human, he stayed human. It was an incredibly humbling process. He didn't claim special privileges. Instead, he lived a selfless, obedient life and then died a selfless, obedient death—and the worst kind of death at that: a crucifixion" (Phil. 2:7–8 MSG).

Let's follow his example. Let's "put on the apron of humility, to serve one another" (1 Pet. 5:5 GNT). Jesus entered the world to serve. . . .

[God] notices the actions of servants. He sent his Son to be one.

—*Cure for the Common Life*

It's not easy watching Jesus wash these feet.

To see the hands of God massaging the toes of men is, well . . . it's not right. The disciples should be washing his feet. Nathanael should pour the water. Andrew should carry the towel. But they don't. No one does. Rather than serve, they argue over which one is the greatest (Luke 22:24).

What disappointment their words must have brought Jesus.

"I'm the number one apostle."

"No, I'm much more spiritual than you."

"You guys are crazy. I brought more people to hear Jesus than
anyone."

As they argue, the basin sits in the corner, untouched. The towel lies
on the floor, unused. The servant's clothing hangs on the wall, unworn.
Each disciple sees these things. Each disciple knows their purpose. But no
one moves, except Jesus. As they bicker, he stands.

But he doesn't speak. He removes his robe and takes the servant's
wrap off of the wall. Taking the pitcher, he pours the water into the basin.
He kneels before them with the basin and sponge and begins to wash.
The towel that covers his waist is also the towel that dries their feet.

It's not right.

Isn't it enough that these hands will be pierced in the morning?
Must they scrub grime tonight? And the disciples . . . do they deserve to
have their feet washed? Their affections have waned; their loyalties have
wavered.

We want to say . . .

Look at John, Jesus. This is the same John who told you to destroy
a city. The same John who demanded that you censure a Christ-follower
who wasn't in your group. Why are you washing his feet?

And James! Skip James. He wanted the seat of honor. He and his
brother wanted special treatment. Don't give it to him. Give him the
towel. Let him wash his own feet. Let him learn a lesson.

And while you are at it, Jesus, you might as well skip Philip. He told
you there wasn't enough food to feed the large crowd. You tested him, and
he flunked. You gave him the chance, and he blew it.

And Peter? Sure, these are the feet that walked on water, but they're
also the feet that thrashed about in the deep. He didn't believe you. Sure
he confessed you as the Christ, but he's also the one who told you that you
didn't have to die. He doesn't deserve to have his feet washed.

None of them do. When you were about to be stoned in Nazareth, did they come to your defense? When the Pharisees took up rocks to kill you, did they volunteer to take your place? You know what they have done.

And what's more, you know what they are about to do!

You can already hear them snoring in the garden. They say they'll stay awake, but they won't. You'll sweat blood; they'll saw logs. You can hear them sneaking away from the soldiers. They make promises tonight. They'll make tracks tomorrow.

Look around the table, Jesus. Out of the twelve, how many will stand with you in Pilate's court? How many will share with you the Roman whip? And when you fall under the weight of the cross, which disciple will be close enough to spring to your side and carry your burden?

None of them will. Not one. A stranger will be called because no disciple will be near.

Don't wash their feet, Jesus. Tell them to wash yours.

That's what we want to say. Why? Because of the injustice? Because we don't want to see our King behaving as a servant? God on his hands and knees, his hair hanging around his face? Do we object because we don't want to see God washing feet?

Or do we object because we don't want to do the same?

Stop and think for a minute. Don't we have some people like the disciples in our world?

Double-tongued promise-breakers. Fair-weather friends. What they said and what they did are two different things. Oh, maybe they didn't leave you alone at the cross, but maybe they left you alone with the bills . . .

or your question

or your illness.

Or maybe you were just left at the altar,

or in the cold,

holding the bag.

Vows forgotten. Contract abandoned.

Logic says: "Put up your fists."

Jesus says: "Fill up the basin."

Logic says: "Bloody his nose."

Jesus says: "Wash his feet."

Logic says: "She doesn't deserve it."

Jesus says: "You're right, but you don't either."

I don't understand how God can be so kind to us, but he is. He kneels before us, takes our feet in his hands, and washes them. Please understand that in washing the disciples' feet, Jesus is washing ours. You and I are in this story. We are at the table. That's us being cleansed, not from our dirt, but from our sins.

And the cleansing is not just a gesture; it is a necessity. Listen to what Jesus said: "If I don't wash your feet, you are not one of my people" (John 13:8 NCV).

Jesus did not say, "If you don't wash your feet." Why not? Because we cannot. We cannot cleanse our own filth. We cannot remove our own sin. Our feet must be in his hands.

Don't miss the meaning here. To place our feet in the basin of Jesus is to place the filthiest parts of our lives into his hands. In the ancient East, people's feet were caked with mud and dirt. The servant of the feast saw to it that the feet were cleaned. Jesus is assuming the role of the servant. He will wash the grimiest part of your life.

If you let him. The water of the Servant comes only when we confess that we are dirty. Only when we confess that we are caked with filth, that we have walked forbidden trails and followed the wrong paths.

We tend to be proud like Peter and resist. "I'm not that dirty, Jesus. Just sprinkle a few drops on me and I'll be fine."

What a lie! "If we say we have no sin, we are fooling ourselves, and the truth is not in us" (1 John 1:8 NCV).

We will never be cleansed until we confess we are dirty. We will never be pure until we admit we are filthy. And we will never be able to wash the feet of those who have hurt us until we allow Jesus, the one we have hurt, to wash ours.

You see, that is the secret of forgiveness. You will never forgive anyone more than God has already forgiven you. Only by letting him wash your feet can you have strength to wash those of another.

Still hard to imagine? Is it still hard to consider the thought of forgiving the one who hurt you?

If so, go one more time to the room. Watch Jesus as he goes from disciple to disciple. Can you see him? Can you hear the water splash? Can you hear him shuffle on the floor to the next person? Good. Keep that image.

John 13:12 says, "When he had finished washing their feet . . ."

Please note, he *finished* washing their feet. That means he left no one out. Why is that important? Because that also means he washed the feet of Judas. Jesus washed the feet of his betrayer. He gave his traitor equal attention. In just a few hours Judas's feet would guide the Roman guard to Jesus. But at this moment they are caressed by Christ.

That's not to say it was easy for Jesus.

That's not to say it is easy for you.

That is to say that God will never call you to do what he hasn't already done.

—A Gentle Thunder

*J*ohn 13 records the events of the final night before Jesus' death. He and his followers had gathered in the Upper Room for Passover. John begins his narrative with a lofty statement: "Jesus knew that the Father had given him authority over everything and that he had come from God and would return to God" (John 13:3 NLT).

Jesus knew the *who* and *why* of his life. Who was he? God's Son.

Why was he on earth? To serve the Father. Jesus knew his identity and authority, "so he got up from the table, took off his robe, wrapped a towel around his waist, and poured water into a basin. Then he began to wash the disciples' feet and to wipe them with the towel he had around him" (John 13:4–5 NLT).

Jesus—CEO, head coach, king of the world, sovereign of the seas—washed feet.

I'm not a fan of feet. Look you in the face? I will. Shake your hand? Gladly. Put an arm around your shoulders? Happy to do so. Rub a tear from the cheek of a child? In a heartbeat. But rub feet? Come on.

Feet stink. No one creates a cologne named Athlete's Foot Deluxe or Gym Sock Musk. Feet are not known for their sweet smell.

Nor their good looks. The businessman doesn't keep a framed photo of his wife's toes on his desk. Grandparents don't carry ankle-down pictures of their grandkids. "Aren't those the cutest arches you've ever seen?" We want to see the face, not the feet.

Feet have heels. Feet have toenails. Bunions and fungus. Corns and calluses. And plantar warts! Some large enough to warrant a zip code. Feet have little piggies that go "wee, wee, wee, all the way home." Forgive me, you people of the ped, society of the sole, but I'm not numbered among you. Feet smell bad and look ugly, which, I believe, is the point of this story.

Jesus touched the stinky, ugly parts of his disciples. Knowing he came from God. Knowing he was going to God. Knowing he could arch an eyebrow or clear his throat, and every angel in the universe would snap to attention. Knowing that all authority was his, he exchanged his robe for the servant's wrap, lowered himself to knee level, and began to rub away the grime, the grit, and the grunge their feet had collected on the journey.

This was the assignment of the slave, the job of the servant. When the master came home from a day spent walking the cobblestone streets, he expected a foot washing. The lowliest servant met him at the door with towel and water.

But in the Upper Room there was no servant. Pitcher of water? Yes. Basin and towel? In the corner on the table. But no one touched them. No one stirred. Each disciple hoped someone else would reach for the basin. Peter thought John would. John thought Andrew would. Each apostle assumed someone else would wash the feet.

And Someone did.

Jesus didn't exclude a single follower, though we wouldn't have faulted him had he bypassed Philip. When Jesus told the disciples to feed the throng of five thousand hungry people, Philip had retorted, "It's impossible!" (see John 6:7). So what does Jesus do with someone who questions his commands? Apparently, he washes the doubter's feet.

James and John lobbied for cabinet-level positions in Christ's kingdom. So what does Jesus do when people use his kingdom for personal advancement? He slides a basin in their direction.

Peter quit trusting Christ in the storm. He tried to talk Christ out of going to the cross. Within hours Peter would curse the very name of Jesus and hightail his way into hiding. In fact, all twenty-four of Jesus' followers' feet would soon scoot, leaving Jesus to face his accusers alone. Do you ever wonder what God does with promise breakers? He washes their feet.

And Judas. The lying, conniving, greedy rat who sold Jesus down the river for a pocket of cash. Jesus won't wash his feet, will he? Sure hope not. If he washes the feet of his Judas, you will have to wash the feet of yours. Your betrayer. Your turkey-throwing misfit and miscreant. That ne'er-do-well, that good-for-nothing villain. Jesus' Judas walked away with thirty pieces of silver. Your Judas walked away with your virginity, security, spouse, job, childhood, retirement, investments.

You expect me to wash his feet and let him go?

Most people don't want to. They use the villain's photo as a dart target. Their Vesuvius blows up every now and again, sending hate airborne, polluting and stinking the world. Most people keep a pot of anger on low boil.

But you aren't "most people." Grace has happened to you. Look at your feet. They are wet, grace soaked. Your toes and arches and heels have felt the cool basin of God's grace. Jesus has washed the grimiest parts of your life. He didn't bypass you and carry the basin toward someone else. If grace were a wheat field, he's bequeathed you the state of Kansas. Can't you share your grace with others?

"Since I, the Lord and Teacher, have washed your feet, you ought to wash each other's feet. I have given you an example to follow. Do as I have done to you" (John 13:14–15 NLT).

To accept grace is to accept the vow to give it.

—Grace

*C*onsider all the titles Jesus could have used to define himself on earth: King of kings, the great I AM, the Beginning and the End, the Lord of All, Jehovah, High and Holy. All of these and a dozen others would have been appropriate.

But Jesus didn't use them.

Instead, he called himself the Son of Man. This title appears eighty-two times in the New Testament. Eighty-one of which are in the gospels. Eighty of which are directly from the lips of Jesus. . . .

To the Jew the Son of Man was a symbol of triumph. The conqueror. The equalizer. The score-settler. The big brother. The intimidator. The Starship *Enterprise*. The right arm of the High and Holy. The king who roared down from the heavens in a fiery chariot of vengeance and anger toward those who have oppressed God's holy people.[1]

The Son of Man was the four-starred general who called his army to invade and led his troops to victory.

For that reason when Jesus spoke of the Son of Man in terms of power, the people cheered.

When he spoke of a new world where the Son of Man would sit on his glorious throne, the people understood.

When he spoke of the Son of Man who would come on the clouds of heaven with great power and authority[2] the people could envision the scene.

When he spoke of the Son of Man seated at the right hand of power,[3] everyone could imagine the picture.

But when he said the Son of Man would suffer . . . the people stood silent. This didn't fit the image . . . it's not what they expected.

Put yourself in their place. You've been oppressed by the Roman government for years. Since your youth you've been taught that the Son of Man would deliver you. Now he's here. Jesus calls himself the Son of Man. He proves he is the Son of Man. He can raise the dead and still a storm. The crowds of followers are growing. You are excited. Finally, the children of Abraham will be set free.

But what's this he's saying? "The Son of Man did not come to be served. He came to serve others." . . .

He is the Son of Man who came to serve and to give his life as a ransom . . . for you.

—And the Angels Were Silent

*J*esus has no room for pecking orders. Love "does not boast, it is not proud" (1 Cor. 13:4 NIV).

His solution to man-made caste systems? A change of direction. In a world of upward mobility, choose downward servility. Go down, not up. "Regard one another as more important than yourselves" (Phil. 2:3 NASB). That's what Jesus did.

He flip-flopped the pecking order. While others were going up, he was going down.

> Your attitude should be the same as that of Christ Jesus: Who, being in very nature God, did not consider equality with God something to be grasped, but made himself nothing, taking the very nature of a servant, being made in human likeness. And being found in appearance as a man, he humbled himself and became obedient to death—even death on a cross! (Phil. 2:5–8 NIV)

Would you do what Jesus did? He swapped a spotless castle for a grimy stable. He exchanged the worship of angels for the company of killers. He could hold the universe in his palm but gave it up to float in the womb of a maiden.

If you were God, would you sleep on straw, nurse from a breast, and be clothed in a diaper? I wouldn't, but Christ did.

If you knew that only a few would care that you came, would you still come? If you knew that those you loved would laugh in your face, would you still care? If you knew that the tongues you made would mock you, the mouths you made would spit at you, the hands you made would crucify you, would you still make them? Christ did. Would you regard the immobile and invalid more important than yourself? Jesus did.

He humbled himself. He went from commanding angels to sleeping in the straw. From holding stars to clutching Mary's finger. The palm that held the universe took the nail of a soldier.

Why? Because that's what love does. It puts the beloved before itself. Your soul was more important than his blood. Your eternal life was more important than his earthly life. Your place in heaven was more important to him than his place in heaven, so he gave up his so you could have yours.

He loves you that much, and because he loves you, you are of prime importance to him.

—A Love Worth Giving

*I*s Jesus not our example? Content to be known as a carpenter. Happy to be mistaken for the gardener. He served his followers by washing their feet. He serves us by doing the same. Each morning he gifts us with beauty. Each Sunday he calls us to his table. Each moment he dwells in our hearts. And does he not speak of the day when he as "the master will dress himself to serve and tell the servants to sit at the table, and he will serve them" (Luke 12:37 NCV)?

If Jesus is so willing to honor us, can we not do the same for others? Make people a priority. Accept your part in his plan. Be quick to share the applause. And, most of all, regard others as more important than yourself. Love does. For love "does not boast, it is not proud" (1 Cor. 13:4 NIV).

—A Love Worth Giving

*F*or some, communion is a sleepy hour in which wafers are eaten and juice is drunk and the soul never stirs. It wasn't intended to be as such.

It was intended to be an I-can't-believe-it's-me-pinch-me-I'm-dreaming invitation to sit at God's table and be served by the King himself.

When you read Matthew's account of the Last Supper, one incredible truth surfaces. Jesus is the person behind it all. It was Jesus who selected the place, designated the time, and set the meal in order. "The chosen time is near. I will have the Passover with my followers at your house."⁴ And at the Supper, Jesus is not a guest, but the host. "And [Jesus] gave to the disciples." The subject of the verbs is the message of the event: "He took . . . he blessed . . . he broke . . . he gave. . . ."

And at the Supper, Jesus is not the served, but the servant. It is Jesus who, during the Supper, put on the garb of a servant and washed the disciples' feet.[5] Jesus is the most active one at the table. Jesus is not portrayed as the one who reclines and receives, but as the one who stands and gives.

He still does. The Lord's Supper is a gift to you.

—And the Angels Were Silent

*W*e see Jesus dining out a few times in the Bible. What did he do?

At the feedings of the four and five thousand, Jesus played chef and asked the disciples to be the waiters (Matt. 15:29–38; 14:13–21).

While communing with the apostles at Passover, he played host and washed their feet. The host became the servant (John 13:1–17).

While Jesus was eating with the Pharisees, a woman with a sinful past anointed him with priceless oil. Jesus kindly allowed her to interrupt his meal and worship him (Luke 7:36–38).

Jesus was rude to only one group of people while eating—the Pharisees, who spoiled his meal with their distasteful treatment of others (Luke 7:39–50).

So what would Jesus leave a waiter?

Encouragement to help him endure the struggles of his job.

Forgiveness despite the mismatched orders and dirty spoon.

Eternity with a spoken word or an invitation to hear more.

Thanks communicated clearly through a satisfactory gratuity of 15 to 20 percent.

Jesus understood what it meant to be a servant, and he would certainly serve the servants with kindness and respect.

—Max on Life

$\mathcal{B}$ehold the most surprising ingredient of a great day: self-denial.

Don't we assume just the opposite? Great days emerge from the soil of self-indulgence, self-expression, and self-celebration. So pamper yourself, indulge yourself, promote yourself. But deny yourself? When was the last time you read this ad copy: "Go ahead. Deny yourself and have the time of your life!"?

Jesus could have written the words. He often goes countercultural, calling us down rather than up, telling us to zig when society says to zag.

In his economy,

+ the least are the greatest (Luke 9:48);
+ the last will be first (Mark 9:35);
+ the chosen seats are the forgotten seats (Luke 14:8–9).

He tells us to

+ honor others above ourselves (Romans 12:10);
+ consider others better than ourselves (Philippians 2:3);
+ turn the other cheek, give away our coats, and walk the second mile (Matthew 5:39–41).

That last instruction surely struck a raw nerve in the Jewish psyche. "Whoever compels you to go one mile, go with him two" (Matthew 5:41 NKJV). Jesus' fellow citizens lived under foreign rule. Roman soldiers imposed high taxes and oppressive laws. This sad state of affairs had existed ever since the Babylonians had destroyed the temple in 586 BC and carried the Judeans into captivity. Though some had returned from geographical exile, the theological and political exile lingered. First-century

Jews were sloshing through a centuries-old morass: oppressed by pagans, looking for the Messiah to deliver them.

Some responded by selling out, working the system to their own advantage. Others got out. The writers of the Dead Sea Scrolls at Qumran chose to separate themselves from the wicked world. Still others decided to fight back. The Zealot option was clear: say your prayers, sharpen your sword, and fight a holy war. Three options: sell out, get out, or fight back.

Jesus introduced a fourth. Serve. Serve the ones who hate you; forgive the ones who hurt you. Take the lowest place, not the highest; seek to serve, not to be served. Retaliate, not in kind but in kindness. He created what we might deem the Society of the Second Mile.

Roman soldiers could legally coerce Jewish citizens into carrying their load for one mile.[6] With nothing more than a command, they could requisition a farmer out of his field or a merchant out of his shop.

In such a case, Jesus said, "Give more than requested." Go two. At the end of one mile, keep going. Surprise the sandals off the soldier by saying, "I haven't done enough for you. I'm going a second mile." Do more than demanded. And do so with joy and grace! . . .

The Society of the Second Mile. Let me tell you how to spot its members. They don't wear badges or uniforms; they wear smiles. They have discovered the secret. The joy is found in the extra effort. The sweetest satisfaction lies not in climbing your own Everest but in helping other climbers.

Second-milers read Jesus' statement that it is better to give than receive (Acts 20:35) and nod their heads. When they hear the instruction "If your first concern is to look after yourself, you'll never find yourself" (Matthew 10:39 MSG), they understand. They've discovered this truth: "Self-help is no help at all. Self-sacrifice is the way, *my* way, to finding yourself, your true self" (Luke 9:24 MSG).

—*Great Day Every Day*

13

Sacrifice

*I*t's nearly midnight when they leave the upper room and descend through the streets of the city. They pass the Lower Pool and exit the Fountain Gate and walk out of Jerusalem. The roads are lined with the fires and tents of Passover pilgrims. Most are asleep, heavied with the evening meal. Those still awake think little of the band of men walking the chalky road.

They pass through the valley and ascend the path that will take them to Gethsemane. The road is steep, so they stop to rest. Somewhere within the city walls the twelfth apostle darts down a street. His feet have been washed by the man he will betray. His heart has been claimed by the Evil One he has heard. He runs to find Caiaphas.

The final encounter of the battle has begun.

As Jesus looks at the city of Jerusalem, he sees what the disciples can't. It is here, on the outskirts of Jerusalem, that the battle will end. He sees the staging of Satan. He sees the dashing of the demons. He sees the Evil One preparing for the final encounter. The enemy lurks as a specter over the hour. Satan, the host of hatred, has seized the heart of Judas and whispered in the ear of Caiaphas. Satan, the master of death, has opened the caverns and prepared to receive the source of light.

Hell is breaking loose.

History records it as a battle of the Jews against Jesus. It wasn't. It was a battle of God against Satan.

And Jesus knew it. He knew that before the war was over, he would be taken captive. He knew that before victory would come defeat. He knew that before the throne would come the cup. He knew that before the light of Sunday would come the blackness of Friday.

And he is afraid. . . .

Never has he felt so alone. What must be done, only he can do. An angel can't do it. No angel has the power to break open hell's gates. A man can't do it. No man has the purity to destroy sin's claim. No force on earth can face the force of evil and win—except God.

"The spirit is willing, but the flesh is weak," Jesus confesses. His humanity begged to be delivered from what his divinity could see. Jesus, the carpenter, implores. Jesus, the man, peers into the dark pit and begs, "Can't there be another way?"

Did he know the answer before he asked the question? Did his human heart hope his heavenly Father had found another way? We don't know. But we do know he asked to get out. We do know he begged for an exit. We do know there was a time when, if he could have, he would have turned his back on the whole mess and gone away.

But he couldn't.

He couldn't because he saw you. Right there in the middle of a world that isn't fair. He saw you cast into a river of life you didn't request. He saw you betrayed by those you love. He saw you with a body that gets sick and a heart that grows weak.

He saw you in your own garden of gnarled trees and sleeping friends. He saw you staring into the pit of your own failures and the mouth of your own grave.

He saw you in your Garden of Gethsemane—and he didn't want you to be alone.

He wanted you to know that he has been there too. He knows what it's like to be plotted against. He knows what it's like to be confused. He knows what it's like to be torn between two desires. He knows what it's like to smell the stench of Satan. And, perhaps most of all, he knows what it's like to beg God to change his mind and to hear God say so gently, but firmly, "No."

For that is what God says to Jesus. And Jesus accepts the answer. At some moment during that midnight hour, an angel of mercy comes over the weary body of the man in the garden. As he stands, the anguish is gone from his eyes. His fist will clench no more. His heart will fight no more.

The battle is won. You may have thought it was won on Golgotha. It wasn't. You may have thought the sign of victory is the empty tomb. It isn't. The final battle was won in Gethsemane. And the sign of conquest is Jesus at peace in the olive trees.

For it was in the garden that he made his decision. He would rather go to hell for you than go to heaven without you.

—*And the Angels Were Silent*

*Y*ou cannot deal with your own sins. "Only God can forgive sins" (Mark 2:7 NCV). Jesus is "the Lamb of God, who takes away the sin of the world!" (John 1:29 NCV). It's not you.

How did God deal with your debt?

Did he overlook it? He could have. He could have burned the statement. He could have ignored your bounced checks. But would a holy God do that? *Could* a holy God do that? No. Else he wouldn't be holy. Besides, is that how we want God to run his world—ignoring our sin and thereby endorsing our rebellion?

Did he punish you for your sins? Again, he could have. He could have crossed your name out of the book and wiped you off the face of the earth.

But would a loving God do that? Could a loving God do that? He loves you with an everlasting love. Nothing can separate you from his love.

So what did he do? "God put the world square with himself through the Messiah, giving the world a fresh start by offering forgiveness of sins. . . . How? you ask. In Christ. God put the wrong on him who never did anything wrong, so we could be put right with God" (2 Cor. 5:19–21 MSG).

Don't miss what happened. He took your statement flowing with red ink and bad checks and put his name at the top. He took his statement, which listed a million deposits and not one withdrawal, and put your name at the top. He assumed your debt. You assumed his fortune. And that's not all he did.

He also paid your penalty. If you are overdrawn at a bank, a fine must be paid. If you are overdrawn with God, a penalty must be paid as well. The fine at the bank is a hassle. But the penalty from God is hell. Jesus not only balanced your account; he paid your penalty. He took your place and paid the price for your sins. "He changed places with us and put himself under that curse" (Gal. 3:13 NCV).

> That's what Christ did definitively: suffered because of others' sins, the Righteous One for the unrighteous ones. He went through it all—was put to death and then made alive—to bring us to God. (1 Pet. 3:18 MSG)

> But he was wounded for the wrong we did; he was crushed for the evil we did. The punishment, which made us well, was given to him, and we are healed because of his wounds. (Isa. 53:5 NCV)

"With one sacrifice [Jesus] made perfect forever those who are being made holy" (Heb. 10:14 NCV). No more sacrifice needs to be made. No more deposits are necessary. So complete was the payment that Jesus used a banking term to proclaim your salvation. "It is finished!" (John 19:30 NKJV). *Tetelestai* was a financial term used to announce the final installment, the ultimate payment.

Now, if the task is finished, is anything else required of you? Of course not. If the account is full, what more could you add? Even saying the phrase "forgive our debts" does not earn grace. We repeat the words to remind us of the forgiveness we have, not to attain a forgiveness we need.

—The Great House of God

Abandon. Such a haunting word. . . .

Abandoned by family.

Abandoned by a spouse.

Abandoned by big business.

But nothing compares to being abandoned by God.

At noon the whole country was covered with darkness, which lasted for three hours. At about three o'clock Jesus cried out with a loud shout, *"Eli, Eli, lema sabachthani?"* which means, "My God, my God, why did you abandon me?" (Matt. 27:45–46 GNT)

By the time Christ screams these words, he has hung on the cross for six hours. Around nine o'clock that morning, he stumbled to the cleft of Skull Hill. A soldier pressed a knee on his forearm and drove a spike through one hand, then the other, then both feet. As the Romans lifted the cross, they unwittingly placed Christ in the very position in which he came to die—between man and God.

A priest on his own altar.

Noises intermingle on the hill: Pharisees mocking, swords clanging, and dying men groaning. Jesus scarcely speaks. When he does, diamonds sparkle against velvet. He gives his killers grace and his mother a son. He answers the prayer of a thief and asks for a drink from a soldier.

Then, at midday, darkness falls like a curtain. "At noon the whole country was covered with darkness, which lasted for three hours" (v. 45 GNT).

This is a supernatural darkness. Not a casual gathering of clouds or a brief eclipse of the sun. This is a three-hour blanket of blackness. Merchants in Jerusalem light candles. Soldiers ignite torches. Parents worry. People everywhere ask questions. From whence comes this noonday night? As far away as Egypt, the historian Dionysius takes notice of the black sky and writes, "Either the God of nature is suffering, or the machine of the world is tumbling into ruin."[1]

Of course the sky is dark; people are killing the Light of the World.

The universe grieves. God said it would. "On that day . . . I will make the sun go down at noon, and darken the earth in broad daylight. . . . I will make it like the mourning for an only son, and the end of it like a bitter day" (Amos 8:9–10 RSV).

The sky weeps. And a lamb bleats. Remember the time of the scream? "At about three o'clock Jesus cried out." Three o'clock in the afternoon, the hour of the temple sacrifice. Less than a mile to the east, a finely clothed priest leads a lamb to the slaughter, unaware that his work is futile. Heaven is not looking at the lamb of man but at "the Lamb of God, who takes away the sin of the world" (John 1:29 RSV).

A weeping sky. A bleating lamb. But more than anything, a screaming Savior. "Jesus cried out with a loud voice" (Matt. 27:46 NASB). Note the sturdy words here. Other writers employed the Greek word for "loud voice" to describe a "roar."[2] Soldiers aren't cupping an ear asking him to speak up. The Lamb roars. "The sun and the moon shall be darkened. . . . The LORD also shall roar out of Zion, and utter his voice from Jerusalem" (Joel 3:15–16 KJV).

Christ lifts his heavy head and eyelids toward the heavens and spends his final energy crying out toward the ducking stars. "*Eli, Eli, lema sabachthani?'* which means, 'My God, my God, why did you abandon me?'" (Matt. 27:46 GNT).

We would ask the same. Why him? Why forsake your Son? Forsake the murderers. Desert the evildoers. Turn your back on perverts and peddlers of pain. Abandon them, not him. Why would you abandon earth's only sinless soul?

Ah, there is the hardest word. *Abandon.* The house no one wants. The child no one claims. The parent no one remembers. The Savior no one understands. He pierces the darkness with heaven's loneliest question: "My God, my God, why did you abandon me?"

Paul used the same Greek word when he urged Timothy: "Be diligent to come to me quickly; for Demas has *forsaken* me, having loved this present world, and has departed for Thessalonica" (2 Tim. 4:9–10 NKJV, emphasis mine).

As Paul looks for Demas, can he find him? No. Forsaken.

As Jesus looks for God, can he find him? No. Forsaken.

Wait a second. Doesn't David tell us, "I have never seen the righteous forsaken" (Ps. 37:25 NIV)? Did David misspeak? Did Jesus misstep? Neither. In this hour Jesus is anything but righteous. But his mistakes aren't his own. "Christ carried our sins in his body on the cross so we would stop living for sin and start living for what is right" (1 Pet. 2:24 NCV).

Christ carried all our sins in his body . . .

May I get specific for a moment? May I talk about sin? Dare I remind you and me that our past is laced with outbursts of anger, stained with nights of godless passion, and spotted with undiluted greed?

Suppose your past was made public? Suppose you were to stand on a stage while a film of every secret and selfish second was projected on the screen behind you?

Would you not crawl beneath the rug? Would you not scream for the heavens to have mercy? And would you not feel just a fraction . . . just a fraction of what Christ felt on the cross? The icy displeasure of a sin-hating God? . . .

Christ carried all our sins in his body . . .

See Christ on the cross? That's a gossiper hanging there. See Jesus? Embezzler. Liar. Bigot. See the crucified carpenter? He's a wife beater. Porn addict and murderer. See Bethlehem's boy? Call him by his other names—Adolf Hitler, Osama bin Laden, and Jeffrey Dahmer.

Hold it, Max. Don't you lump Christ with those evildoers. Don't you place his name in the same sentence with theirs!

I didn't. *He* did. Indeed he did more. More than place his name in the same sentence, he placed himself in their place. And yours. With hands nailed open, he invited God, "Treat me as you would treat them!" And God did. In an act that broke the heart of the Father, yet honored the holiness of heaven, sin-purging judgment flowed over the sinless Son of the ages.

And heaven gave earth her finest gift. The Lamb of God who took away the sin of the world.

"My God, my God, why did you abandon me?" Why did Christ scream those words?

So you'll never have to.

—*Next Door Savior*

The maître d´ wouldn't change his mind. He didn't care that this was our honeymoon. It didn't matter that the evening at the classy country club restaurant was a wedding gift. He couldn't have cared less that Denalyn and I had gone without lunch to save room for dinner. All of this was immaterial in comparison to the looming problem.

I wasn't wearing a jacket.

Didn't know I needed one. I thought a sport shirt was sufficient. It was clean and tucked in. But Mr. Black-Tie with the French accent was unimpressed. He seated everyone else. Mr. and Mrs. Debonair were given a table. Mr. and Mrs. Classier-Than-You were seated. But Mr. and Mrs. Didn't-Wear-a-Jacket?

If I'd had another option, I wouldn't have begged. But I didn't. The hour was late. Other restaurants were closed or booked, and we were hungry. "There's got to be something you can do," I pleaded. He looked and me, then at Denalyn, and let out a long sigh that puffed his cheeks.

"All right, let me see."

He disappeared into the cloakroom and emerged with a jacket. "Put this on." I did. The sleeves were too short. The shoulders were too tight. And the color was lime green. But I didn't complain. I had a jacket, and we were taken to a table. (Don't tell anyone, but I took it off when the food came.)

For all the inconvenience of the evening, we ended up with a great dinner and an even greater parable.

I needed a jacket, but all I had was a prayer. The fellow was too kind to turn me away but too loyal to lower the standard. So the very one who required a jacket gave me a jacket, and we were given a table.

Isn't this what happened at the cross? Seats at God's table are not available to the sloppy. But who among us is anything but? Unkempt morality. Untidy with truth. Careless with people. Our moral clothing is in disarray. Yes, the standard for sitting at God's table is high, but the love of God for his children is higher. So he offers a gift.

Not a lime-colored jacket but a robe. A seamless robe. Not a garment pulled out of a cloakroom but a robe worn by his Son, Jesus. . . .

The character of Jesus was a seamless fabric woven from heaven to earth . . . from God's thoughts to Jesus' actions. From God's tears to Jesus' compassion. From God's word to Jesus' response. All one piece. All a picture of the character of Jesus. But when Christ was nailed to the cross, he took off his robe of seamless perfection and assumed a different wardrobe, the wardrobe of indignity.

The indignity of nakedness. Stripped before his own mother and loved ones. Shamed before his family.

The indignity of failure. For a few pain-filled hours, the religious leaders were the victors, and Christ appeared the loser. Shamed before his accusers.

Worst of all, he wore *the indignity of sin.* "He himself bore our sins in his body on the tree, so that we might die to sins and live for righteousness" (1 Pet. 2:24 NIV).

The clothing of Christ on the cross? Sin—yours and mine. The sins of all humanity.

I can remember my father explaining to me the reason a group of men on the side of the road wore striped clothing. "They're prisoners," he said. "They have broken the law and are serving time."

You want to know what stuck with me about these men? They never looked up. They never made eye contact. Were they ashamed? Probably so.

What they felt on the side of the road was what our Savior felt on the cross—disgrace. Every aspect of the crucifixion was intended not only to hurt the victim but to shame him. Death on a cross was usually reserved for the most vile offenders: slaves, murderers, assassins, and the like. The condemned person was marched through the city streets, shouldering his crossbar and wearing a placard about his neck that named his crime. At the execution site he was stripped and mocked.

Crucifixion was so abhorrent that Cicero wrote, "Let the very name of the cross be far away, not only from the body of a Roman citizen, but even from his thoughts, his eyes, his ears."[3] Jesus was not only shamed before people, he was shamed before heaven.

Since he bore the sin of the murderer and adulterer, he felt the shame of the murderer and adulterer. Though he never lied, he bore the disgrace of a liar. Though he never cheated, he felt the embarrassment of a cheater. Since he bore the sin of the world, he felt the collective shame of the world.

It's no wonder that the Hebrew writer spoke of the "disgrace he bore" (Heb. 13:13 NLT).

While on the cross, Jesus felt the indignity and disgrace of a criminal. No, he was not guilty. No, he had not committed a sin. And, no, he did not deserve to be sentenced. But you and I were, we had, and we did. We were left in the same position I was with the maître d'—having nothing to offer but a prayer. Jesus, however, goes further than the maître d'. Can you imagine the restaurant host removing his tuxedo coat and offering it to me?

Jesus does. We're not talking about an ill-fitting, leftover jacket. He offers a robe of seamless purity and dons my patchwork coat of pride, greed, and selfishness. "He changed places with us" (Gal. 3:13 NCV). He wore our sin so we could wear his righteousness.

Though we come to the cross dressed in sin, we leave the cross dressed in the "coat of his strong love" (Isa. 59:17 NCV) and girded with a belt of "goodness and fairness" (Isa. 11:5 NCV) and clothed in "garments of salvation" (Isa. 61:10 NIV).

Indeed, we leave dressed in Christ himself. "You have all put on Christ as a garment" (Gal. 3:27 NEB).

It wasn't enough for him to prepare you a feast.

It wasn't enough for him to reserve you a seat.

It wasn't enough for him to cover the cost and provide the transportation to the banquet.

He did something more. He let you wear his own clothes so that you would be properly dressed.

He did that . . . just for you.

—He Chose the Nails

*C*hrist exchanged hearts with you. Yes, your thieving, lying, adulterous, and murderous heart. He placed your sin in himself and invited God to punish it. "The LORD has put on him the punishment for all the evil we have done" (Isa. 53:6 NCV). . . .

Though healthy, Jesus took our disease upon himself. Though diseased, we who accept his offer are pronounced healthy. More than pardoned, we are declared innocent. We enter heaven, not with healed hearts, but with his heart. It is as if we have never sinned. Read slowly the announcement of Paul: "If anyone is in Christ, he is a new creation; the old has gone, the new has come!" (2 Cor. 5:17 NIV).

We enjoy the same status as Bertram Campbell. He spent three years and four months in prison for a forgery he did not commit. When the real criminal finally confessed, the governor declared Campbell, not just pardoned, but innocent.[4] God does for us exactly the same. "God made him who had no sin to be sin for us, so that in him we might become the righteousness of God" (2 Cor. 5:21 NIV).

This is no transplant, mind you, but a swap. The holy and the vile exchange locations. God makes healthy what was sick, right what was wrong, straight what was crooked.

—3:16: The Numbers of Hope

"*T*he Lord . . . dressed them."

Oh, for a glimpse of that moment. Adam and Eve are on their way out of the garden. They've been told to leave, but now God tells them to stop. "Those fig leaves," he says, shaking his head, "will never do." And he produces some clothing. But he doesn't throw the garments at their feet and tell them to get dressed. He dresses them himself. "Hold still, Adam. Let's see how this fits." As a mother would dress a toddler. As a father would zip up the jacket of a preschooler. As a physician would place a lab coat over a frightened girl. God covers them. He protects them.

Love always protects.

Hasn't he done the same for us? We eat our share of forbidden fruit. We say what we shouldn't say. Go where we shouldn't go. Pluck fruit from trees we shouldn't touch.

And when we do, the door opens, and the shame tumbles in. And we hide. We sew fig leaves. Flimsy excuses. See-through justifications.

We cover ourselves in good works and good deeds, but one gust of the wind of truth, and we are naked again—stark naked in our own failure.

So what does God do? Exactly what he did for our parents in the garden. He sheds innocent blood. He offers the life of his Son. And from the scene of the sacrifice the Father takes a robe—not the skin of an animal—but the robe of righteousness. And does he throw it in our direction and tell us to shape up? No, he dresses us himself. He dresses us with himself. "You were all baptized into Christ, and so you were all clothed with Christ" (Gal. 3:26–27 NCV).

The robing is his work, not ours. Did you note the inactivity of Adam and Eve? They did nothing. Absolutely nothing. They didn't request the sacrifice; they didn't think of the sacrifice; they didn't even dress themselves. They were passive in the process. So are we. "You have been saved by grace through believing. You did not save yourselves; it was a gift from God. It was not the result of your own efforts, so you cannot brag about it. God has made us what we are" (Eph. 2:8–10 NCV).

We hide. He seeks. We bring sin. He brings a sacrifice. We try fig leaves. He brings the robe of righteousness. And we are left to sing the song of the prophet: "He has covered me with clothes of salvation and wrapped me with a coat of goodness, like a bridegroom dressed for his wedding, like a bride dressed in jewels" (Isa. 61:10 NCV).

—A Love Worth Giving

*E*xactly what did God give up when he gave his Son to the world?

I've decided I cannot know. Why? Because I have never been to heaven. When God gave us his Son, his Son gave up heaven. Try to imagine that sacrifice. What if you were to leave your home and become homeless or leave the human race and become a mosquito or a wasp? Would that be comparable to God's becoming human? Jesus, whose address in heaven was Everywhere, limited himself to a human body in a map-dot town on the fringe of the Roman Empire.

Of course, as you said, he did this "for a time." Maybe that is part of the sacrifice. God is timeless, unbound by clocks or calendars. And for a time he entered time.

But as I said, I've never lived in heaven, and I've never been eternal, so I can't understand what he gave up.

Nor have I been sinless, so I can't imagine what it was like to become sin. This is the heart of the Christian gospel. That he who had no sin took on sin (2 Cor. 5:21). That Christ on the cross became a sinner in the eyes of heaven. That he experienced the pain and punishment due to every rapist, thief, mass murderer, and despot.

He paid the price for sin by becoming a sinner. Since I've always been a sinner, I can't appreciate this sacrifice.

And I've never given my child for evil people. I might give myself or a bit of myself to help evil people. But sacrifice one of my daughters? No way. Even if I knew I would see her again, I wouldn't do it. But God did.

It seems to me that God gave more than we could ever ask.

—Max on Life

*O*ur inability to finish what we start is seen in the smallest of things:

A partly mowed lawn.
A half-read book.
Letters begun but never completed.
An abandoned diet.
A car up on blocks.

Or, it shows up in life's most painful areas:

An abandoned child.
A cold faith.
A job hopper.
A wrecked marriage.
An unevangelized world.

Am I touching some painful sores? Any chance I'm addressing someone who is considering giving up? If I am, I want to encourage you to remain. I want to encourage you to remember Jesus' determination on the cross.

Jesus didn't quit. But don't think for one minute that he wasn't tempted to. Watch him wince as he hears his apostles backbite and quarrel. Look at him weep as he sits at Lazarus's tomb or hear him wail as he claws the ground of Gethsemane.

Did he ever want to quit? You bet.

That's why his words are so splendid.

"It is finished."

Stop and listen. Can you imagine the cry from the cross? The sky is dark. The other two victims are moaning. The jeering mouths are silent. Perhaps there is thunder. Perhaps there is weeping. Perhaps there is silence. Then Jesus draws in a deep breath, pushes his feet down on that Roman nail, and cries, "It is finished!"

What was finished?

The history-long plan of redeeming man was finished. The message of God to man was finished. The works done by Jesus as a man on earth were finished. The task of selecting and training ambassadors was finished. The job was finished. The song had been sung. The blood had been poured. The sacrifice had been made. The sting of death had been removed. It was over. A cry of defeat? Hardly. Had his hands not been fastened down I dare say that a triumphant fist would have punched the dark sky. No, this is no cry of despair. It is a cry of completion. A cry of victory. A cry of fulfillment. Yes, even a cry of relief.

The fighter remained. And thank God that he did. Thank God that he endured.

—No Wonder They Call Him the Savior

*G*od, motivated by love and directed by divinity, surprised everyone. He became a man. In an untouchable mystery, he disguised himself as a carpenter and lived in a dusty Judaean village. Determined to prove his love for his creation, he walked incognito through his own world. His callused hands touched wounds and his compassionate words touched hearts. He became one of us.

Have you ever seen such determination? Have you ever witnessed such a desire to communicate? If one thing didn't work, he'd try another. If one approach failed, he'd try a new one. His mind never stopped. "In the past God spoke . . . at *many* times and in *various* ways," writes the author of Hebrews, "but in these last days he has spoken to us by his Son."[5]

But as beautiful as this act of incarnation was, it was not the zenith. Like a master painter God reserved his masterpiece until the end. All the earlier acts of love had been leading to this one. The angels hushed and the heavens paused to witness the finale. God unveils the canvas and the ultimate act of creative compassion is revealed.

God on a cross.

The Creator being sacrificed for the creation. God convincing man once and for all that forgiveness still follows failure.

I wonder if, while on the cross, the Creator allowed his thoughts to wander back to the beginning. One wonders if he allowed the myriad of faces and acts to parade in his memory. Did he reminisce about the creation of the sky and sea? Did he relive the conversations with Abraham and Moses? Did he remember the plagues and the promises, the wilderness and the wanderings?

We don't know.

We do know, however, what he said.

"It is finished."

The mission was finished. All that the master painter needed to do was done and was done in splendor. His creation could now come home.

"It is finished!" he cried.

And the great Creator went home.

(He's not resting, though. Word has it that his tireless hands are preparing a city so glorious that even the angels get goosebumps upon seeing it. Considering what he has done so far, that is one creation I plan to see.)

—*No Wonder They Call Him the Savior*

14

Savior

I have a sin nature.

So do you. (Merry Christmas.) Under the right circumstances you will do the wrong thing. You won't want to. You'll try not to, but you will. Why? You have a sin nature.

You were born with it. We all were. Our parents didn't teach us to throw temper tantrums; we were born with the skill. No one showed us how to steal a cookie from our sibling; we just knew. We never attended a class on pouting or passing the blame, but we could do both before we were out of our diapers.

Each one of us entered the world with a sin nature.

God entered the world to take it away. Christmas commemorates the day and the way God saved us from ourselves.

Look carefully at the words the angel spoke to Joseph.

Joseph son of David, do not be afraid to take Mary home as your wife, because what is conceived in her is from the Holy Spirit. She will give birth to a son, and you are to give him the name Jesus, because he will save his people from their sins. (Matt. 1:20–21 NIV)

We may not see the connection between the name *Jesus* and the phrase "save his people from their sins," but Joseph would have. He was familiar with the Hebrew language. The English name *Jesus* traces its origin to the Hebrew word *Yeshua*. *Yeshua* is a shortening of *Yehoshuah*, which means "Yahweh saves."[1]

Who was Jesus? *God* saves.

What did Jesus come to do? God *saves*.

God saves. Jesus was not just godly, godlike, God hungry, God focused, or God worshipping. He was God. Not merely a servant of God, instrument of God, or friend of God, but Jesus was God.

God *saves*, not God empathizes, cares, listens, helps, assists, or applauds. God saves. Specifically "he will save his people from their sins" (v. 21). Jesus came to save us, not just from politics, enemies, challenges, or difficulties. He came to save us from our own sins.

Here's why. God has high plans for you and me. He is recruiting for himself a people who will populate heaven. God will restore his planet and his children to their gar-den of Eden splendor. It will be perfect. Perfect in splendor. Perfect in righteousness. Perfect in harmony.

One word describes heaven: *perfect*.

One word describes us: *imperfect*.

God's kingdom is perfect, but his children are not, so what is he to do? Abandon us? Start over? He could. But he loves us too much to do that.

Will he tolerate us with our sin nature? Populate heaven with rebellious, self-centered citizens? If so, how would heaven be heaven?

He had a greater plan. "God was pleased for all of him-self to live in Christ" (Col. 1:19 NCV).

All the love of God was in Jesus. All the strength of God was in Jesus. All the compassion and power and devotion of God were, for a time, in the earthly body of a carpenter.

No wonder the winds obeyed when Jesus spoke; he was *God speaking*.

No wonder the bacteria fled when Jesus touched the wounds; he was *God touching*.

No wonder the water held him as he walked; he was *God walking*.

No wonder the people stood speechless as he taught; he was *God teaching.*

And no wonder ten thousand angels stood in rapt attention as Jesus was nailed to the cross; he was *God dying.*

He let people crucify him, for goodness' sake! He became sin for our sake. "He made Him who knew no sin to be sin for us" (2 Cor. 5:21 NKJV). What started in the Bethlehem cradle culminated on the Jerusalem cross.

But that's not all.

Jesus not only did a work *for* us; he does a work *within* us. "The mystery in a nutshell is just this: Christ is in you" (Col. 1:27 MSG).

He commandeers our hands and feet, requisitions our minds and tongues. "He decided from the outset to shape the lives of those who love him along the same lines as the life of his Son" (Rom. 8:29 MSG).

Having paid sin's penalty, Christ defuses sin's power. The punk within diminishes, and the Christ within flourishes. God changes us day by day from one level to the next. We'll never be sinless, but we will sin less.

And when we do sin, we have this assurance: the grace that saved us also preserves us. We may lose our tempers, our perspective, and our self-control. But we never lose our hope. Why? Because God has his hold on us. He "is able to keep you from stumbling, and to present you faultless before the presence of His glory with exceeding joy" (Jude v. 24 NKJV).

The believer has been saved from the guilt of sin, is being saved from problems of sin, and, upon the return of Christ, will be saved from the punishment for sin. Complete and full-service salvation.

God saves!

And *only* God saves. If we could save ourselves, why would we need a Savior? Jesus did not enter the world to help us save ourselves. He entered the world to save us from ourselves.

As a Boy Scout, I earned a lifesaving merit badge. I never actually saved anyone. In fact, the only people I saved were other Boy Scouts who didn't need to be saved. During training I would rescue other trainees.

We took turns saving each other. But since we weren't really drowning, we resisted being rescued.

"Stop kicking and let me save you," I'd say.

It's impossible to save those who are trying to save themselves.

You might save yourself from a broken heart or going broke or running out of gas. But you aren't good enough to save yourself from sin. You aren't strong enough to save yourself from death. You need a Savior.

Because of Bethlehem you have one.

—Because of Bethlehem

We need someone to save us from meaninglessness and meanness. We are lost and need to be found and taken home. We need a Savior. The Christmas promise is this: we have a Savior, and his name is Jesus.

His time on earth was a search-and-rescue mission. He rescued a woman hiding in Samaria. Five husbands had dumped her like the morning garbage. The sixth wouldn't marry her. She was the town scamp. She filled her water bucket in the heat of the day to avoid the stares of the people. Christ went out of his way to help her.[2]

He rescued a demoniac in the caves. Evil spirits had driven the man to mutilate himself, slashing himself with stones. One word from Christ stopped the hurting.[3] He spotted pint-size Zacchaeus in Jericho. The tax collector had swindled enough people to stockpile his retirement. Yet he would have given it all for a clean conscience and a good friend. One lunch with Jesus and he found both.[4]

Jesus' ministry went on like this for three years. He changed person after person; no one quite knew how to respond to this carpenter who commanded the dead. His healing hands had calluses; his divine voice had an accent. He tended to doze off on boats and grow hungry on trips. Yet he scared the hell out of the possessed and gave hope to the dispossessed. Just when he seemed poised for a crown, he died on a cross. . . .

"God . . . loved us and sent His *unique* Son *on a special mission* to become an atoning sacrifice for our sins" (1 John 4:10 The Voice). Jesus took on our sin. He was covered by the rebellion that separated us from God. He endured what we should have endured. He paid the price to save us.

When we were still powerless, Christ died for the ungodly. (Rom. 5:6 niv)

Christ . . . died for sins once for all, the righteous for the unrighteous, that he might bring us to God. (1 Peter 3:18 rsv)

In the manger God loves you; through the cross God saves you.
—*Because of Bethlehem*

Team Hoyt consists of a father-son squad: Dick and Rick. They race. They race a lot. Sixty-four marathons. Two hundred and six triathlons. Six triathlons at Ironman distance. Two hundred and four 10K runs. Since 1975, they've crossed nearly a thousand finish lines. They've even crossed the USA. It took them forty-five days to run and pedal 3,735 miles, but they did it.

Team Hoyt loves races. But only half of Team Hoyt can run. Dick, the dad, can. But Rick's legs don't work, nor does his speech. At his birth in 1962, the umbilical cord wrapped around his neck, starving oxygen from his brain, stealing coordination from his body. Doctors gave no hope for his development.

Dick and his wife, Judy, disagreed with the prognosis. Rick couldn't bathe, dress, or feed himself, but he could think. They knew he was bright. So they enrolled him in public school. He graduated. He entered college and graduated again.

But Rick wanted to run. At age fifteen, he asked his dad if they could enter a five-mile benefit race. Dick was not a runner, but he was a father, so he loaded his son in a three-wheeled wheelchair, and off they went. They haven't stopped since.

Young Rick Hoyt relies on his dad to do it all: lift him, push him, pedal him, and tow him. Other than a willing heart, he makes no contribution to the effort. Rick depends entirely on the strength of his dad.[5]

God wants you to do the same. "Whoever believes *in him* shall not perish but have eternal life" (John 3:16 NIV).

The phrase "believes *in him*" doesn't digest well in our day of self-sufficient spiritual food. "Believe *in yourself*" is the common menu selection of our day. Try harder. Work longer. Dig deeper. Self-reliance is our goal.

And tolerance is our virtue. "In him" smacks of exclusion. Don't all paths lead to heaven? Islam, Hinduism, Buddhism, and humanism? Salvation comes in many forms, right? Christ walks upriver on this topic. Salvation is found, not in self or in them, but *in him*.

We bring to the spiritual race what Rick Hoyt brings to the physical one. Our spiritual legs have no strength. Our morality has no muscle. Our good deeds cannot carry us across the finish line, but Christ can. "To the one who does not work, but believes *in Him* who justifies the ungodly, his faith is credited as righteousness" (Rom. 4:5 NASB).

Paul assures salvation to the most unlikely folks: not to the worker, but to the trust-er; not to the able-bodied, but to the unable; not to the affluent saint, but to the bankrupt and unemployable—the child who will trust with Rick Hoyt reliance. "Trusting-him-to-do-it is what gets you set right with God, by God. Sheer gift" (Rom. 4:5 MSG).

We bring what Rick brings. And God does what Dick does. He takes start-to-finish-line responsibility for his children. "I give them eternal life, and they shall never perish; no one can snatch them out of my hand" (John 10:28 NIV).

Jesus fortified this language with the strongest possible negation, leading the Amplified Bible translators to translate: "And I give them eternal life, and they shall never lose it or perish throughout the ages. [To all eternity they shall never by any means be destroyed.] And no one is able to snatch them out of My hand" (John 10:28).

We parents understand God's resolve. When our children stumble, we do not disown them. When they fall, we do not dismiss them. We may punish or reprimand, but cast them out of the family? We cannot. They are biologically connected to us. Those born with our DNA will die with it.

God, our Father, engenders the same relationship with us. Upon salvation we "become children of God" (John 1:12 ESV). He alters our lineage, redefines our spiritual parenthood, and, in doing so, secures our salvation. To accomplish the mission, he seals us with his Spirit. "Having believed, you were marked in him with a seal, the promised Holy Spirit" (Eph. 1:13 NIV). A soul sealed by God is safe. . . .

God vacuum-seals us with his strongest force: his Spirit. He sheathes his children in a suit of spiritual armor, encircles us with angels, and indwells us himself. The queen of England should enjoy such security.

Christ paid too high a price to leave us unguarded. "Remember, he has identified you as his own, guaranteeing that you will be saved on the day of redemption" (Eph. 4:30 NLT).

What a difference this assurance makes.

An air force pilot told me of the day he forgot to secure himself into the seat of his high-powered jet. He completed every other preliminary act. He satisfied his checklist from beginning to end. Yet he forgot to buckle his seat belt. His jet was configured in such a way that once the plane was airborne, the belt could not be secured. Ejection from the plane meant separation from his seat, and separation from his seat meant separation from his parachute and a face-plant at 120 mph. That'll suck the joy out of the journey. Can you imagine flying a jet without a parachute?

Many do. Eternal insecurity extracts joy from many people. Only Christ guarantees a safe landing. . . .

No one but Jesus "buckles you in." You may slip—indeed you will—but you will not fall. Hence the invitation to believe "in him." Don't believe in you; you can't save you. And don't believe in others; they can't save you.

Some historians clump Christ with Moses, Muhammad, Confucius, and other spiritual leaders. But Jesus refuses to share the page. He declares, "I am the way, and the truth, and the life; no one comes to the Father, but by me" (John 14:6 RSV). He could have scored more points in political correctness had he said, "I *know* the way," or "I *show* the way." Yet he speaks not of what he does but of who he is: I *am* the way.

His followers refused to soften or shift the spotlight. Peter announced: "There is salvation in no one else! God has given no other name under heaven by which we must be saved" (Acts 4:12 NLT).

Many recoil at such definitiveness. John 14:6 and Acts 4:12 sound primitive in this era of broadbands and broad minds. The world is shrinking, cultures are blending, borders are bending; this is the day of inclusion. All roads lead to heaven, right?

But can they? The sentence makes good talk-show fodder, but is it accurate? Can all approaches to God be correct?

Islam says Jesus was not crucified. Christians say he was. Both can't be right.

Judaism refuses the claim of Christ as the Messiah.[6] Christians accept it. Someone's making a mistake.

Buddhists look toward Nirvana, achieved after no less than 547 reincarnations.[7] Christians believe in one life, one death, and an eternity of enjoying God. Doesn't one view exclude the other?

Humanists do not acknowledge a creator of life. Jesus claims to be the source of life. One of the two speaks folly.

Spiritists read your palms. Christians consult the Bible. Hindus perceive a plural and impersonal God.[8] Christ-followers believe "there is only one God" (1 Cor. 8:4 NLT). Somebody is wrong.

And, most supremely, every non-Christian religion says, "You can save you." Jesus says, "My death on the cross saves you." How can all religions lead to God when they are so different? We don't tolerate such illogic in other matters. We don't pretend that all roads lead to London or all ships sail to Australia. All flights don't land in Rome. Imagine your response to a travel agent who claims they do. You tell him you need a flight to Rome, Italy, so he looks on his screen.

"Well, there is a flight to Sydney, Australia, departing at 6:00 A.M."

"Does it go to Rome?"

"No, but it offers wonderful in-flight dining and movies."

"But I need to go to Rome."

"Then let me suggest Southwest Airlines."

"Southwest Airlines flies to Rome?"

"No, but they have consistently won awards for on-time arrivals."

You're growing frustrated. "I need one airline to carry me to one place: Rome."

The agent appears offended. "Sir, all flights go to Rome."

You know better. Different flights have different destinations. That's not a thickheaded conclusion but an honest one. Every flight does not go to Rome. Every path does not lead to God. Jesus blazed a stand-alone trail void of self-salvation. He cleared a one-of-a-kind passageway uncluttered by human effort. Christ came, not for the strong, but for the weak; not for the righteous, but for the sinner. We enter his way upon confession of our need, not completion of our deeds. He offers a unique-to-him invitation in which he works and we trust, he dies and we live, he invites and we believe.

We believe *in him.* "The work God wants you to do is this: Believe the One he sent" (John 6:29 NCV).

Believe in yourself? No. Believe in him.

Believe in them? No. Believe in him.

And those who do, those who believe "in him shall not perish but have eternal life" (John 3:16 NIV).

How do we begin to believe? We do what young Rick Hoyt did. We turn to our Father for help.

When Dick and Rick Hoyt cross finish lines, both receive finisher medals. Post-race listings include both names. The dad does the work, but the son shares in the victory. Why? Because he believes. And because he believes, both celebrate the finish.

May you and your Father do the same.

—3:16: The Numbers of Hope

"Come to me, all you who are weary and burdened, and I will give you rest."⁹

Come to me. . . . The invitation is to come to him. Why him? He offers the invitation as a penniless rabbi in an oppressed nation. He has no political office, no connections with the authorities in Rome. He hasn't written a best-seller or earned a diploma.

Yet, he dares to look into the leathery faces of farmers and tired faces of housewives and offer rest. He looks into the disillusioned eyes of a preacher or two from Jerusalem. He gazes into the cynical stare of a banker and the hungry eyes of a bartender and makes this paradoxical promise: "Take my yoke upon you and learn from me, for I am gentle and humble in heart, and you will find rest for your souls."¹⁰

The people came. They came out of the cul-de-sacs and office complexes of their day. They brought him the burdens of their existence, and he gave them not religion, not doctrine, not systems, but rest.

As a result, they called him Lord.

As a result, they called him Savior.

Not so much because of what he said, but because of what he did.

What he did on the cross during six hours, one Friday.

—Six Hours One Friday

*A*ccording to the Bible, it is possible to "know beyond the shadow of a doubt that you have eternal life" (1 John 5:13 MSG).

How do we know that? "If you confess with your mouth, 'Jesus is Lord,' and believe in your heart that God raised him from the dead, you will be saved" (Rom. 10:9 NIV).

First, confess that Jesus is Lord. Say it out loud or quietly in your heart—either way. Just mean it.

Then believe that Jesus was resurrected. He's not a man in the grave but God in the flesh with the power over death.

Confess and believe . . . and you will have salvation.

Catch what Romans 10:9 does not say—live perfectly, be nice to everyone, don't mess up, don't doubt, always smile . . . and you will be saved. Can't do it.

Impossible.

Just confess and believe. Salvation will follow.

It's so easy . . . yet so hard.

God wants us to know we are saved, for saved people are dangerous people, willing to face off with the world, unafraid of the consequences since they know that, whatever happens, they will have eternal life.

"Therefore, there is now no condemnation for those who are in Christ Jesus" (Rom. 8:1 NIV). Watch out, world!

—Max on Life

*I*t's the ultimate question of the Christ: whose son is he?

Is he the son of God or the sum of our dreams? Is he the force of creation or a figment of our imagination?

When we ask that question about Santa, the answer is the culmination of our desires. A depiction of our fondest dreams.

Not so when we ask it about Jesus. For no one could ever dream a person as incredible as he is. The idea that a virgin would be selected by God to bear himself. . . . The notion that God would don a scalp and toes and two eyes. . . . The thought that the King of the universe would sneeze and burp and get bitten by mosquitoes. . . . It's too incredible. Too revolutionary. We would never create such a Savior. We aren't that daring.

When we create a redeemer, we keep him safely distant in his faraway castle. We allow him only the briefest of encounters with us. We permit him to swoop in and out with his sleigh before we can draw too near. We wouldn't ask him to take up residence in the midst of a contaminated people. In our wildest imaginings we wouldn't conjure a king who becomes one of us.

But God did. God did what we wouldn't dare dream. He did what we couldn't imagine. He became a man so we could trust him. He became a sacrifice so we could know him. And he defeated death so we could follow him.

It defies logic. It is a divine insanity. A holy incredibility. Only a God beyond systems and common sense could create a plan as absurd as this. Yet it is the very impossibility of it all that makes it possible. The wildness of the story is its strongest witness.

For only a God could create a plan this mad. Only a Creator beyond the fence of logic could offer such a gift of love.

What man can't do, God does.

—And the Angels Were Silent

*W*hen Christ is great, our fears are not.

As awe of Jesus expands, fears of life diminish. A big God translates into big courage. A small view of God generates no courage. A limp, puny, fireless Jesus has no power over cancer cells, corruption, identity theft, stock-market crashes, or global calamity. A packageable, portable Jesus might fit well in a purse or on a shelf, but he does nothing for your fears.

This must be why Jesus took the disciples up the mountain. He saw the box in which they had confined him. He saw the future that awaited them: the fireside denial of Peter, prisons of Jerusalem and Rome, the demands of the church, and the persecutions of Nero. A box-sized version of God simply would not work. So Jesus blew the sides out of their preconceptions.

May he blow the sides out of ours.

Don't we need to know the transfigured Christ? One who spits holy fires? Who convenes and commands historical figures? Who occupies the loftiest perch and wears the only true crown of the universe, God's beloved Son? One who takes friends to Mount Hermon's peak so they can peek into heaven?

Ascend it. Stare long and longingly at the Bonfire, the Holy One, the Highest One, the Only One. As you do, all your fears, save the fear of Christ himself, will melt like ice cubes on a summer sidewalk. You will agree with David: "The LORD is my light and my salvation; whom shall I fear?" (Ps. 27:1 NKJV).

In the book *Prince Caspian*, Lucy sees Aslan, the lion, for the first time in many years. He has changed since their last encounter. His size surprises her, and she tells him as much.

> "Aslan," said Lucy, "you're bigger."
>> "That is because you are older, little one," answered he.
>> "Not because you are?"
>> "I am not. But every year you grow, you will find me bigger."[11]

And so it is with Christ. The longer we live in him, the greater he becomes in us. It's not that he changes but that we do; we see more of him. We see dimensions, aspects, and characteristics we never saw before, increasing and astonishing increments of his purity, power, and uniqueness. We discard boxes and old images of Christ like used tissues. We don't dare place Jesus on a political donkey or elephant. Arrogant certainty becomes meek curiosity. Define Jesus with a doctrine or confine him to an opinion? By no means. We'll sooner capture the Caribbean in a butterfly net than we'll capture Christ in a box.

In the end we respond like the apostles. We, too, fall on our faces and worship. And when we do, the hand of the carpenter extends through the tongue of towering fire and touches us. "Arise, and do not be afraid" (Matt. 17:7 NKJV).

—Fearless

"*For* in Christ there is all of God in a human body" (Col. 2:9 TLB). Jesus was not a godlike man, nor a manlike God. He was God-man.

Midwifed by a carpenter.

Bathed by a peasant girl.

The maker of the world with a belly button.

The author of the Torah being taught the Torah.

Heaven's human. And because he was, we are left with scratch-your-head, double-blink, what's-wrong-with-this-picture? moments like these:

Bordeaux instead of H_2O.

A cripple sponsoring the town dance.

A sack lunch satisfying five thousand tummies.

And, most of all, a grave: guarded by soldiers, sealed by a rock, yet vacated by a three-days-dead man.

What do we do with such moments?

What do we do with such a *person?* We applaud men for doing good things. We enshrine God for doing great things. But when a man does God things?

One thing is certain, we can't ignore him.

Why would we want to? If these moments are factual, if the claim of Christ is actual, then he was, at once, man and God. There he was, the single most significant person who ever lived. Forget MVP; he is the entire league. The head of the parade? Hardly. No one else shares the street. Who comes close? Humanity's best and brightest fade like dime-store rubies next to him.

Dismiss him? We can't.

Resist him? Equally difficult. Don't we need a God-man Savior? A just-God Jesus could make us but not understand us. A just-man Jesus could love us but never save us. But a God-man Jesus? Near enough to touch. Strong enough to trust. A next door Savior.

A Savior found by millions to be irresistible. Nothing compares to "the surpassing worth of knowing Christ Jesus my Lord" (Phil. 3:8 RSV). The reward of Christianity is Christ.

—Next Door Savior

If there was anything that Jesus wanted everyone to understand it was this: a person is worth something simply because he is a person. That is why he treated people like he did. Think about it. The girl caught making undercover thunder with someone she shouldn't—he forgave her. The untouchable leper who asked for cleansing—he touched him. And the blind welfare case that cluttered the roadside—he honored him. And the wornout old windbag addicted to self-pity near the pool of Siloam—he healed him!

And don't forget the classic case study on the value of a person by Luke. It is called "The Tale of the Crucified Crook."

If anyone was ever worthless, this one was. If any man ever deserved dying, this man probably did. If any fellow was ever a loser, this fellow was at the top of the list.

Perhaps that is why Jesus chose him to show us what he thinks of the human race.

Maybe this criminal had heard the Messiah speak. Maybe he had seen him love the lowly. Maybe he had watched him dine with the punks, pickpockets, and potmouths on the streets. Or maybe not. Maybe the only thing he knew about this Messiah was what he now saw: a beaten, slashed, nail-suspended preacher. His face crimson with blood, his bones peeking through torn flesh, his lungs gasping for air.

Something, though, told him he had never been in better company. And somehow he realized that even though all he had was prayer, he had finally met the One to whom he should pray.

"Any chance that you could put in a good word for me?" (Loose translation.)

"Consider it done."

Now why did Jesus do that? What in the world did he have to gain by promising this desperado a place of honor at the banquet table? What in the world could this chiseling quisling ever offer in return? I mean, the Samaritan woman I can understand. She could go back and tell the tale. And Zacchaeus had some money that he could give. But this guy? What is he going to do? Nothing!

That's the point. Listen closely. Jesus' love does not depend upon what we do for him. Not at all. In the eyes of the King, you have value simply because you are. You don't have to look nice or perform well. Your value is inborn.

Period.

Think about that for just a minute. You are valuable just because you exist. Not because of what you do or what you have done, but simply because you are. Remember that. Remember that the next time you are left bobbing in the wake of someone's steamboat ambition. Remember that the next time some trickster tries to hang a bargain basement price tag on your self-worth. The next time someone tries to pass you off as a cheap buy, just think about the way Jesus honors you . . . and smile.

I do. I smile because I know I don't deserve love like that. None of us do. When you get right down to it, any contribution that any of us makes is pretty puny. All of us—even the purest of us—deserve heaven about as much as that crook did. All of us are signing on Jesus' credit card, not ours.

And it also makes me smile to think that there is a grinning ex-con walking the golden streets who knows more about grace than a thousand theologians. No one else would have given him a prayer. But in the end that is all that he had. And in the end, that is all it took.

No wonder they call him the Savior.

—No Wonder They Call Him the Savior

15

Hope

The angel sat on the dislodged tombstone. He did not stand in defiance or crouch in alertness. He sat. Legs crossed and whistling? In my imagination at least. The angel sat upon the *stone*. Again, the irony. The very rock intended to mark the resting place of a dead Christ became the resting place of his living angel And then the announcement:

"He is risen."

Three words in English. Just one in Greek. *Ēgerthē*. So much rests on the validity of this one word. If it is false, then the whole of Christianity collapses like a poorly told joke. Yet, if it is true, then God's story has turned your final chapter into a preface. IF the angel was correct, then you can believe this: Jesus descended into the coldest cell of death's prison and allowed the warden to lock the door and smelt the keys in a furnace. And just when the demons began to dance and prance, Jesus pressed pierced hands against the inner walls of the cavern. From deep within he shook the cemetery.

And out he marched, the cadaver turned king, with the mask of death in one hand and the keys of heaven in the other. *Ēgerthē!* He is risen!

Not risen from sleep. Not risen from confusion. Not risen from stupor or slumber. Not spiritually raised from the dead; *physically* raised. The women and disciples didn't see a phantom or experience a sentiment. They saw Jesus in the flesh. "It is I myself!" he assured them (Luke 24:39 NIV).

The Emmaus-bound disciples thought Jesus was a fellow pilgrim. His feet touched the ground. His hands touched the bread. Mary mistook him for a gardener. Thomas studied his wounds. The disciples ate fish that he cooked. The resurrected Christ did phys8cal deeds in a physical body. "I am not a ghost" he explained (Luke 24:39 NLT). "Handle me and see, for a spirit does not have flesh and bones as you see I have" (verse 39 NKJV).

The bodily resurrection means everything. If Jesus lives on only in spirit and deeds, he is but one of a thousand dead heroes. But if he lives on in flesh and bone, he is the King who pressed his heel against the head of death. What he did with his own grace he promises to do with yours: empty it. . . .

Death is not the final chapter in your story. In death you will step into the arms of the One who declared, "I am the resurrection and the life. The one who believes in me will live, even though they die; and whoever lives by believing in me will never die" (John 11:25–26 NIV).

—God's Story, Your Story

A party was the last thing Mary Magdalene expected as she approached the tomb on that Sunday morning. The last few days had brought nothing to celebrate. The Jews could celebrate—Jesus was out of the way. The soldiers could celebrate—their work was done. But Mary couldn't celebrate. To her the last few days had brought nothing but tragedy.

Mary had been there. She had heard the leaders clamor for Jesus' blood. She had witnessed the Roman whip rip the skin off his back. She had winced as the thorns sliced his brow and wept at the weight of the cross. . . .

She was there. She was there to hold her arm around the shoulder of Mary the mother of Jesus. She was there to close his eyes. She was there.

So it's not surprising that she wants to be there again.

In the early morning mist she arises from her mat, takes her spices and aloes, and leaves her house, past the Gate of Gennath and up to the hillside. She anticipates a somber task. By now the body will be swollen. His face will be white. Death's odor will be pungent.

A gray sky gives way to gold as she walks up the narrow trail. As she rounds the final bend, she gasps. The rock in front of the grave is pushed back.

"Someone took the body." She runs to awaken Peter and John. They rush to see for themselves. She tries to keep up with them but can't.

Peter comes out of the tomb bewildered and John comes out believing, but Mary just sits in front of it weeping. The two men go home and leave her alone with her grief.

But something tells her she is not alone. Maybe she hears a noise. Maybe she hears a whisper. Or maybe she just hears her own heart tell her to take a look for herself.

Whatever the reason, she does. She stoops down, sticks her head into the hewn entrance, and waits for her eyes to adjust to the dark.

"Why are you crying?" She sees what looks to be a man, but he's white—radiantly white. He is one of two lights on either end of the vacant slab. Two candles blazing on an altar.

"Why are you crying?" An uncommon question to be asked in a cemetery. In fact, the question is rude. That is, unless the questioner knows something the questionee doesn't.

"They have taken my Lord away, and I don't know where they have put him."

She still calls him "my Lord." As far as she knows his lips were silent. As far as she knows, his corpse had been carted off by graverobbers. But in spite of it all, he is still her Lord. Such devotion moves Jesus. It moves him closer to her. So close she hears him breathing. She turns and there he stands. She thinks he is the gardener.

Now, Jesus could have revealed himself at this point. He could have called for an angel to present him or a band to announce his presence. But he didn't.

"Why are you crying? Who is it you are looking for?"[1]

He doesn't leave her wondering long, just long enough to remind us that he loves to surprise us. He waits for us to despair of human strength and then intervenes with heavenly. God waits for us to give up and then—surprise!

Has it been a while since you let God surprise you? It's easy to reach the point where we have God figured out.

We know exactly what God does. We break the code. We chart his tendencies. God is a computer. If we push all the right buttons and insert the right data, God is exactly who we thought he was. No variations. No alterations. God is a jukebox. Insert a tithe. Punch in the right numbers and—bam—the divine music we want fills the room. . . .

Have you got God figured out? Have you got God captured on a flow-chart and frozen on a flannelboard? If so, then listen. Listen to God's surprises.

Hear the rocks meant for the body of the adulterous woman drop to the ground.

Listen as Jesus invites a death-row convict to ride with him to the kingdom in the front seat of the limo.

Listen as the Messiah whispers to the Samaritan woman, "I who speak to you am he."

Listen to the widow from Nain eating dinner with her son who is supposed to be dead.

And listen to the surprise as Mary's name is spoken by a man she loved—a man she had buried.

"Miriam."[2]

God appearing at the strangest of places. Doing the strangest of things. Stretching smiles where there had hung only frowns. Placing twinkles where there were only tears. Hanging a bright star in a dark sky. Arching rainbows in the midst of thunderclouds. Calling names in a cemetery.

"Miriam," he said softly, "surprise!"

Mary was shocked. It's not often you hear your name spoken by an eternal tongue. But when she did, she recognized it. And when she did, she responded correctly. She worshiped him.

The scene has all the elements of a surprise party—secrecy, wide eyes, amazement, gratitude. But this celebration is timid in comparison with the one that is being planned for the future. It will be similar to Mary's, but a lot bigger. Many more graves will open. Many more names will be called. Many more knees will bow. And many more seekers will celebrate.

It's going to be some party. I plan to make sure my name is on the guest list. How about you?

> *"No eye has seen, no ear has heard,*
> *no mind has conceived*
> *what God has prepared for those who love him."*[3]
>
> —*Six Hours One Friday*

*T*homas would die for Christ. Surely he'd die for the chance to see the risen Christ. But he wasn't about to be fooled. He'd buried his hopes once, thank you. Not about to bury them again. No matter what the others said, he needed to see for himself. So for seven days he sat. Others rejoiced; he resisted. They celebrated; he was silent. Thomas needed firsthand evidence. So Jesus gave it. First one hand, then the other, then the pierced side. "Put your finger here and see my hands. Put your hand into the wound in my side. Don't be faithless any longer. Believe!" (John 20:27 NLT).

And Thomas did. "My Lord and my God!" (v. 28).

Only a God could come back from the dead. And only a God of love would come back for a doubter.

Desert God—he'll still love you.

Deny God—he'll still love you.

Doubt God—he'll still love you.

Paul was convinced. Are you? Are you convinced that you have never lived a loveless day? Not one. Never unloved. Those times you deserted Christ? He loved you. You hid from him; he came looking for you.

And those occasions you denied Christ? Though you belonged to him, you hung with them, and when his name surfaced, you cursed like a drunken sailor. God let you hear the crowing of conscience and feel the heat of tears. But he never let you go. Your denials cannot diminish his love.

Nor can your doubts. You've had them. You may have them even now. While there is much we cannot know, may never know, can't we be sure of this? Doubts don't separate doubters from God's love.

The jail door has never closed. God's love supply is never empty. "For his unfailing love toward those who fear him is as great as the height of the heavens above the earth" (Ps. 103:11 NLT).

The big news of the Bible is not that you love God but that God loves you; not that you can know God but that God already knows you! He tattooed your name on the palm of his hand. His thoughts of you outnumber the sand on the shore. You never leave his mind, escape his sight, flee his thoughts. He sees the worst of you and loves you still. Your sins of tomorrow and failings of the future will not surprise him; he sees them now. Every day and deed of your life has passed before his eyes and been calculated in his decision. He knows you better than you know you and has reached his verdict: he loves you still. No discovery will disillusion him; no rebellion will dissuade him. He loves you with an everlasting love. . . .

The greatest discovery in the universe is the greatest love in the universe—God's love. "Nothing can ever separate us from his love" (Rom.

8:38 NLT). Think what those words mean. You may be separated from your spouse, from your folks, from your kids, from your hair, but you are not separated from the love of God. And you never will be. Ever.

—Come Thirsty

*T*his is the promise of Christ: "Don't let your hearts be troubled. Trust in God, and trust also in me. There is more than enough room in my Father's home. If this were not so, would I have told you that I am going to prepare a place for you? When everything is ready, I will come and get you, so that you will always be with me where I am" (John 14:1–3 NLT).

While Jesus' words sound comforting to us, they sounded radical to his first-century audience. He was promising to accomplish a feat no one dared envision or imagine. He would return from the dead and rescue his followers from the grave.

Traditional Judaism was divided on the topic of resurrection. "For Sadducees say that there is no resurrection—and no angel or spirit; but the Pharisees confess both" (Acts 23:8 NKJV). The Sadducees saw the grave as a tragic, one-way trip into Sheol. No escape. No hope. No possibility of parole. "The living know that they will die, but the dead know nothing" (Eccl. 9:5 NIV).

The Pharisees envisioned a resurrection, yet the resurrection was spiritual, not physical. "There are no traditions about prophets being raised to a new bodily life. . . . However exalted Abraham, Isaac, and Jacob may have been in Jewish thought, nobody imagined they had been raised from the dead."[4]

Ancient Greek philosophy used different language but resulted in identical despair. Their map of death included the River Styx and the boatman Charon. Upon death, the soul of the individual would be ferried across the river and released into a sunless afterlife of bodiless spirits, shades, and shadows.

This was the landscape into which Jesus entered. Yet he walked into this swamp of uncertainty and built a sturdy bridge. He promised, not just an afterlife, but a better life.

"There are many rooms in my Father's home, and I am going to prepare a place for you." We Westerners might miss the wedding images, but you can bet your sweet chuppah that Jesus' listeners didn't. This was a groom-to-bride promise. Upon receiving the permission of both families, the groom returned to the home of his father and built a home for his bride. He "prepared a place."

By promising to do the same for us, Jesus elevates funerals to the same hope level as weddings. From his perspective the trip to the cemetery and the walk down the aisle warrant identical excitement. . . .

Weddings are great news!

So, says Jesus, are burials. Both celebrate a new era, name, and home. In both the groom walks the bride away on his arm. Jesus is your coming groom. "I will come and get you . . ." He will meet you at the altar. Your final glimpse of life will trigger your first glimpse of him.

—Fearless

*M*any Christians . . . live with a deep-seated anxiety about eternity. They *think* they are saved, *hope* they are saved, but still they doubt, wondering, *Am I really saved?*

This is not merely an academic question. Children who accept Christ ask it. Parents of prodigals ask it. So do friends of the wayward. It surfaces in the heart of the struggler. It seeps into the thoughts of the dying. When we forget our vow to God, does God forget us? Does God place us on a standby list?

Our behavior gives us reason to wonder. We are strong one day, weak the next. Devoted one hour, flagging the next. Believing, then unbelieving. Our lives mirror the contours of a roller coaster, highs and lows.

Conventional wisdom draws a line through the middle of these fluctuations. Perform above this line, and enjoy God's acceptance. But dip below it, and expect a pink slip from heaven. In this paradigm a person is lost and saved multiple times a day, in and out of the kingdom on a regular basis. Salvation becomes a matter of timing. You just hope you die on an upswing. No security, stability, or confidence.

This is not God's plan. He draws the line, for sure. But he draws it beneath our ups and downs. Jesus' language couldn't be stronger. "And I give them eternal life, and they shall never lose it or perish throughout the ages. [To all eternity they shall never by any means be destroyed.] And no one is able to snatch them out of My hand" (John 10:28 AMPC).

Jesus promised a new life that could not be forfeited or terminated. "Whoever hears my word and believes him who sent me has eternal life and will not be condemned; he has crossed over from death to life" (John 5:24 NIV). Bridges are burned, and the transfer is accomplished. Ebbs and flows continue, but they never disqualify. Ups and downs may mark our days, but they will never ban us from his kingdom. Jesus bottom-lines our lives with grace.

Even more, God stakes his claim on us. "By his Spirit he has stamped us with his eternal pledge—a sure beginning of what he is destined to complete" (2 Cor. 1:22 MSG). You've done something similar: engraved your name on a valued ring, etched your identity on a tool or iPad. Cowboys brand cattle with the mark of the ranch. Stamping declares ownership. Through his Spirit, God stamps us. Would-be takers are repelled by the presence of his name. Satan is driven back by the declaration: *Hands off. This child is mine! Eternally, God.*

On-and-off salvation never appears in the Bible. Salvation is not a repeated phenomenon. Scripture contains no example of a person who was saved, then lost, then resaved, then lost again.

Where there is no assurance of salvation, there is no peace. No peace means no joy. No joy results in fear-based lives. Is this the life God creates? No. Grace creates a confident soul who declares, "I know whom I have believed, and am convinced that he is able to guard what I have entrusted to him for that day" (2 Tim. 1:12 NIV).

Of all we don't know in life, we know this: we hold a boarding pass. "These things I have written to you who believe in the name of the Son of God, that you may know that you have eternal life" (1 John 5:13 NKJV). Trust God's hold on you more than your hold on God. His faithfulness does not depend on yours. His performance is not predicated on yours. His love is not contingent on your own. Your candle may flicker, but it will not expire.

—Grace

*W*hy do Jesus and his angels rejoice over one repenting sinner? Can they see something we can't? Do they know something we don't? Absolutely. They know what heaven holds. They've seen the table, they've heard the music, and they can't wait to see your face when you arrive. Better still, they can't wait to see you.

When you arrive and enter the party, something wonderful will happen. A final transformation will occur. You will be just like Jesus. Drink deeply from 1 John 3:2: "We have not yet been shown what we will be in the future. But we know that when Christ comes again, *we will be like him*" (NCV, emphasis mine).

Of all the blessings of heaven, one of the greatest will be you! You will be God's magnum opus, his work of art. The angels will gasp. God's work will be completed. At last, you will have a heart like his.

You will love with a perfect love.

You will worship with a radiant face.

You will hear each word God speaks.

Your heart will be pure; your words will be like jewels; your thoughts will be like treasures.

You will be just like Jesus. You will, at long last, have a heart like his. Envision the heart of Jesus and you'll be envisioning your own. Guiltless. Fearless. Thrilled and joyous. Tirelessly worshiping. Flawlessly discerning. As the mountain stream is pristine and endless, so will be your heart. *You will be like him.*

And if that were not enough, everyone else will be like him as well. "Heaven is the perfect place for people made perfect."[5] Heaven is populated by those who let God change them. Arguments will cease, for jealousy won't exist. Suspicions won't surface, for there will be no secrets. Every sin is gone. Every insecurity is forgotten. Every fear is past. Pure wheat. No weeds. Pure gold. No alloy. Pure love. No lust. Pure hope. No fear. No wonder the angels rejoice when one sinner repents; they know another work of art will soon grace the gallery of God. They know what heaven holds.

—Just Like Jesus

*H*ow can we be sure there is life after death?

The Bible says so. "Because Jesus was raised from the dead, we've been given a brand-new life and have everything to live for, including a future in heaven—and the future starts now!" (1 Peter 1:3–4 MSG).

Jesus said so. "This is what is written: The Christ will suffer and rise from the dead on the third day, and repentance and forgiveness of sins will be preached in his name to all nations, beginning at Jerusalem. You are witnesses of these things" (Luke 24:46–48 NIV).

The angel said so. "Do not be afraid, for I know that you are looking for Jesus, who was crucified. He is not here; he has risen, just as he said. Come and see the place where he lay" (Matt. 28:5–6 NIV).

Witnesses said so. "He was seen by Peter and then by the twelve apostles. After that, Jesus was seen by more than five hundred of the believers at the same time" (1 Cor. 15:5–6 NCV).

Even the rolled-away stone testifies to Christ's rising from the dead (Matt. 28:1–7). No barrier will keep us locked inside the grave. Christ was the first example that we will all follow.

While we wait for this glorious resurrection, what are our spirits doing? Jesus spoke of death as sleep when talking to the disciples about Lazarus:

> After he had said this, he went on to tell them, "Our friend Lazarus has fallen asleep; but I am going there to wake him up."
>
> His disciples replied, "Lord, if he sleeps, he will get better." Jesus had been speaking of his death, but his disciples thought he meant natural sleep. (John 11:11–13 NIV)

Is death a time of unconscious, REM-driven snoozing? In the story of the rich man and Lazarus (a different Lazarus) in Luke 16, Jesus described a conscious death with an awareness of events, people, and identity. So it can't be sound-asleep sleep.

When we are asleep, our bodies transition into a different state, just like death. Still, motionless, the body lies there, yet the brain keeps working in an altered state of consciousness. In death, consciousness also shifts as the spirit leaves the body behind. The body waits for its own moment at the resurrection when it will be stirred awake by the alarm clock call of the final trumpet and rise anew from its tomb to be reunited with its still-conscious spirit and the Person who conquered death before us all.

—Max on Life

*"W*hen the dove returned to him in the evening, there in its beak was a freshly plucked olive leaf!" (Gen. 8:11 NIV).

An olive leaf. Noah would have been happy to have the bird . . . but to have the leaf! This leaf was more than foliage; this was promise. The bird brought more than a piece of a tree; it brought hope. For isn't that what hope is? Hope is an olive leaf—evidence of dry land after a flood. Proof to the dreamer that dreaming is worth the risk.

Don't we love the olive leaves of life?

"It appears the cancer may be in remission."

"I can help you with those finances."

"We'll get through this together."

What's more, don't we love the doves that bring them? When the father walks his son through his first broken heart, he gives him an olive leaf. When the wife of many years consoles the wife of a few months, when she tells her that conflicts come and all husbands are moody and these storms pass, you know what she is doing? She is giving an olive leaf.

We love olive leaves. And we love those who give them.

Perhaps that's the reason so many loved Jesus.

He stands near a woman who was yanked from a bed of promiscuity. She's still dizzy from the raid. A door slammed open, covers were pulled back, and the fraternity of moral police barged in. And now here she stands. Noah could see nothing but water. She can see nothing but anger. She has no hope.

But then Jesus speaks, "If any one of you is without sin, let him be the first to throw a stone at her" (John 8:7 NIV). Silence. Both the eyes and the rocks of the accusers hit the ground. Within moments they have left, and Jesus is alone with the woman. The dove of heaven offers her a leaf.

"Woman, where are they? Has no one condemned you?"

"No one, sir," she said.

"Then neither do I condemn you," Jesus declared. "Go now and leave your life of sin." (vv. 10–11 NIV)

Into her shame-flooded world he brings a leaf of hope.

He does something similar for Martha. She is bobbing in a sea of sorrow. Her brother is dead. His body has been buried. And Jesus, well, Jesus is late. "If you had been here, my brother would not have died." Then I think she might have paused. "But I know that even now God will give you whatever you ask" (John 11:21–22 NIV). As Noah opened his hatch, so Martha opens her heart. As the dove brought a leaf, so Christ brings the same.

"I am the resurrection and the life. He who believes in me will live, even though he dies; and whoever lives and believes in me will never die. Do you believe this?"

"Yes, Lord," she told him, "I believe that you are the Christ, the Son of God, who was to come into the world." (John 11:25–27 NIV)

How could he get by with such words? Who was he to make such a claim? What qualified him to offer grace to one woman and a promise of resurrection to another? Simple. He had done what the dove did. He'd crossed the shoreline of the future land and journeyed among the trees. And from the grove of grace he plucked a leaf for the woman. And from the tree of life he pulled a sprig for Martha.

And from both he brings leaves to you. Grace and life. Forgiveness of sin. The defeat of death. This is the hope he gives. This is the hope we need.

—*A Love Worth Giving*

Notes

CHAPTER 1: CREATOR

1. "Whirlpool Galaxy Facts," Space Facts, http://space-facts. com/whirlpool -galaxy/.
2. Tim Sharp, "How Big Is the Sun?/Size of the Sun," Space. com, August 8, 2012, www.space.com/17001-how-big-is-the-sun-size-of-the-sun.html.
3. Space.com staff, "Supergiant Star's Rainbow Nebula Revealed," Space.com, June 23, 2011, http://www.space. com/12051-bright-nebula-photo-supergiant-star-betelgeuse. html.
4. Miriam Kramer, "Supergiant Star Betelgeuse to Crash into Cosmic 'Wall,'" Space.com, January 25, 2013, http://www. space.com/19415-supergiant-star -betelgeuse-crash-photo. html.
5. Genesis 1:1 NIV.
6. Genesis 1:31 NIV.
7. Mark 15:34 NIV.
8. Spiros Zodhiates, ed., *Hebrew-Greek Key Word Study Bible: Key Insights into God's Word, New International Version* (Chattanooga, TN: AMG Publishers, 1996), #5770, p. 2122.
9. Ibid., #1919, p. 2072.

CHAPTER 2: IMMANUEL

1. Luke 1:33 NIV.
2. John 11:1–36; Matthew 14:22–33; John 8:1–11.
3. Allaahuakbar.net, "Shirk: The Ultimate Crime," http://www.allaahuakbar.net /shirk/crime.htm.
4. Mark 12:31 NIV.
5. Mark 10:29.
6. Matthew 5:44 NIV.

7. Matthew 28:20 NIV.

8. 1 Corinthians 15:51–52, NKJV.

Chapter 3: Friend

1. Colossians 4:11.

2. Acts 13:6.

3. Matthew 27:17; William Barclay, *Jesus As They Saw Him* (Grand Rapids, Mich.: Wm. B. Eerdmans).

4. Matthew 1:21.

5. Hebrews 4:15 NIV.

6. Matthew 28:20 NIV.

7. Hebrews 13:5 NIV.

8. Thanks to Landon Saunders for sharing this story with me.

9. Gerhard Kittel and Gerhard Friedrich, eds., *Theological Dictionary of the New Testament*, trans. Geoffrey W. Bromiley (Grand Rapids: Eerdmans Publishing Co., 1971), 9:483.

Chapter 4: Example

1. Alfred Edersheim, *The Life and Times of Jesus the Messiah*, unabr. ed. (Peabody, MA: Hendrickson Publishers, Inc., 1993), 62–63.

2. Luke 4:16 NCV, emphasis added.

Chapter 5: Teacher

1. See Matthew 10:1–28.

2. Matthew 10:21–22 NIV.

3. Matthew 10:26–31 NIV.

4. Matthew 10:26 NIV.

5. Matthew 24:45–51.

6. Matthew 25:1–13.

7. Matthew 25:14–30.

8. Matthew 24:42 NCV.

9. Matthew 24:30.

10. Matthew 24:44 NCV.

11. Acts 1:11 NIV.

12. Hebrews 9:28 NCV.

13. 1 Thessalonians 5:2 NIV.

14. Matthew 25:32–33 NCV.

15. Matthew 7:24–27.

16. Matthew 7:13–14.

17. Larry Dixon, *The Other Side of the Good News* (Wheaton, IL: Victor Books, 1992), 133.

CHAPTER 6: HEALER

1. Matthew 15:29–32 NIV.
2. Matthew 20:29–34 NKJV.
3. Frederick Dale Bruner, *Matthew: A Commentary by Frederick Dale Bruner*, vol. 2, *The Churchbook: Matthew 13–28* (Dallas: Word, 1990), 747.

CHAPTER 8: VICTOR

1. Robert Jeffress, *Hell? Yes! . . . and Other Outrageous Truths You Can Still Believe* (Colorado Springs, CO: WaterBrook Press, 2004), 73.
2. John Blanchard, *Whatever Happened to Hell?* (Wheaton, IL: Crossway Books, 1995), 105.
3. W. E. Vine, *Expository Dictionary of New Testament Words: A Comprehensive Dictionary of the Original Greek Words with Their Precise Meanings for English Readers* (McClean, VA: MacDonald Publishing Company, n.d.), 867.

CHAPTER 9: LIFE

1. W. E. Vine, *Expository Dictionary of New Testament Words: A Comprehensive Dictionary of the Original Greek Words with Their Precise Meanings for English Readers* (McClean, VA: MacDonald Publishing Company, n.d.), 676.
2. Luke 7:15 NCV.
3. Luke 7:16 NCV.
4. Luke 23:39 TLB.

CHAPTER 10: FORGIVER

1. Charles W. Slemming, *He Leadeth Me: The Shepherd's Life in Palestine* (Fort Washington, Pa.: Christian Literature Crusade, 1964), quoted in Charles R. Swindoll, *Living Beyond the Daily Grind, Book 1: Reflections on the Songs and Sayings in Scripture* (Nashville: W Publishing Group, 1988), 77–78.

CHAPTER 11: INTERCESSOR

1. John 17:20–21, author's paraphrase.
2. Jim Reimann, *Victor Hugo's Les Misérables* (Nashville, TN: Word Publishing, 2001), 16.
3. Ibid., 29–31.
4. Charles J. Rolls, *Time's Noblest Name: The Names and Titles of Jesus Christ* (Neptune, NJ: Loizeaux Brothers, 1985), 84–86.

CHAPTER 12: SERVANT LEADER

1. For further reference consider the Book of Enoch, an intertestamental book completed sometime around 70 BC. This ancient manuscript tells us what picture came to the minds of people when they heard the title "the Son of Man."

   Note these phrases excerpted from the Book of Enoch.

   And this Son of Man whom thou hast seen shall put down the kings from their thrones,

   And shall loosen the reins of the strong

   And break the teeth of sinners.

   And he shall put down the kings from their thrones and kingdoms because they do not extol and praise him . . . (Enoch 46).

   When they see that Son of Man

   Sitting on the throne of his glory.

   And the kings and the mighty and all who possess the earth shall

   bless and glorify and extol him who rules over all, who was hidden.

   . . . all the elect shall stand before him on that day.

   And all the kings and the mighty and the exalted and those who rule the earth

   Shall fall before him on their faces,

   And worship and set their hope on the Son of Man,

   And petition him and supplicate for mercy at their hands.

   . . . he will deliver them to the angels for punishment,

   to execute vengeance on them because they have oppressed his children and his elect (Enoch 62).

   For that Son of Man has appeared,

   And has seated himself on the throne of his glory,

   And all evil shall pass away before his face,

   And the word of that Son of Man shall go forth

   And be strong before the Lord of Spirits (Enoch 69).

2. Matthew 24:30; Mark 13:26; Luke 17:26–30.

3. Matthew 26:64.

4. Matthew 26:18 NCV.

5. John 13:4–5.

6. Frederick Dale Bruner, *The Christbook: Matthew—A Commentary*, rev. and exp. ed. (Dallas: Word Publishing, 1987), 210.

CHAPTER 13: SACRIFICE

1. Matthew Henry, *Matthew to John*, vol. 5 of *Matthew Henry's Commentary on the Whole Bible* (Old Tappan, NJ: Fleming H. Revell, 1985), 428.

2. Walter Bauer, *A Greek-English Lexicon of the New Testament*, trans. William F. Arndt and F. Wilbur Gingrich (Chicago: University of Chicago Press, 1979), 50.

3. Isabel McHugh and Florence McHugh, trans., *The Trial of Jesus: The Jewish and Roman Proceedings against Jesus Christ Described and Assessed from the Oldest Accounts*, by Josef Blinzler (Westminster, MD: The Newman Press, 1959), 103.

4. Donald Grey Barnhouse, *Let Me Illustrate: More Than 400 Stories, Anecdotes & Illustrations* (Grand Rapids: Fleming H. Revell, 1967), 196.

5. Hebrews 1:1–2 NIV, italics mine.

CHAPTER 14: SAVIOR

1. Frederick Dale Bruner, *Matthew: A Commentary*, vol. 1, *The Christbook: Matthew 1–12*, rev. and exp. ed. (Grand Rapids: William B. Eerdmans, 2004), 29–30.

2. John 4:4–29.

3. Mark 5:1–15.

4. Luke 19:1–10.

5. David Tereshchuk, "Racing Towards Inclusion," Team Hoyt, http://www .teamhoyt.com/history.shtml.

6. Peter Cotterell, *London Bible College Review*, Summer 1989, quoted in Peter Lewis, *The Glory of Christ* (London: Hodder and Stoughton, 1992), 461.

7. Michael Green, *You Must Be Joking: Popular Excuses for Avoiding Jesus Christ* (London: Hodder and Stoughton, 1981), 43, quoted in Lewis, *The Glory of Christ*, 461.

8. Green, *You Must Be Joking*, 43, quoted in Lewis, *The Glory of Christ*, 461.

9. Matthew 11:28 NIV.

10. Matthew 11:29 NIV.

11. C. S. Lewis, *Prince Caspian: The Return to Narnia* (New York: Macmillan Publishing, 1951), 136. Copyright " C. S. Lewis Pte. Ltd. 1942, 1943, 1944, 1952. Extract reprinted by permission.

CHAPTER 15: HOPE

1. John 20:1–18 NIV.

2. "Miriam" is the Aramaic form of "Mary."

3. 1 Corinthians 2:9 NIV.

4. N. T. Wright, *Christian Origins and the Question of God*, vol. 3, *The Resurrection of the Son of God* (Minneapolis: Fortress Press, 2003), 205–6.

5. Charles Spurgeon's sermon entitled "The Sympathy of Two Worlds," quoted in John MacArthur, *The Glory of Heaven* (Wheaton, IL: Crossway Books, 1996), 118.

Sources Index

All the material in *Jesus* was originally published in books authored by Max Lucado. All copyrights to the original works are held by Max Lucado.

And the Angels Were Silent (Nashville: Thomas Nelson, 2013), 13–16, 22–26, 82–83, 110–13, 121–26, 128–30.

Anxious for Nothing (Nashville: Thomas Nelson, 2017), 55–57, 134–39, 148.

Applause of Heaven, The (Nashville: Thomas Nelson, 2013), 65–66, 80–83.

Because of Bethlehem (Nashville: Thomas Nelson, 2016), 15–18, 26–31, 111–12, 123–25.

Before Amen (Nashville: Thomas Nelson, 2014), 5–6, 54–56, 78–79, 95–100.

Come Thirsty (Nashville: W Publishing Group, 2004), 11–14, 140–41.

Cure for the Common Life (Nashville: Thomas Nelson, 2007), 65–66, 99–100, 102, 105–106, 109, 130–32.

Facing Your Giants (Nashville: Thomas Nelson, 2013), 26–27, 33, 100, 162–63.

Fearless (Nashville: Thomas Nelson, 2012), 47–48, 94–95, 117–19, 169–71.

Gentle Thunder, A (Nashville: Thomas Nelson, 2012), 22–23, 26–30, 84–86, 112–16, 152–53.

Glory Days (Nashville, Thomas Nelson, 2015), 43–44, 85.

God Came Near (Nashville: Thomas Nelson, 2008), 3–5, 7–8, 31–32, 37–39, 44–45, 47–50.

God's Story, Your Story (Grand Rapids: Zondervan, 2011), 99–103.

Grace (Nashville: Thomas Nelson, 2012), 15–21, 18–20, 48–50, 52, 91–92, 110–11, 111–12.

Great Day Every Day (Nashville: Thomas Nelson, 2012), 21–23, 31–33, 64–70, 97–99.

Great House of God, The (Nashville: Thomas Nelson, 2013), 68–69, 100–102, 139–40, 146–49.

He Chose the Nails (Nashville: Thomas Nelson, 2007), 23–27, 71–74, 92–94.

He Still Moves Stones (Nashville: Thomas Nelson, 2009), 56–60, 95–98, 101, 107–10, 125–27, 129–31, 141, 155–62, 174–78.

In the Eye of the Storm (Nashville: Thomas Nelson, 2012), 59, 151–52, 158, 160–63, 171–77.

In the Grip of Grace (Nashville: Thomas Nelson, 2014), 49–50, 55–56, 142.

Just Like Jesus (Nashville: Thomas Nelson, 2013), 3–4, 57–58, 91, 132–33, 140–44, 157–58.

Love Worth Giving, A (Nashville: Thomas Nelson, 2014), 25–30, 49–50, 54, 130–31, 153–54.

Max on Life (Nashville: Thomas Nelson, 2011), 8, 13, 18, 19, 49, 55, 201–202.

Next Door Savior (Nashville: Thomas Nelson, 2012), 4–5, 17–22, 37–42, 54–57, 77–80, 91–92, 108–12, 129–34, 151, 153–55.

No Wonder They Call Him the Savior (Nashville: Thomas Nelson, 2009), 17–18, 35–36, 38–39.

On the Anvil (Wheaton, IL: Tyndale, 1991), 105–107.

Outlive Your Life (Nashville: Thomas Nelson, 2010), 100–102, 118, 144–45, 160.

Six Hours One Friday (Nashville: Thomas Nelson, 2012), 17–18, 93, 104–106, 107–109, 129–33.

3:16: The Numbers of Hope (Nashville: Thomas Nelson, 2014), 2–4, 37–40, 47–49, 52–59, 68–73, 77–78, 82–83, 97–103.

Traveling Light (Nashville: Thomas Nelson, 2011), 117–21.

When Christ Comes (Nashville: Word Publishing, 1999), 92–94

When God Whispers Your Name (Nashville: Thomas Nelson, 2009), 55–56, 22–26